UNBELIEVABLE... YET TRUE

UNBELIEVABLE... YET TRUE

BY THERESA D'SOUZA GREENHOUGH

WITH BARBARA CAVANESS

UNBELIEVABLE... YET TRUE
Published by Harvester

International Standard Book Number: 0-9749539-2-X

Cover design by IFLE Creative, LLC, Springfield, MO
Book design by Jennifer S. Hall, Springfield, MO

DEDICATION

David and I would like to dedicate this book to the poor children of the world, especially the ones under our care. They have brought out the best in us. They have helped us to walk in the school of the Spirit and hear from the Master. Each of the children is so unique and were it not for them, we would not have had such a hunger and passion for the heartbeat of God.

God bless you, children! Uncle and Auntie love you and will always be there for you.

TABLE OF CONTENTS

FOREWORD

LUKE RECORDS FOR US IN THE BOOK OF ACTS THE OUTPOURING of the Holy Spirit on the Day of Pentecost. We read, shortly thereafter, of the healing of the lame man in the name of Jesus by Peter and John; the "great wonders and miracles" done by Stephen who was "full of faith and power;" and the "special miracles" God did through Paul (Acts 3:8, 6:8, 19:11). They lived the fulfillment of Jesus' promise that believers would do "greater works" than He had done (John 4:12).

Acts seems to end very abruptly with Paul continuing to preach and teach about Jesus Christ to the Gentiles in Rome. The fact is the Book of Acts is not finished yet. We carry on in the footsteps of the apostles and early Christians as the Holy Spirit bestows His gifts in and through us—messages of wisdom and knowledge, faith, gifts of healing, miraculous powers, prophecy, discerning of spirits, tongues, and the interpretation of tongues. All are distributed by the Holy Spirit today, just as they were then (1 Cor. 12:8-12).

I first met this woman of God in 1999 at the "Pentecost, Prophecy & Power" conference convened by the Assemblies of God Theological Seminary. An evangelist from India, she gave the keynote address and one of the plenary sessions. I marveled at her command of the Scriptures, yet greatly admired her humble spirit as she preached under great anointing. Pastors, evangelists, missionaries, and students alike lingered in the sanctuary following her messages, skipped workshops, and "did business" with God as Theresa moved in the Spirit and ministered to individuals through His gifts. Many testified that their lives would never be the same.

The book in your hands reads like the twenty-ninth chapter of Acts. You will hardly be able to put it down. The true stories will move you to laughter at times and tears at other times. If you have longed and prayed for God to use you in Holy Spirit power in the same way He used the Early Church Christians, Theresa's testimonies and life experiences will inspire you and encourage you to believe for the "greater works" in your life too.

GEORGE O. WOOD, General Superintendent
General Council of the Assemblies of God
Springfield, Missouri
2010

ACKNOWLEDGMENTS

I THANK GOD FOR MY PARENTS WHO PRAYED ME INTO THE Kingdom and for my brothers and sisters who encouraged me from day one.

I am also grateful for the Redemptorist Fathers, the Loreto nuns, and the Jesuit priests, who to this day are my friends. They never stifled my spiritual growth, but brought the best out of me.

Appreciation is due to the Eastern Pentecostal Bible College, Peterborough, Ontario, Canada, whose faculty and students accepted and supported me in more ways than one.

I want to thank the Burlington Assembly of God staff, its members, and especially Pastor Paul Graban, who saw the anointing on my life. They went out of their way to promote my ministry.

I appreciate Joyce and Joe who, along with their three dogs, made it possible for me to have the upstairs of their home for myself, rent-free, from 1995 to this day so that I could hear from God and work on the messages He was inspiring me to put together.

Special thanks to my in-laws Harry and Mary Greenhough who have backed us 100 percent and never cease to bless us.

I'm very grateful to Barbara for responding to God's voice and assisting me to put my life's stories, *Unbelievable, Yet True*, in our first book together. I thank God that she took up the challenge of not only crossing cultural borders, but traveled across the globe to work with me and to put into writing this next chapter of the unconcluded 'Book of Acts of the Holy Spirit.'

Finally, I'd like to thank David, who helped in the editing, not just of this book, but also my life. I thank God for David's patience for fourteen months before I said, "I do," but whom I'll be running after for the rest of my life. "Thanks Hon, for truly being a "man after God's own heart." Without you and all the others, this book would not have been written."

CHAPTER 1

EARLY YEARS

"Before you were born I set you apart" (Jer. 1:5).

JUST AS GOD KNEW JEREMIAH BEFORE HE WAS FORMED IN HIS mother's womb, I believe God knew me before my actual birth. My humble, down-to-earth parents already had five children; they didn't really need another mouth to feed. But being God-fearing Roman Catholics, they welcomed each new baby as God's gift to them.

My father worked at a silk mill, Jagdamba Fabrics, as a hard-working engineer overseeing 32 huge machines for over 30 years. He awoke to pray at 3:00 a.m. and left at 4:00 a.m. to take three sets of trains on the long journey to his workplace. We lived on the family property near Bombay (now Mumbai). My grandma was a housewife and my grandpa had a weaving business. He was a member of the St. Vincent De Paul Society at Our Lady of Perpetual Succour Church and gave most of his property to the Redemptorist Fathers. The church had over 10,000 members.

I had a very close relationship with both my father and mother. In my early twenties, when I was suffering from migraines and severe allergies, a prayer warrior friend of mine discerned that I had suffered a shock in my mother's womb. When I met my mom on the next holiday and asked her about my birth, she started crying, though she was not angry or upset. She related this story: "You were my sixth pregnancy in eleven years. We didn't have much money for anything; I even pawned my wedding band. The doctor told me to abort you, that I was too weak to manage another delivery. We couldn't afford another child either, but I decided to go on with the pregnancy. I was under a lot of stress. After you were born, 11 January 1958, I took you to church and placed you on the altar even before taking you home. I told God, 'This child is yours.'"

My mother named me Theresa, meaning 'harvester.' My full name was Theresa Maria Magdalene. My family called me 'Maggie' all my growing-up years.

I was my father's 'pet.' Even though he was very strict, I loved him deeply. He was a perfectionist, very particular about his clothes. He had been raised in Mangalore in the state of Karnataka. He had not been educated. The first time he went to school, he arrived late and the teacher hit him on the top of his head with a slate. He never went back, so he could not read or write, though he spoke five Indian languages. He spoke Konkani, the Mangalore dialect, and insisted that we kids know it in order to communicate with our grandparents. Though he could not speak much English, he wanted all his children to be educated in the Roman Catholic school system. He worked hard to pay our tuition fees and buy uniforms and books. It cost more than the government schools, but the teaching was better.

My mom was educated only to the eighth grade. Her father was an Anglo-Indian from Calicut. She had learned Marathi and Hindi on her own and tutored students in those languages. She was always counseling and praying for people. My older siblings were Harry, Christine, Philomena, Mina, and Tony. Those younger than me were Steve, Gerald, and Anita.

The Charismatic Movement spread to my country and my parents were baptized in the Holy Spirit, speaking in unknown tongues, when I was little. Mother composed songs and even preached in that movement in the Roman Catholic Church. We kids attended a half-hour mass every morning before school.

One day, when I was still a toddler in arms, my family attended a wedding on the sixth floor of a building. The more than 700 guests were given confetti to throw on the bridal party as they entered. Suddenly Dad couldn't find me. Then all he saw were my toes inside the building and my body hanging outside the window and waving to people. He nearly panicked as he got hold of my ankles and dragged me back through the window. I was not scared of heights.

As a child I wasn't content to walk anywhere. Even before I started school, I skipped and jumped and ran everywhere. I loved to whistle; I was a perfect tomboy. I climbed trees, went biking, took hikes, swam in the ocean—all the daredevil things of those days. I had so much energy. I always wore shorts under my school clothes or party clothes, just in case I needed to climb. I was always up to something. My brothers and sisters tolerated and loved me in spite of it all.

When I was very small, I had a fair complexion and was the favorite of our Anglo-Indian neighbor, Mrs. Bramblebee. She was overprotective of me and would scold my brothers and sisters if they weren't caring for me properly. I played a lot and partied a lot. I made up games and played hide-and-seek with my friends. Once I hid on the terrace inside the water tank. For hours I stood or sat on the heavy rod in the cement tank, waiting for someone to find me. If I had fallen, I would no doubt have drowned.

As a little girl I loved to go to school and I had many friends. We saw few cars and met on the road to walk to school. When it was sunny we would walk, when passing under chilly shade trees we would run. Our walk to school every day took about 15 minutes, with a low-lying area toward the end of the way. Every year the monsoon rains came and that area flooded. We kids loved to walk in water and had great fun. We would get our shoes and clothes muddy and wet. We loved getting drenched and looking like scarecrows. It didn't matter what we looked like because everyone looked the same. We thrived on it and couldn't care less where the water came from.

When we left for school, Mother would give strict orders to the older ones to take care of the younger ones. One area always got very flooded in the rains, with the water literally waist deep at times. One day I was sitting on my big brother Harry's shoulder. He was helping me with my school bag, while holding a big umbrella in his other hand. All of a sudden the water rose and I was looking around and toppled off his shoulder into the water. The current was pulling me under. Harry took the big umbrella and fished me out of the water. He was my hero and loved me so much. He got a caning that night at home because of what had happened to me. Now I know we have a bigger brother, Jesus, making intercession for us at God's right hand. If we slip or fall, anywhere at all, He will pick us up.

After Grandpa gave his property to the church, we moved to an apartment building. The attic was for sleeping, without room to stand. When we had overnight guests, I even slept under the dining room table.

Mom was a seamstress. She took orders to sew the uniforms of the students of the Loreto Convent, which had about 1,000 students at that time. She also cooked all the meals for the family and had only one elderly woman to wash the dishes and swab the floors. Mom suffered from asthma most of her life. We had no washing machine for the piles of muddy clothes from so many kids. The clothes were soaked in pails of water in the bathroom and scrubbed by Dad after he came home from work.

As a small girl I used to tease my older sisters, because I did what all the boys did. No dolls or playing house or teacher games for me. I liked outdoor games mostly. One day my Uncle Valerian (Mom's older brother) saw me teasing them until they cried, so he chased me with a sickle—out of the neighborhood and beyond.

One day I was cycling around the high wall of the school with my friend, Angelina Sequeira, sitting on the front handlebar. As I rode into the intersection, I did not notice a taxi coming on my right. It hit us and Angelina fell off. Her head landed right between the wheels of the taxi, but she was unharmed. It was a rented bicycle and had gotten badly twisted. My Aunt Rosie took the cycle and had it fixed, without scolding me or telling my parents.

Another time my sister Christine put on a gray, black, and white jumpsuit, with sequin trim. I told her she looked like a crow. Sobbing and crying bitterly, she took off the outfit and refused to go out with the friends who were waiting for her. Mother chased me around the house with a broom, until I ran to the loft and took the atlas, pretending to study. Mom wanted to punish me, but instead she put her arm around my shoulders. I wept and never did that again.

I loved to give 'news bulletins.' In other words, I was a tattletale. My younger brother Gerald took a rubber lizard and put it in the Class Attendance Register of the teacher. The teacher came that day with a tight skirt on and all 60 boys in the class were watching closely. She stepped onto her platform, opened the book, and the lizard fell out. Her skirt tore as she jumped back. Everyone screamed as Gerald picked up the lizard and threw it out on the parapet wall. He then went out the window of the top floor himself and jumped to the ground—the 'hero,' though he had been responsible for the prank. The other boys got caned by the principal, Father Fonsecca, and Gerald brought the lizard home.

The older woman who helped mother was doing dishes in the wash area. She brought the dishes to the counter and piled them one on top of the other. Gerald and Steve decided to place that lizard on the top dish. Then they called her, "Aji Bai." When she came and saw the lizard, she dropped what she was carrying and all the metal plates and dishes clattered to the floor. Mom yelled at them, but Dad would have whipped them if he had found out. They were all scared that I would tell him.

I could always see Dad coming home from work as he walked across the cricket field behind the house. I was very fond of him, so I would run out and walk with him, telling him all the day's news. I wanted him to laugh, why should he miss out on the fun? So I told him all about it. He scolded the boys, but we all laughed together too.

Another day, Dad had received a bonus plus his salary. He had bought gifts and sweets for us kids. While he was waiting for the next train, he fell asleep on the bench at one of the railway platforms. Thieves robbed him of his train pass, the money, and the gifts. Then when Dad did get on the train, the ticket collector nabbed him for not having a ticket and put him behind bars. I refused to eat until Dad came home. I knew something was seriously wrong. In the morning Mom called his company, and they reported he had left the previous day to go home. Mr. Baretto, a friend of the family in town with a top position in the railways, learned what had happened and helped to get Dad released. He had spent the night in jail with no food, no money, and lots of bugs.

Dad was an honest God-fearing man of integrity. When he notified the company of his retirement, the owner of the company, Jagdamba Fabrics, came all the way to our home and pleaded with him to come back. This Sikh gentleman said, "No one smokes cigarettes, drinks alcohol, uses drugs, or even uses a swear word because of their high esteem and respect for you, Mr. D'Souza. You know all those 32 machines and the 'personality' of each one." But my father declined, as my oldest sister Christine had asked him to give up working. The journey had gotten too strenuous—three hours one way. He was in his early sixties, and it was exhausting for him.

As a schoolgirl I loved playing basketball. I always found it easy to make friends, so I had a group of followers. The headmistress knew that I had an inborn talent for sports and she encouraged me. I participated in competitions with other schools. By secondary school I had become somewhat 'professional' in athletics. I took part in long-distance running and high jumps. On Saturdays and Sundays I represented my school at area, district, state, and interstate meets. I had no coach to train me, just innate talent. I always wore shorts under my knee-length skirt—our uniform was a gray pinafore with a light blue blouse. I had to repeat the coursework of the eighth grade because I had been gone too much. I competed in hurdles, basketball, throwball (similar to volleyball), and 'rounders' (similar to baseball). During physical education period I would bat the ball into the boys' compound, so I had to go around and get it. All my classmates would hang out with me and we would miss part of the next class which was Math, not my favorite subject.

Concentrating on one event, I set the all-India record in high jumps in 1975, my final year (11th grade). I knew I was on my way to Olympic competition! I entered Khalsa College—a Sikh school—and trained every day for four-to-six hours to be a professional athlete. My coach then was Jaswant Singh, a good man. He would ask me three questions: "Did you sleep well? Eat well? Pray well?" During training I could attend no funerals or weddings, no excuses! I wanted to work for what I received. I had to deny myself and live a disciplined life, with no smoking, no drinking, and no boyfriends. I had set a goal and I intended to reach it. I ran six miles some days. Other days I ran in knee-deep water to strengthen my muscles. I worked for longer strides as I trained with Sikh male runners. News reports called me the 'Queen of the Track.'

Though I did not realize it, God knew the distances I would have to run and the hurdles I would have to cross in my life: "'For I know the plans I have for you,' declares the Lord, 'plans to prosper you and not to harm you, plans to give you hope and a future'" (Jer. 29:11). Christ has a mission, a calling, for each person. The Holy Spirit wants to let each one know that plan, that destiny God has for him or her. Each individual is unique, a masterpiece God has created in His image.

My oldest sister, Christine, received a scholarship for photography and went to a German university while I was still in school. So as a teenager I had everything anyone could want—money, friends, and a family who loved me. My sister sent me clothes and shoes. I seemed to have no enemies, even though stories about me appeared in the newspapers and TV news of a country of more than 900 million people.

I was a troublesome girl as a teenager. In fact, I was spoiled as the 'favorite' of my aunts, uncles, and grandparents. For 15 years the priests and nuns in our church and schools allowed me to grow in maturity and stature with their encouragement and approval. They never stifled me. I can still speak very highly of them. My parents gave me more freedom than my older siblings ever had. They all worked as tutors to help out with the family finances.

I witnessed people healed of cancer when mom prayed. Our home became a house of prayer where people came every day for intercession. It was a cradle of love. God's presence was so real at home; I never heard my parents argue or belittle each other. As a child I had told my mom, "One day you will see me star on TV!" She responded gently, "Child, remember that every good and perfect gift comes from God. Give the glory to Him."

We went to church almost every day of my life! Before going to school, I had to go to church. On Sundays Mom sat at one end of the pew and Dad at the other—nine kids in between. I always had to sit next to Mom, because she pinched my thigh if I was caught giggling or turning around. I was a spoiled kid, the brat in the family. My older brothers and sisters would say to my parents, "You're going out today? You take that brat with you. We'll babysit any of the rest." But God had a plan for my life.

Each of the nine children born into the family was molded with love. They had unique gifts and were allowed to fulfill the dreams of God, not the dreams of their parents. It took time, but all have learned to give God the glory where they live and minister, scattered around the world. It happened because my parents believed in God's dreams. Unless you believe in

God's dreams, you cannot see them fulfilled in your children. As you learn to receive God's love, you will learn how to properly love your children. Allow God to use you as a channel of His love and glory, not only to your own physical children, but also to the spiritual 'little ones' around you.

In my 10th and 11th grades I had gotten involved in social work. I had a great love for lepers. Every Saturday, after school let out around 11:00 a.m., I went to my grandmother's for snacks and to leave my books there. Then I used to ride my bike with about ten of my friends to a town called Mankhurd on the outskirts of Bombay. We would mingle with the lepers in Mother Teresa's home for lepers. Our parents didn't know, but we had a great time strumming on the guitars for them, making them sing, and acting for them. Every week we came with new tricks and stunts.

One day near Christmas we gave our parents a surprise. We had taught the lepers to act out the Christmas story and invited our parents to watch. They didn't realize their children would be part of the drama too, right on stage with the lepers. That was a beautiful day for my parents and their friends—to know that their children were not mingling with the drug addicts, prostitutes, and brawlers of this world, but with these children of God. They said it was the best Christmas gift we ever gave our families. That desire to minister to the lepers did not come from a human point of view, but it came from God. When you first see a leper it's gruesome and everything in you is repulsed. Nothing in your natural self wants to approach such a person. But divine love in you reaches out and embraces even a leper.

You and I were lepers spiritually until Jesus came and embraced us. His blood cleansed us from the leprosy of sin that afflicted us. Today we are meant to do the same for drug addicts and HIV/AIDS victims—in fact, all whom society rejects. God calls believers to embrace them in the arms of love. We must be in tune with the Holy Spirit, and pray, "Holy

Spirit, do with me what you know is best. Take away my will; walk with me and lead me."

CHAPTER 2

CONVERSION

Not to win a crown that fades, but one of unfailing glory (1 Cor. 9:25).

MY CHARISMATIC PARENTS FAITHFULLY ATTENDED A Catholic church, but by age 18, I was living a "backslidden" life. I went to church only because I had to go with the rest of the family, knowing God existed but not living a life committed to Him.

My concentration focused on the things of the world more than the things of God. Studying for my B.A. at the Khalsa College in Mumbai, I attended lectures from 6:30 to 10:00 a.m. Then I would go to work for the Indian Navy each day. The next year I worked for the Western Railway Board of India. As a somewhat famous athlete in India, I got everything placed at my feet, not really having to work hard for it.

As mentioned earlier, I was a long-distance runner and high jumper. All my childhood I had sailed over gates, fences, and walls. It just came naturally to me—God's gift. If no one was looking, I jumped over the pews in the church! I used to say my brains were in my toes. I had even broken national records.

By this time I was training six hours a day for the Olympic trials. My girlfriend, Valentine, and I were jogging together one evening when we heard the whistle of a train. So I said, "It's time to run!" Instead of going over the bridge to the railway platform to catch the train home, we decided on the spur of the moment to take a shortcut. We ducked through a huge hole in the wall which was meant to keep people from the tracks. (Poor people had taken the bricks from the wall to use in their own houses or to sell.) We decided to cut across the nine sets of tracks to reach the station more quickly.

When my feet touched the very first set of tracks, my body went limp and I was unable to move at all. It felt like electricity flowing through those tracks. Around my body I felt a layer of cold air; around that was hot steam engine air. The train that was coming was not a local train, but a high-tech express train on its way into the city. Ordinarily it did not stop at that local station.

Suddenly people were screaming down from the bridge, "Don't commit suicide!" The train had just slammed on its brakes. When it came to a stop, the engine driver climbed down. My girlfriend, who couldn't see me, thought I was under the train and was crying her heart out. The engineer picked me up bodily from where I was still standing almost paralyzed on the tracks and set me on my feet between the two sets of tracks. He looked straight into my eyes and said, "My child, I don't know which god you worship, but your God has spared your life today. I didn't stop that train."

I didn't worship any god. I came from the country of many gods. Of course I knew about Jesus, but knowledge of Jesus is not going to get anyone into the Kingdom of God. It has to be a relationship! I didn't have a relationship with Jesus Christ at that time as I have today. In the night, when I would wake from sleep to get up to go to the washroom, I would find Dad kneeling by my bed. He was by *my* bed—out of all the other eight children's beds—with his arms stretched up to heaven. He would be crying silently, tears running down his cheeks. My dad never cried, only when he was in prayer. He cried for my conversion. (Parents, don't give up praying for your children! I'm the product of my parents' prayers.)

God spared me from that speeding train. If I had died, where would I have gone? Into the fires of hell forever and ever. There is no mid-state called purgatory, no in-between state after death. You can pray to Mary, make novenas, and pray the rosary. I had done all that most of my life growing up, but I know the Word of God today and no one can deceive me. Read God's

Book of books—His love letter to us—and let the living Word set you free!

The Indian train driver turned to me and addressed the whole crowd that had gathered. In a shocked voice he said, "You know what? I'm near retirement. I know this engine inside out. It takes a few minutes of monitoring this engine before it can come to a perfect halt. Today this train stopped of its own accord! I didn't touch one button in that engine."

Friend, there is a God who holds back the hand of the enemy in your life and in mine. You are reading this book not by chance or coincidence. God has a plan for your life. He wants you to know that He loves you unconditionally. God wants to give you hope and a wonderful future.

Sitting in my parents' bedroom one night, I began shaking in repentance. "God, I'm a sinner," I cried. "I'm not worthy." I rushed from there into the kitchen, so as not to wake the family, and stayed there for hours. That night, June 6, 1977, I was truly born again and baptized in the Holy Spirit. It was a tremendous encounter with Christ. I didn't see Him in person, but from 10 p.m. until 2 a.m. I sang and worshiped Him in tongues. I was so full of God; I became a changed person! I realized I was singing so beautifully, and it was in a language I had not heard. I felt so clean. Then I offered myself for service to the Lord.

As a young woman I had such great ambitions for myself. I wanted to be an Olympic runner. I knew I would be if I trained two more years. I had been dating a fellow sportsman for two years. I planned to marry him, have six children, and train them all to be athletes. God had other plans.

I also wanted to stay in India, to be the only child in the family never to leave our country. In keeping with Indian culture I revered my parents, so I vowed never to get a passport. Most of my brothers and sisters had gone to Germany, Switzerland, and Denmark, to universities abroad. They had married foreigners and came back to India only to visit the beaches. India's more than one billion people need committed persons to reach them for Christ, and I was not a committed person until after I had been baptized in the Holy Spirit.

From that night on, the things of this world ceased to matter to me. All I wanted was to know Christ and to thank Him. When we want to thank someone we give them something we value. When we know the mind of the Spirit, we understand that it is not worth giving God what we like. We've got to know what He likes. God wanted me to thank Him by doing His will for the rest of my life—a thanksgiving offering that pleases Him. I no longer went inside movie theaters, no longer hung out with the wrong friends or skipped college lectures. I began to realize there was much more to life than all the trash I had been living with.

When we put ourselves first, we have blocked God and made an idol out of self. The devil comes as an angel of light, subtle and sneaky, convincing us of what is in our 'best interests.' So we then do what the heathen of this world do, those who do not know the one true God. We claim to be Christians, to be Spirit-filled, but because Satan creeps in we put religion in the place of God. Other priorities take the place of the things of God. If we feed our minds with the wrong things of the world, via books, television, or Internet, we don't come to know God nor have the fullness we are meant to have in Christ. We need to tune into God's wavelength through the power of the Holy Spirit. He will tell us what to do, where to go. On that night of the sixth of June, 1977, I said to Jesus, "Take me. Do with me what you will."

The following day I returned from work early and skipped sports training at the college. I went straight to the Roman Catholic church where I was a member. We as a family had very close ties with the Redemptorist Fathers. Arriving at the Presbytery I rang the doorbell and waited. Father Franklin Lobo came to the door. I was not expecting him at all. I was hesitant and lied to him, saying that a girl in my office wanted Mother Teresa's address. He, being a Spirit-filled priest, turned round and said, "That address is for you, isn't it?" I slammed the door in his face, jumped back on my bicycle, and scooted out of there.

The next day, once again, I was back ringing the same doorbell at the Presbytery. To my horror, there was Father Franklin once again. I had expected an elderly priest to show up, someone that I could confide in. I had no choice but to say, "Yes, Father, that address was for me." He asked me to join him inside and we sat down to talk.

Father Franklin had a way of testing the spirits. He turned to me and said, "Are you wanting to join Mother Teresa and do what she does? Look at you; you're always dressed to kill. You're the one who brings the fashions into town." Most of the clothes I wore in those days were from Switzerland and Germany, as my older sisters who had settled abroad used to bring them for me. I must admit I was very vain. I would never answer the door at home unless I had matching nail polish and lipstick on. My purses and shoes had to match what I was wearing.

Father Franklin went on, "When you go on your sports trips, you have porters to carry your suitcases. Well, you'll have only a pail to put all your belongings in and you will have to carry it yourself. Isn't it true that you decide for yourself whether you're going to participate in a particular event and even decide whether you want to travel or not? When you join Mother Teresa, you will have no choices to make and you will have to do as you are told." He decided to challenge me even further by saying, "I've tasted the grand meals your mother cooks at home. At Mother Teresa's you will be eating dry *chappatis* (Indian flat bread)."

I was a determined young woman and when Father Franklin had finished talking, I said, "Father, when a girl falls in love with a guy, she'll do almost anything for the man she loves. Well, I have fallen in love with Jesus and I'm willing to do anything for Him."

He responded warmly, "Now we can talk in depth!" This wise man explained to me that I had a true call from the Lord, but that I would have to pray and wait on the Lord to know more of what God wanted me to do. To be frank, I had never prayed to discern God's will for my life. I was pretty impulsive.

I went home and said to Jesus, "Lord, I'm giving you exactly one month, not more, to show me what you want me to do for you. If you do not show me very clearly what it is that you want of me, then I will continue with my university studies, my work at the Western Railway Board of India, my career as a sports woman and socializing with my friends and boyfriend." I was very content with him, so why lose him? I also told the Lord that I would make sure to go to church daily for that one month and be led of the Holy Spirit.

A few days later I was back again at the Presbytery door. I met with Father Franklin and told him I wanted so much to follow Jesus. He counseled me that it was time for me to inform my parents about my desire to follow Jesus. I told him I was scared to approach my dad, as he was a disciplinarian and I was not sure about what exactly I was to do next. I asked Father Franklin to come home and inform my parents himself of my decision to follow Jesus.

That same evening my mother had happened to meet me at the Presbytery entrance. She was a leader in the Charismatic Movement at the church and had come for a leadership meeting. I had always been very open with both my parents. But when she asked me if I would be going home with her, I did not know what to say. Father Franklin had to speak up for me, saying, "Mrs. D'Souza, you can go ahead. I will be bringing Theresa home tonight." I'm sure my mother wondered what trouble her daughter must have gotten herself into that I could not confide in her, but had to stay on at the church to be counseled by a priest.

That evening on my way back home with Father Franklin cycling beside me, I was pretty nervous imagining what the scene at home would be like with my hot-tempered dad. My dad and I had a great relationship. He never denied me anything and was always there for me. He was proud of me as an athlete and always backed me. But still, I made sure to stay as close as possible to the main entrance of the house, just in case I had to run out if Dad got out of control that night.

Father Franklin called both my parents and the four of us sat down to talk. He started the conversation saying, "Your daughter has had a real experience with God and wants to dedicate her life to following Jesus, but she does not know where and when as of yet."

My dad was the first to speak up; I was very anxious as to what he was going to do or say. But instead, he said tenderly, "My child, your mother and I have given you whatever you wanted up to this day and if that is what you want in life, we will surely pray with you and give you whatever God wants for you."

My mom, in turn, added, "Look at all these trophies and cups on the shelves. They are not going to last, but what you do for Jesus will last for eternity." At that stage the three of us were huddled together crying in each others' arms. I wasn't even aware that Father Franklin had slipped out of the room.

So that night when I was filled with the Spirit I prayed, "Lord, you know I'm the kind of person who can't wait. I have to know things immediately, because I am so fast at everything. June sixth to July sixth is what I give you, Jesus. Please show me clearly what it is you want of me or I will continue on with my life as it is." I realized deep down, though, that I was a new person. The old had gone, as Paul writes (2 Cor. 5:17). There was a change; a new creation was beginning to develop in me. My friends noticed the difference; I praise God for that. They asked, "Theresa, what is it? Are you going on an international sports trip? Are you dating someone new? What is it? There's a newfound joy that you're radiating!"

Since I had been a child, I had enjoyed whistling. One evening while returning from the church on my bicycle, only a few days after explaining my intentions to my parents, I was whistling the tune of, "I have decided to follow Jesus, no turning back, no turning back. The cross before me, the world behind me … no turning back, no turning back." All of a sudden I stopped whistling and said, "Holy Spirit, tonight you must show me what it is that you want of me."

As I walked into the house, on the dining table I saw a little book that I had never seen before and I have no idea where it is now. I opened the book to the Table of Contents and then I called out to my mom, who was in the kitchen, "Mom, there's a book here with the names of 26 different congregations and the work they do. Today I'm going to cut 26 little slips of paper, number each of them, and fold them. Whichever number you pick up, I'm going to go and join that congregation and do the work they are doing."

Well, in my family I would be the first one to object to such foolishness, but I was very serious about this procedure. My mom stopped cooking and came into the bedroom. She called for my younger brothers, Steve and Gerald, to join us along with Dad. I remember Steve holding the slips of paper in his hand, all of us standing in a circle. Dad led us in prayer; Mom picked out slip number 12 and I looked it up. That number stood for the Loreto Congregation. I had no clue that this had to do with 'nuns,' but I felt the Holy Spirit burst into joy within me. I was excited. Little did I realize that I was going to join a convent and become a nun. I just wanted to follow Jesus. I turned to my mom and said, "Mom, tomorrow you go and meet the nuns and tell them your daughter is interested in joining them and working with them. Let me know what they say."

As usual I went about my hectic routine, but couldn't wait to get back home and hear from Mom about her meeting with the nuns. She knew these nuns well, as she sewed the uniforms for the Loreto students in Mumbai. Upon talking with Mom, I learned that the nuns were excited and wanted to meet with me. Now I was not ready for this and asked my mom why they wanted to meet me. It was a tug-of-war. My natural self was at war with my spirit. All my student life I had been raised in a convent school, but had done my best to avoid the nuns, since I was a tomboy. If I saw the nuns coming down the street, I'd cycle in the opposite direction from them. I could never see myself in a nun's garb. The nuns who taught us always had their eyes on three of my older sisters, hoping that one of them would have joined the convent.

I remember having so many questions for Mom. I did not know what to wear, if I was to go and meet the nuns. I wore mainly pantsuits for work and sports training, but now I had an interview to go to in a convent. I chose a nice yellowish dress which I thought was long enough, as it came to just above my knees—only to be told years later by Sister Ursula, "I still remember you walking into the convent in your minidress!"

On the way to the convent I kept saying to my mom, "If the nuns are stiff and starchy, even I'll keep my distance from them." But then my mom calmed my fears by asking me to just be myself and let the Holy Spirit who called me, guide me. Sister Evelyn was the Mother Superior. As we entered her office, Sister Ursula happened to be there. These Irish nuns made me feel at home with them right from the start. They were so pleasant and joyful that I forgot all my fears and relaxed. Those Irish eyes were truly smiling and I just couldn't wait to join these nuns. When they asked me when exactly I'd like to join them, I remember saying that I was ready right away. They said they'd have to inform the Provincial, Sister Patricia Hickey, in Kolkata, and then get back to me.

The Loreto nuns soon let me know that there was another postulant (candidate) in Mumbai by the name of Ubaldine (later to be called Sister Asha), who had come from Goa to join Loreto in Kolkata. If I was willing, we could travel together. My dad, of course, wanted to go with us to Kolkata and see where his daughter was going to spend the rest of her life. I asked the nuns to go ahead and book our train tickets, which they booked for the 6th of July 1977. This was exactly one month, to the day, from the date I had been born again and filled with the Holy Spirit. I had given Jesus just one month to show me what He wanted me to do and He was faithful, being an on-time God!

When you have an encounter with Jesus, you cannot put it into words. It's unique. You feel so full, from deep within, that words don't suffice, but tears of joy just come at times. To get to know God on that level is beautiful; it's wholesome. And that is what God was doing with me. I no longer was found on dance floors, neither ballroom dancing nor the overnight sessions at the discotheque. Everything changed. What God was doing in me was wonderful. I could say with Paul, "Whatever were gains to me I now consider loss ... that I may gain Christ and be found in him .... I want to know Christ—yes, to know the power of his resurrection and participation in his sufferings, becoming like him" (Phil. 3:7-10). Then I will know the truth of His glory in eternity. I thank God for that tremendous encounter with Christ that night.

Instead of my daredevil adventures and pleasure seeking, I sought to come closer to God. As much as I had challenged myself on the sports field, I challenged myself from then on to understand the things of heaven. All the pop songs I knew and the heroes in my life faded. The man in my life became the Man Christ Jesus. He took the place of everything else. Nothing else was important to me.

When you walk with Jesus and have that *dunamis* power inside you, you begin to realize that you are so small in your own eyes. Whatever you do has to be of the Lord, for we can never function without God. We are humbled when we see that God can use us—the scum of society. John the Baptist said, "He must increase; but I must decrease" (John 3:30, KJV). The more I die to self, the more I can see the power of God infuse me.

Many people were not informed as to why I was leaving college. My friends would have tried to stop me. My coach was a Sikh, a good athlete who was also faithful to his faith, never cutting his hair and wearing it under a turban. When I told the principal about joining the convent, I remember him saying, "Theresa, you are going for a noble cause. God bless you!" That was another Sikh speaking! That's how I could go, relieved of my responsibility. I told only my coach, the principal of my college, and my family the truth. No one else knew where I was going.

Even the company that I was working with did not know that I was going to join the convent. They had sponsored me as an athlete in exchange for my working afternoons for them—in between morning lectures and evening training. They offered me double my salary and unlimited perks, telling me I didn't even have to work. They would send my checks to my house. You say, "Hey, wait a minute. You're training for the Olympics and the next moment you're in the convent? Can anything good come out of a convent?" I sent my letter of resignation to the company from the convent.

I want you to know that Joseph stayed in a pit for a long time. (What does the PIT stand for? Nothing but 'prophet-in-training.') Then Joseph was put in Potiphar's jail, and that's where he learned to meet God face to face (Gen. 37-40). There's a waiting period. That's what Jesus said. He called them to "be with him" before sending them out (Mark 3:14). Did they go to Bible college or to seminary? No. That does not negate training, but when you have the Holy Spirit, He will direct your path. The critics scoffed, "Who are these unschooled, unlettered guys?" The scripture says, "They were astonished and took note that these men had been with Jesus" (Acts 3:13). See the difference! Being with Jesus gives you power, an anointing, and authority in the Spirit.

When you feel the heartbeat of the Master, there's no telling what you're going to do next. Get excited. He chose you from the foundations of the earth. He put His seal on you. He says, "Child, there's no knowing what I'm going to do through you. You're going to shake this world." Don't look back; just look ahead and know that He "who calls you is faithful, and he will do it" (1 Thess. 5:24).

Exactly a month later, the sixth of July, I found myself joining a Roman Catholic convent. You may be surprised, but I wasn't. When I was a girl in school I kept away from nuns. They were very fond of my family and thought very highly of us children. The nuns actually spoiled me too, but I always wanted to be an independent female. Mind you, I'm not so independent in many ways now. I depend totally on God.

See, God knows what He's doing. I gave up sports, gave up all the novels I used to read, gave up everything. I didn't miss it, now that I had a newfound joy. I had a satisfaction, a peace beyond compare. I started filling my mind, my heart, my spirit, with the Word of God. Then in the convent I learned to pray, to meditate, to wait on the Lord, so that one day He could use me—at the right time.

Those nuns were surprised when I joined the convent, but God knew what He was doing. I had given Him exactly one month to show me His perfect will and He did so in many clear unmistakable ways.

Leaving my home in Mumbai, I traveled by train with my father to Kolkata. I changed my name from Theresa to Helen, since another nun in the convent had the same first and last name as me.

Thus began the next unbelievable chapter of my life—unbelievable, yet true!

CHAPTER 3

IN THE SCHOOL OF THE SPIRIT

"Teach me your ways so I may know you" (Ex. 33:13).

I WALKED INTO THE CONVENT, NOT THE ONE I HAD BEEN educated through, but one that was run by the British and the Irish nuns in India. The Loreto congregation ran about 18 privately organized schools and colleges. The elite of India went to these institutions and paid high fees to do so. Soon I found myself very comfortable in that convent. I hadn't known what it was to wear a dress. I had always worn shorts, jogging suits, or trousers. Gradually, God was making a lady out of me. He was pruning me, working in my life.

I admired and appreciated everything about my new life. All that I lacked was the four-to-six hours of training that I used to put in every day. I found no more time for those things. My body craved the exercise and my muscles cramped, but God gave me the grace to put up with the physical pain of not exercising my body and led me to exercise my heart in things of higher reality instead. I thank God!

We have to deny ourselves. Everything does not come easily for us. If we're going to walk with Jesus, we have to learn to deny ourselves, take up our cross daily, and follow Him. (See Luke 9:23.) I admired the nuns who had dedicated their lives fully to God. They were all educated women. That particular order never admitted someone until they had at least a B.A. degree. I thank God that I had that, in order to join them. In former days they had admitted only foreigners, English or Irish women to head their schools and colleges. Gradually they had begun to accept educated Indians.

As a child I had never fallen sick. I could eat anything. But soon after joining the convent I entered a period of intense spiritual warfare involving my physical body. During the first six months of postulancy (probationary candidate status), I suffered three attacks of malaria, a bout of paratyphoid, and one of yellow fever. I became allergic to all foods except soup and dry toast. Anything else would make me break out in a rash and bright red hives. There were times when the nuns took me to the emergency room (ER) at the nearest hospital. I wouldn't be able to speak. I could hear them in the ER, but I couldn't speak. I was choking to that extent with allergies. I could hardly breathe at times. I was also allergic to sulfa and penicillin.

I tried homeopathic medicines. The doctor administered 149 allergy tests. Almost everything infected me—dust, mites, grass, vegetables, meats, etc. My blood pressure would drop so low the doctors wondered how I could survive. I used to drink three cups of coffee before 10 o'clock in the morning. Yet I had no strength. I would go to take a shower and black out, because I was so weak. My bruises were the only way I knew I had fallen. The attack of the enemy was so strong, yet deep down I had a great peace. I didn't care about what was happening. I had decided to follow Jesus and I was not turning back! When you don't have a clue what's wrong, you know who's wrong. The liar! The truth is that divine healing is available. I used to keep going, quoting the same scripture for 18 years, "God, I thank you that by your stripes, I'm healed!" (See Isa. 53:5.)

After six months as a postulant came two years of being a novice (candidate for membership in the religious congregation), which was a period of intense prayer and study of the religious lifestyle—Ignatian spirituality. While still in this training I was assigned to Loreto Entally, a school attached to the training center, to teach one or two courses.

One course was seventh grade Roman Catholic Catechism. Even though we had a textbook, I felt led by the Holy Spirit not to open it but to teach directly from the Bible. My class was always packed with students, though no roll was taken. (Roll was taken first period by the class teacher.) Most of the Loreto schools catered to children of India's elite, but this one served daughters of the pavement dwellers from the slums. It had 500 boarders plus day students, many from broken homes and problem backgrounds. Some were older—15-17 years old—because they had dropped behind in their studies. (This was the school Mother Teresa had left before moving into the slums to start the Missionaries of Charity congregation.) The language was English and I always started class with fun, games, and tricks.

One day as I prayed in the Spirit in the corridor on the way to class, God told me that evil spirits were in the classroom. I said, "Lord, I'm available; you're on!" I went in and kept my Bible on the table. When I stood in front of the class I told them we would not have games that day; we would stand up and pray instead. Karina McKenzie, age 17, spoke up, "No, tell us about Free Masonry first." I didn't know anything about that subject, but I said, "Karina, right now we're going to pray. When I'm done with this class, you can meet me outside and I'll tell you all you want to know about it." Not to be deterred, Karina continued, "But everyone in my family has gone to the wall, banged their heads, and died...."

I turned around and said, "Karina, stop it right now!" When she had opened her mouth, her demeanor and countenance had changed. The classroom had windows on each side and two doors into the corridor. She began speaking again in a rough gruff voice; actually some kind of hideous creature was speaking through her. The other 45 girls in the class were screaming. Some jumped out of the windows and some ran through the doors to the basketball courts and the fields. I had never understood the power of Satan, but I felt him and heard her screams that shook the whole area. Four huge buildings on the campus emptied immediately. Sister Teresa McKlingie, the principal, was the only one who had not left the building. She was a tall Irish nun, a beautiful person.

I should have been the first to leave, but I was filled with compassion. I went to Karina, standing in the middle of the room, and held her by the shoulders. "Karina," I commanded, "say 'Jesus.'" A voice said, "We are not here for Karina. It is you we want. When we have you, we have this whole organization." Only then was I convinced I was encountering demonic spirits. I said, "Satan, I'm not getting out of this place. You get out of here, in Jesus' name!" The atmosphere in the room had changed from extreme heat to ice cold air, like a morgue. When I took authority and bound Satan and his demons in Jesus' name, the cold air seemed to go out of Karina's body and through the window opposite her. The air in the room returned to normal.

Karina fell to the ground and started frothing at the mouth. The principal came to see if I was all right, since I was only a novice. That night no one wanted to go into the dorms. The nuns had sent Karina home and were praying and counseling with the other girls.

During my novitiate training my novice mistress called me to her office. I had a phone call from my brother Gerald to say that my mom had suffered a stroke and had lost the use of her right side. Somehow she was able to communicate to them that if I would come home and anoint her with oil and pray she would be healed. Up until then I had never prayed for anyone in this way, though I had seen my mom and dad do it many times. They were very strong in the Charismatic Movement in Mumbai. I agreed to go.

When I arrived I went to the kitchen for some oil. We didn't have olive oil in those days, just coconut oil. That would do. I took it to her bedside, anointed her, and prayed the prayer of faith. Immediately she was totally healed and started moving around to prepare food for us in the kitchen. Christ said, "If you have faith as small as a mustard seed, you can say to this mountain, 'Move from here to there,' and it will move. Nothing will be impossible for you" (Matt. 17:20). He also said, "Whatever you bind on earth will be bound in heaven, and whatever you loose on earth will be loosed in heaven" (Matt. 16:19). My mother's faith and mine, in agreement, had brought about a healing miracle. God was teaching me more about the power of prayer.

Years later I was the boarding mistress at Loreto Entally, with 110 girls from the fifth to seventh grade under my care. We had about 500 boarders altogether. I lived there and had a matron to assist with the dormitory duties and clothes of the boarders. The students nicknamed her 'Poison,' because of her strictness. They were wild and would do anything to get her attention. She had one key to open the shower and turn on the water. She turned on the water, the students got themselves wet, then she turned off the water and they soaped themselves. Then she'd start the water again for them to rinse themselves. One Sunday afternoon two girls came into the bath area. One was inside the bath with a metal pail, and ran out of water. The second girl dropped a pail on the first one's head, slitting it open. She was bleeding profusely so we rushed her to the emergency room. I had come to expect the unexpected.

Another night the 110 boarders all stood in the passageway for evening prayers. We were on the third floor with big open windows on one side, no mesh, no bars. Down the corridor and outside the dorm was my room. Curfew was imposed from about 8:30 or 9:00 p.m. with no talking allowed until the 7:30 a.m. breakfast. As I was praying, the Holy Spirit dropped a student's name in my mind—Celestina Nathan. (I can truly say God never gives me the whole gist of anything at one time. Only as I obey, do I get the next step.) So I said, "Celestina Nathan, come out here." She took medication for epileptic seizures.

Then I went on to say, “Matron, you are off duty completely. Girls, if anything should happen tonight, please do not knock on Matron’s door. Tonight, should Celestina get one of her seizures, come and wake me up. I know exactly how to handle her. All I have to do is throw her out one of those windows and go back to bed.” I didn’t know what this was all about, but found out later that she was going to pretend to have a seizure to keep the matron awake half the night. She knew how to bring it on to get attention. She would sleep all day the following day, but Matron had to get up and work. From that night on, Celestina never had another seizure.

I was so madly in love with Jesus, I could just walk by the bedsides of sick girls in the dorm and the fever would leave them. It was not my power that healed, but the power of God in me. Nun’s training had moments of fun and humor too. As a novice I enjoyed helping the students every evening with sports. In a nun’s garb with a veil on my head, I wore knee-length shorts underneath so I could shoot baskets with them and do high jumps. I could clear a bar higher than my height. The small kids were so amused. When the Provincial, Sister Patricia, came visiting, they told her that Sister Helen had ‘flied.’

After morning mass, the nuns would break silence at breakfast. One day, all 50 nuns were cackling like chickens. We had one motherhouse for six schools, one B.A. college, and a teachers’ training center in Kolkata. I asked them what they were talking about. They wanted to know where I had been the previous night when they had all come out of the building. Apparently the building had shaken when an earthquake struck and they all had run out, frightened. I had a room on the third floor with a big metal bed. I had wondered how my bed had gotten to the middle of the floor when I had gotten up that morning. I thought maybe I had moved it and just forgot. I couldn’t remember. After hearing their story, I realized it had moved with the tremor. I had a clear conscience and could sleep through anything.

During this whole time, four or five years, I struggled with my health. When I became a principal the enemy would accuse me, "You are a cheat. You have not revealed the truth of your health to the authorities. You are not fit to lead." He was attacking my mind.

I traveled to the Bangalore area in the south of India to attend a 40-day conference for heads of schools at Kristu Jyothi College run by the Salesian Fathers. There, near the elevator one day, I met a Christian brother who was known for the gift of healing. God had used him to pray for many people and he offered to pray for me. I was still shy and didn't want people laying hands on me, so I just asked him to pray when he had the time. He said, "I will fast and pray for you for 24 hours, with my companion. Give me your name and address. We'll write and tell you what God tells us."

I went on with the conference and forgot about him. After I returned to Kolkata I received a letter from this man, written after he had prayed for me for 24 hours, detailing all I had gone through with my health. He listed my symptoms, even knew that I often felt like I was losing consciousness due to allergies and severe migraine headaches. He said there were cells in my brain that had a vacuum and that only powerful prayer could help me. He said I had suffered a shock while still in my mother's womb.

To challenge the devil's taunts, I took the letter to Sister Stella Lahiry, the Provincial of the Loreto nuns in India, at the motherhouse. She was pretty shocked and anxious for what I had gone through, receiving this letter. "This brother should have mailed this to me," she said as she rose to comfort me. I told her I was not anxious, but I wanted her to know that I had really suffered these symptoms since I had joined the convent. "Do you still want me to be heading one of your institutions?" I asked.

She replied, "Even if you were a vegetable, Sister Helen, we would want you." She proposed calling in Father Jim Borst and

Sister Usha, well-known, powerful, Charismatic prayer warriors who had been instrumental in bringing the Charismatic Movement to India in the 1970s.

"No, I don't need anyone to fly in," I said. "God can heal me wherever I am. If there are cells in my brain that have a vacuum, then there is more room for the Holy Spirit."

"Sister Helen, if you ever need me, I'm here for you," Sister Stella promised. Like Joseph I had favor with God and favor with people wherever I went. I continued as a nun and the attacks continued too—no turning back, no turning back....

On Wednesday evenings after school ended, I would cut across the Irish Christian brother's premises next door and visit the local government hospital in Asansol to pray for the sick and minister to them. Every time I made an attempt to reach out to the sick, I had an intense attack of indigestion, vomiting until my feet touched the steps of the hospital. The enemy would whisper to me, "You don't want to do what you've got to do; you have dozens of books to mark." Or, "even Jesus sent people out two by two, and here you are going on your own. You know nothing about medical science and you're trying to play physician." Or, "your body is not healed and you are trying to go pray for the sick." Those food allergies and headaches were Satan's attempt to stop me from doing God's work. Though my body seemed weak, my spirit was yielded to the Holy Spirit. I allowed Him to tell me what to do.

The moment I stepped onto the hospital steps, all I had was a burden for the suffering. I forgot myself. The hospital was poorly kept without proper accommodations for the patients. Patients lay on the floors of the corridors and a stench pervaded. I couldn't take strong smells in the natural, but I hardly noticed when I was on God's mission. No one stopped me from ministering to the sick. The authorities were excited to see me. At times the doctors would come with the patient's file and ask me what exactly was wrong with the patient.

One time I sat on the side of the bed of a very elderly man with a towel draped around his head, though not like a Sikh. He was in tears and his body was shaking. In the natural I didn't understand his Bhojpuri dialect, but when I held his hand and began praying in the Spirit, it seemed as if he were replying to what I was saying in tongues. He had been seriously ill for a very long time in that hospital and I was crying with him. Before long a sweet countenance appeared on his face. How refreshing to see the release from the pain and distress he had gone through! He got out of bed, put on his sandals, took his belongings and was discharged that evening with no traces of the disease he had suffered for years. God had touched him. I realized that the Holy Spirit had enabled me to give him the salvation message in his own dialect.

In the same hospital as I came in one day, the doctors told me about a burn case. A woman had attempted suicide by dumping kerosene on herself and lighting a match. She was burned over 85 percent of her body. They told me her flesh was rotting and smelled very bad, so I shouldn't go near her. They had her under a white mosquito net and every part of her body that was visible was burned. She was of the Muslim faith with four children and a drunken husband. Led of the Holy Spirit, I knelt at her bedside at an angle so that she could see my face and I could see hers. I did not notice the horrible smell. I spoke to her in Hindi about the love of God. As I ministered the Lord spoke through me and reminded her of her past—as a girl being raised in a convent school. She had read from the Bible and had learned how Christ sacrificed himself on Good Friday to become the Savior of the world—and how He rose again after three days and ascended to intercede for us for eternity. Then I asked her, "Would you like to give your life to Christ? It's never too late. Jesus loves you immensely and He wants to set you free from pain and agony and forgive your sins. He doesn't want you to carry the guilt of all these years." She had tried to commit suicide three times.

Her lips and face were so badly burned that she could not speak. The only things not burned that I could see were the index fingers on each hand. I gently took hold of her right index finger under the net. "I need to know if you have received Jesus in your heart. Can you give me a sign?" She was staring into space and had not moved her eyelids at all, but tears started flowing from her eyes. With much pain, she slowly lifted her burned arm in front of her chest and touched her two index fingers together in the shape of a cross. Then she moved her arms back again. By this she showed me she had invited the crucified Lord into her life as her Savior. I told her I would return the following day and read to her from the Hindi Bible. The next day I couldn't make it to the hospital, but I knew in my spirit that she had gone to be with the Lord in the wee hours of the morning. I thank God that He took me to her to bring her into His kingdom.

From Kolkata I went to be the principal of the high school at Darjeeling. I traveled by train and bus. It was my first visit to the mountains of northern India. When I got out of the bus, something fell from one of the trees onto my back—a shower of snow. I was so surprised, since I had not encountered real snow before. I had seen it only on TV and in movies. The same evening, late, the school lost power due to a snowstorm. We had no hot water, no heaters, just blankets to sleep under. I slept so soundly. The next morning after mass everyone was talking at the same time. "What's wrong?" I asked.

They looked at me strangely and said, "What's wrong with you? Didn't you hear what happened in the night?" A crazy man had broken the glass doors and come into the convent. He had destroyed pictures, porcelain items, and paintings in the parlors. Sister Francis Michael had rung the gong 60 times to get help, but I had not heard a sound. I slept through it all.

I had been transferred to this school because of ethnic tension there between the English-medium section on the hill and the Nepali-medium section closer to the valley. The two schools never mingled for anything, though they had occupied the same premises for years. The English snobs would not cooperate. Sister Christine, principal of the Nepali section, and I decided to interact and do things together. Every Saturday, we formed 'clubs,' encouraging the hundreds of students to interact. We conducted races on the hills and cross-country events. We led exercises and the staff of the two schools had to mingle too. Eventually we broke years of the English looking down on the Nepali, even though both schools were run by the same organization.

Several years later I was sent to be the principal at the Loreto High School in Shillong, in the northeast hills of India. I was suffering from a sore throat and took a small 25-milligram tablet about 7:30 p.m., not realizing I was allergic to the sulfa in it. The same night I started choking. My body swelled up to twice its size and turned red and itchy all over. I prayed and cried, walking up and down in my room. I didn't want to disturb anyone; no one else could drive. I read a whole book to distract myself from tearing at my flesh. In the morning I didn't go to mass or to breakfast. My superior, Sister Elizabeth D'Souza, came to check, thinking I had overslept.

She realized something was terribly wrong. She did not realize I could not talk. The doctor came by 11:00 a.m., but I had been suffering all night and the injection he gave me only provided a little relief. He told me to sleep, but 15 minutes later, I was back where I had started. This continued until 3:00 p.m., with the terrible itching. By that evening I was found unconscious and rushed to the emergency room. I could hear, but not speak. The doctor was angry, saying to Sister Elizabeth, "Why didn't you bring her coffin as well?"

For the next week my hands and feet were tied to the bed in the intensive care unit (ICU). Each time the Hindu doctors came in, they said, "She is suffering so much, but she has such peace." When we cannot pray, the Holy Spirit intercedes for us with wordless groans—according to the will of God (Rom. 8:26-27). I had such moments of intimacy with Christ, though I could not speak. Just one tablet did that. When I got out of the ICU after one week, I learned that Jesus never fails. He had a job for me to do.

Every morning an elderly Nepalese gentleman, whom we called 'Mali,' came to work as the head gardener for the school and community. His wife and children lived in Nepal. I didn't know where Mali lived. He was the first worker to arrive in the morning and the last to leave at night. Every morning he brought flowers into the office with a big smile. I loved coming early to let the children sit on my lap or play games on the floor. This was a nursery to tenth grade day school, not a boarding school.

For two days Mali the gardener did not show up. This was highly unusual. I went to the kitchen and asked Sister Pauline if she had seen him. She called the 27 domestic staff that lived together down the hill and asked if they knew where he was. After the second day, I sent someone to locate his home in the town, to see if he was sick or needed anything. They found he had been sharing a room in town with other men. We had had a snowfall, and they thought he had stayed at the convent those two days. He usually walked the few miles to and from the school.

I called the police and gave them a missing person report. The police came and I went with them to check the hospitals. We went to first one, then another, then the third big hospital. We couldn't find his name anywhere in their records. I was standing by the police Jeep under a tree, when God gave me a word of knowledge. I told them, "Mali is in this hospital." They said, "No, we went from bed to bed with two of your men. He's not here. It's not possible, Sister."

I said, "OK, follow me." I went to the back of the hospital and saw a big building with a garage-type entrance on the premises. The hospital superintendent told me that that was not a ward, but a morgue! I told him Mali was in there. He lay dead on the stone-cold floor. Someone clearing the snow had picked up his corpse and brought it to the morgue, not registering any name. He had apparently fallen in the snow and died on the street. I sent word to his family in Nepal and his relatives in Shillong.

Because of my people skills, my superiors put me in charge of the Leadership Training Service (LTS) which worked with the Khasi Students' Union (KSU) in Shillong. The town had political tension, and an Indian was needed, not a foreigner. Every evening I would leave the convent and walk the streets, burdened for the youth of the Khasi tribe. I met a girl named Bloody Mary. She looked very sad. Other young people's names were Chalice, Malice, Callous, and Solar Eclipse (a boy born during an eclipse). They indulged in drinking, drugs, sexual immorality, and promiscuity. The wives were the heads of families and the laborers; the men were often weak and lazy. If a wife put her husband's sandals outside the door, it meant, "I'm done with you."

The Salesian Fathers, who ran the youth center in town, conducted a weekend seminar on sex education. Sixty youngsters attended on Friday, 80 on Saturday morning, 100 that night, and 120 on Sunday. Afterward I handed out evaluation sheets, asking them whether such a seminar should be conducted again. The Khasi and Nepali young people in the town did not get along, but this had brought them together. Other questions asked if the sessions had benefitted them and invited suggestions for future seminars.

One answer read, "Simply fantastic. We are happy to know that someone is doing something for the Khasi youth in this town." It was signed, Bull Lyndoh. He was the president of the KSU, and a person the police wanted to arrest. They held him responsible for past riots, but he always hid in caves in the nearby hills. The priests were surprised he had been at the seminar, and even more surprised that he had sent that response.

Curfews were common, as were bombings in the market, riots, and closed shutters. One day I got locked in one of the stores when fighting broke out between the police and the KSU youth. Another day, as I sat in my office, two young men brought a message from Bull Lyndoh. It said that in one hour, bombs would be thrown into the area. I was to evacuate the children and the staff for protection. I asked, "When exactly will these bombs be thrown?" They replied, "As soon as we return and give the word." I explained that it was impossible to send the little children home; their parents would be working. I started witnessing to these young men and the Holy Spirit came on me. I told them about eternal life and asked them if they were ready to face God; where would they end up?

Both of them started crying like babies. They gave their lives to Christ a few hours later and never went back to the gang. No bombs came that day; God had different plans!

One day God gave me a vision of a little girl in Bangladesh. She was poorly dressed in a short skirt and blouse, and had straight black hair and olive skin. The Spirit was telling me to meet her, but I had no passport, so how was I to go to her? My friend and superior, Anne-Marie Brown, agreed to make a road trip with me from Shillong to the northeast hill area that bordered Bangladesh. One of the parents from the school loaned us a car filled with gas and a Hindu driver to take us on the 13-hour journey. We rode down the cliffs to the border area and then asked the driver to stop. He assumed we were just going to relieve ourselves in the bushes. I said to Anne-Marie, "You don't need your passport; come with me." The border guards watched as we approached and they walked toward us. I can understand Bengali, but I do not speak much of it. I only knew a little, but I used it, saying to the immigration officer, "How about tea and snacks? We've had a long journey."

He replied, "Sure, join us." I whispered to Anne-Marie to follow him while I ducked under the long pole across the road, used to stop trucks for inspection. I went toward the bushes and suddenly there appeared the very girl I had seen in my vision. She was saying to me, "A man who called himself Jesus told me to come and be here. He said you would come." She was speaking in the Bangladeshi dialect. For 15 minutes the Holy Spirit enabled me to share with her about Christ. Afterward I went back out of the bushes, got in the car, and we returned the 13 hours to Shillong. I have no idea what has happened to her, but I followed the leading of the Spirit and I am confident He is taking care of the rest.

Sister Helen (Theresa) as the principal of the Loreto Convent High School, Darjeeling.

CHAPTER 4

MOTHER TERESA AT LORETO CONVENT

"Not as I will, but as you will" (Matt. 26:39).

AFTER TWO YEARS OF NOVITIATE TRAINING, I DID A BACHELOR of Arts degree in English at the University of Kolkata. In 1983, while still a junior nun (six-year period between novitiate and final vows), I was walking along a path one Sunday morning in Asansol, West Bengal. I had brought the boarders back from the church where we had attended mass. It would be another hour or so before lunch, so I had decided to walk along a path with two huge fish ponds on either side.

All of a sudden the power of God fell all over me. I felt like Isaiah in the throne room, "Woe is me, a man of unclean lips" (Isa. 6:5), and yet God enabled me to come into His presence. I was not worthy. Through my tears and praying in the Spirit, I cried out, "Jesus, what am I doing in this elite educational institution, catering to the rich of the world, when there are 13 million lepers in my country whom society has rejected? I'm so content with the way things are going, but is there anything else you want of me? Is it time for me to work with the lepers? I've dedicated my whole life to you. Show me what it is that you want of me."

I had a hunger to go out and work among the lepers. Loreto was a posh congregation with elite students whose parents were real VIPs in India. The schools were established mainly for the British and other business people, who had maids and servants in their homes. They had chauffeurs to drive their children to school, to bring hot lunches for them, and to wait for them until school finished. Irish and English nuns ran the Loreto schools and colleges and they were very careful not to take too many Indians into the organization, unless they were highly qualified and educated. I'm not saying I was highly qualified; previously I had my brains in my toes. But when the Holy Spirit came, the brains moved into the right place. God put things in order.

When I was a school girl I was never one of the top ten. I just barely passed as all my time was spent out on the sports field. Weekends I was competing for different organizations, clubs, and events. I made it through, only because I was very attentive in class when I was there. I listened closely, but I didn't do my homework as such. When the Holy Spirit came, what a change! My grades went to a 4.0 grade point average, because of the anointing and determination.

So in 1983 I wondered what I was doing giving my life to the service of the wealthy while most of my countrymen were living below the poverty line. I found myself talking to God at all times about this. One, two, three hours was not enough. I needed to be in communion with God day and night. I hungered for God. And God touched my soul in ways that were unknown to most human beings. My name, 'Theresa,' means 'harvester.' He's called me to bring in the end-time harvest. I remember walking to my classroom to give a lecture and having the Holy Spirit fall heavily upon me in the corridor. There were times I would say, "God, I cannot contain you. You're doing something in my life, but humanly speaking, I cannot be seen by the public in this state. I'm too fragile; I'll break."

I used to hide myself in my room or in the washroom and cry tears of joy, because God was doing something to my spirit. He was changing me, sanctifying me. I was drinking of His Spirit, bathing in Him. I had such a hunger for God and the things of the Spirit. I had been baptized in the Spirit before becoming a nun, but we never sang or spoke in tongues in chapel. It was only when I was alone that the power of God would just fall all over me.

My eyes were swollen from the tears; my face was blotchy red from the desperate pleading with the Lord that Sunday morning. I felt I had to make a change, had to get out of that particular place of service. I prayed, "God, plant me where you know I can be the best use to you and to humanity. I want to be serving, maybe lepers. God, I don't mind being a leper. Take me and use me. Not my will, but let yours be done." Since I was interested in working with lepers, it was my intention to find a way to approach Mother Teresa and ask her if there was a place for me with the Missionaries of Charity, where I could dedicate the rest of my life to work with her lepers. I had observed one such establishment as a teenager.

Mother Teresa, who later won the Nobel Peace Prize, had started out as a Loreto nun, at the same institution I was then involved with. She had served as a Loreto nun for the first 20 years of her religious life, until God showed her another vision and moved her to start her own congregation of the Missionaries of Charity. Around the world you will find the Missionaries of Charity working for the destitute, the dying, the suffering, the lepers, the poor, the blind, the lame, the maimed—all those whom society rejects.

I was in my room that Sunday afternoon, busy on some projects for the school, tears running out of my eyes. I was praying in the Spirit, unaware that Mother Teresa had arrived at the convent. (There were about 12 of us in the community.) She had been traveling in one of the local trains from Kolkata to one of the leper colonies she had established. The train happened to stop in Asansol, West Bengal, near enough for her to visit the convent. Mother Teresa felt led of the Spirit to get off the train, even though she had not reached her destination. She decided to come and visit our convent.

As a teenager Mother Teresa had come from Yugoslavia with another nun by the name of Sister Magdalene. Mother did not know that Sister Magda, who happened to be in our convent at that time, was at death's door, but God had brought Mother Teresa to visit her friend that Sunday afternoon.

Everyone was having kind of a Sunday nap; it's very hot in India. When they heard that Mother Teresa had come, the whole community rushed to visit her and to make sure to have her shadow sort of fall on them. They were overjoyed at seeing this great saint of God and sharing fellowship with her. They hailed from England, Ireland, Australia, Yugoslavia, and India. They could not wait to get Mother's attention for themselves that day. Naturally, we all would do that.

She went and visited her friend Magda and prayed for her. The power of God fell on Mother Teresa in that room. Suddenly she looked around and said to the other nuns, "There is one more young nun I have not met. Where is she?" Everyone was excited and answered that all were present. Mother Teresa kept turning and asking, stressing three times, "There is one more...." Mind you, she had never met the young nun before. They had never known each other, although this young sister was in awe of Mother Teresa, had read about her, had seen her on TV, and was mentally aping her as a child. That young nun was someone by the name of Sister Helen (the name I had chosen when I had entered the convent).

Mother Teresa was looking for me though she did not know me. My superior, an English nun by the name of Mary Ross, came to my door. She said, "Believe it or not, Mother Teresa would like to meet with you personally." I said, "I'll be there." Before I could even leave my room, there stood Mother Teresa at my door. See how minutely God thinks about you? He takes time to answer the cry of your heart. She took my hand in hers, rubbing the back of my hand very gently, and looking straight into my eyes. She gave me this message: "My child, the time has not yet come for you to leave the convent. When the time comes, God himself will reveal His plan to you. For right now, stay where you are."

So I continued, in obedience, to work at the school. What a confirmation! It was as if God were saying, "Don't work for the lepers as yet. Stay where you are. This is your waiting period. At the right time God will use you among the lepers or wherever He has planned...."

Why was there need for an all-holy, Almighty God, who knew the cries of my heart, to respond to me in a way that I would accept—a way that I could understand, in human terms, His specific direction to me? This same God desires to communicate with you at your level. If you are open, He comes to you. He is omnipresent—everywhere present. You don't have to wait to go to a mountain peak to have that special meeting with God. You don't have to wait to shut yourself in your washroom so no one can see the tears running down your face. Enjoy God where you are; learn to hear the voice of the Holy Spirit. Look into the face of God and receive grace upon grace, cleansing, refreshing, renewal, from His loving hand. Even in the parking lot, you can have a moment of intimacy with the Lord Jesus Christ.

If anyone has any doubts about Mother Teresa's anointing, you're mistaken. She knew Jesus. The Bible teaches us that you will know them by their fruit. (See Luke 6:44.) You could sense the fruit of the Holy Spirit in that woman. I'm speaking to you as a first-hand reference, because since the experience I'm describing, I have walked the streets of Kolkata with her. I knew her personally. She would tell the big-moneyed people, "Don't thank me; go thank Jesus." Now someone who's constantly pointing people to Jesus, that's the fruit of the Spirit. They have an anointing—fruit that abides. (See John 15:16.) Many of us tend to look at the rosary beads, scapulas, and medals and make wrong judgments, but God looks at the heart of a person.

For 13½ years I waited in the convent, seeing miracles, healings, and deliverances of people possessed by demons. I heard myself speak in languages I had never learned. I gave medical advice and shared the Good News in hospitals, when I did not even have a clue about medical science. I'm talking about living and moving and having our being in God, as we learn to yield to His Spirit. As Paul said, "He is not far from any one of us" (Acts 17:28).

CHAPTER 5

NEAR DROWNING AS A NUN

Let Christ "be exalted in my body, whether by life or by death" (Phil. 1:20).

I STAYED ON AT LORETO AND PREPARED TO MAKE MY FINAL VOWS in February of 1986. In a Roman Catholic congregation, every nun makes three vows for life. At the end of a nine-year period of intense religious training, of my own free will, I was to make a vow of poverty. This meant I would not hold any wealth in my name, that I would not have a private bank account. The second vow, chastity, meant that I would not get married. Of my own free will I chose to follow Christ and be a totally committed and dedicated person, living a chaste, pure, and holy life. The last vow, obedience, meant that I would follow the given constitutions of that organization and that I would obey my local superiors and anyone placed above me. Above all I would obey Christ and do His will for my life.

Now no one is forced to make these vows. A person makes them of her own free choice. But both parties see if you're ready for that. The congregation and the person come together to dialogue and see if you're fit for that kind of a commitment.

So near the end of 1985 I made a 30-day retreat in a place called Goa, on the west coast of India. It used to be a Portuguese colony and boasts beautiful beaches, similar to Hawaii. Every day I spent 10-15 hours with God, communing with Him. I would sit in the cleft of a rock and meditate on His Word. I was hungry for God with a deep spiritual hunger. I thirsted for God! I would sit on the rocks with my feet in the water and be lost in God. I didn't know what it was to crave for bread or food. It felt like a honeymoon period between me and God, but even that wasn't enough. I found myself waking up at 2:00 a.m., going out, sitting on the top of a hill, and just crying tears of joy. I wanted to come closer to God, and He honored the desire of my heart. He gave me such fullness.

Every afternoon I went to the ocean to swim. The Retreat House was perched atop the hill and down below was a private beach with the vast ocean in view. Being an athlete, I found a great thrill in nature and the ocean was my birthplace, as it were. One beautiful day my friend and I went to that secluded beach. My friend was taller than me. Her name is Shanti, meaning 'peace' in the Indian language. She was a social worker, a committed person, who would be giving the rest of her life to God and to the poor. She sat on the shore with her Bible, meditating on the Scriptures.

That day I swam way out into the ocean. Shanti was lost in the Word, not really paying attention to me. In that ocean I hit a rock, but she didn't know what was happening to me. My left knee was bleeding and my right leg got a cramp. All of a sudden I felt like I was drowning. I couldn't swim anymore, though I was a good swimmer. The current took me to the bottom of the ocean—deep under water.

I felt excited because I was so close to God. I said, "God, I thank you. My life has been totally committed to you ever since I met Jesus. Here I am. You've come for me; I'm so grateful. You didn't wait for me to backslide, but you came for me at this opportune moment...."

But God was not finished with me. He brought me up to the surface with only my arm out of the water. Then He took me back to the bottom. I panicked then. There was no more gloryland; I knew I was in the depths and already unconscious. From my subconscious I prayed, "God, save me! Save me for the sake of my parents." Though I had committed my life and had turned my back on family and the things of the world, I found myself begging God, screaming to Him to rescue me. Why? When my brother, the oldest in the family, was 18 years old, he had drowned in that very ocean. That death had left such a tremendous vacuum in our lives, that we couldn't forget what had happened to him. For years we dealt with that. For a long time my mother would get sick and even become unconscious, remembering that incident.

So I prayed, "God, don't do this to Mom and Dad again. Don't do this to the family." For the third time I was thrown to the bottom of the ocean and for the third time I came up again. It was like being sent to the furnace—the fire—and you come out purified and whole. This third time was different and I cried, "God if there's anything good that's going to come out of my life, save me! If not, take me, here I am."

I think that's what God wants from you and me. He wants us to reach that point of transparency with Him when we say, "God, if there is anything good in me, use me. You have wanted nothing but my wellbeing. God keep me as yours. If not, cleanse me, purify me, break me, mold me, fill me, and use me for your work." Let that be your prayer.

Shanti, who was sitting on the shore, was busy with God, but she told me this story afterwards. Suddenly, down the hill on the right side, came two men dressed in slacks and jackets. Now you don't find guys dressed like that on the beaches in India, or on beaches anywhere else in the world, for that matter. She saw them coming because from where she sat, she could view a wide expanse of the shore. They came and stood beside her and said, "Do you realize that your friend out there is drowning?" Shanti had never swum in her life! Moreover she was terrified of the water. She liked to sit on the shore, but had never ever stepped into the water in her life. The next thing she realized, the men beside her were gone. She turned around, shocked that they were nowhere in sight. Now you can see people in broad daylight if they make a move, but there were no footprints on the sand—

nothing! They were there no more. The next she knew, she was way out in the ocean offering me her hand. The two of us sailed back, like professional swimmers, back to the shore.

We stood on the shore and cried our hearts out. We had seen God perform a miracle—one woman who had nearly drowned and another, who didn't know what it was to ever step into the water, had rescued her. To God be the glory! As the Scripture says, "Where can I go from your Spirit? Where can I flee from your presence? If I go up to the heavens, you are there; if I make my bed in the depths, you are there. If I rise on the wings of the dawn, if I settle on the far side of the sea, even there your hand will guide me, your right hand will hold me fast" (Psa. 139:7-10).

Do not believe anyone who tries to infiltrate your mind with secular humanism or New Age thinking that tells you there is no God. He is there! He is here—wherever His people are. Are you hungry and thirsty for Him? He will offer you the wellsprings of life, so that you in turn can be a fountain of life to others.

I can be a convincing witness because I know that He who lived, died, and rose from the dead continues to live on in every circumstance of my life. He is always in control of every situation. I plead with you. Let go of the reins of your life; give them to the Holy Spirit. Don't cling to them; cling to Him. Let God show you the path you are to take.

After finishing the retreat I traveled from Goa to Mumbai, prior to making my final vows. During nine years of training, I had made only this one 30-day retreat. I felt so full of life and in tune with God. I found a letter waiting for me from my Provincial Stella Lahiry (head of the Loreto nuns' organization). She was requesting me to transfer from the hill stations of Shimla to Kolkata—to the Mother House—as House Mistress. My responsibility was to oversee all the guests and the maintenance of several buildings that housed 60 nuns, the high school, the degree college, and the B.Ed. Teachers' Training Center. I was a very young nun and very nervous at that stage, because I recalled that that position had always been given to nuns with much experience, and prior to me, always foreigners. I didn't think I could live up to my predecessors' standards. That afternoon I was to visit my parents. Just the thought of having to take on this particular position at the convent had given me a temperature.

My mom knew something was up. I opened up to her and she asked in return, "What role does the Holy Spirit play in all of this? You just came out of a 30-day retreat and you're not willing to trust God for this too?" That put me back on track. I accepted my transfer and as far as I can recall, those were some of the best years of my time as a nun. When you walk with God one step at a time, you cannot go wrong!

Within the next two months, in February 1986, I found myself going in for my final vows. My vows were made to God, not to a congregation, not to the Pope, though I respected the Pope very highly and believed he was a man of God. I also believed in Mother Teresa and her ministry. Thousands of others like them are committed to the cause of Christ. Looking at him and others from a human point of view, we're bound to judge them, but we have no right to judge anyone. There is only one Judge, and that is Christ.

After becoming a fully-professed nun in the Roman Catholic Church, I continued to walk in the Spirit. Four times every day, I would recite the Psalms, meditating on the Word of God. I worked 16-18 hours a day as I moved from position to position, from headmistress of huge institutions—schools and colleges with very high standards—to being the principal of the Lucknow Intermediate College. I was only 23 years old when I was first made a school principal.

Most of the time I had people on the faculty who were more highly qualified than me, but my qualification was that I had the Holy Spirit, the Giver of all wisdom, all understanding, and all knowledge. That's why the leaders—priests, nuns, police—could look and see a person who had wisdom beyond her years. It was not me; it was the One in me who was at work. I do not want the glory to go to me; the glory has to go to God! It's not you—it is the One working in you. "Jesus Christ is the same yesterday and today and forever" (Heb. 13:8). Give the glory to Him and no other.

CHAPTER 6

FINAL YEARS IN THE CONVENT

"Give glory to God" (Luke 17:18, KJV).

IN THE LATE 1980s, I SERVED AS PRINCIPAL OF LORETO Dharamtala in Kolkata. I had also been appointed as the Convener for 60 of the Indian Certification of Secondary Education (ICSE) Schools Examination Board. It so happened that I had to put a stop to the exams, because one of the schools was responsible for the leaking of the exam questions to certain students. Immediately this decision became a big issue with the politicians and the media all getting involved. My secretaries at the school were nervous, even about answering the phone. Press reporters had been calling and harassing them. It was turning into a nightmare for everyone.

The ICSE Board and some of us decided to postpone these exams so that we could get the next set of questions ready and make sure they were sealed and leakproof. The exam papers were held in Delhi.

At that stage, the politicians tried to 'make hay while the sun shone.' Some were not in favor of Christian schools and wanted to give the Christians a bad name. One day while I was sitting in my office, the senior class chemistry teacher came running in. Her husband, who worked in a government position in town, had informed her that a huge mob was coming with slogans and banners to attack me. Politicians were leading the mob. So he requested his wife to get me out of the school and hide me. My life was in danger because I had stood my ground in wanting the exams to be fair play for all.

I decided not to run away. I told her I had done nothing wrong. I thank God that a month prior to joining the convent I had been born again and filled with the Holy Spirit. And "the Spirit God gave us does not make us timid, but gives us power, love and self-discipline" (2 Tim. 1:7). I told the staff members and faculty over the intercom, "Don't be anxious. Make sure to keep all students inside the classrooms and not let a single one out. Man your classrooms; stay with your kids."

Then I told the security at the gate to let the mob into the courtyard. The crowd rushed in and stood on the basketball court where we had student assembly every morning. I took my usual place in front on a small platform. They were shouting and yelling. I looked at them with so much love and compassion, because I knew they had been misled.

All of a sudden there was pin-drop silence. I began to speak and asked them to give me just two minutes of their time. Then I told them the truth about the reason for postponing the citywide exams. I started by saying, "When I'm done speaking, I won't be running away. I will be right here. You can do with me what you have decided is best." I thought to myself, "If God is for us, who can be against us?" (Rom. 8:31).

The Holy Spirit had spoken through me with such love and compassion for them, that the whole atmosphere had changed. The people who were there decided to turn and attack the politicians, who had intentionally misrepresented the facts to them. Their representative said to me, "Sister, you can go ahead and do as you have planned for us. We students will stand by your decisions." God knows how to scatter our enemies and let truth alone triumph.

One day, after transferring to Loreto Lucknow, I went to the convent kitchen to get a glass of juice and noticed that the cook, Kundan, was really long-faced for some reason. I asked him what the reason was. He said his 17-year-old son, Ashok, was dying because his heart valves were not working right.

On the next college holiday I followed Kundan to his home. Open sewage ditches ran on either side of the road and I had a weak stomach. His family of six children lived in a little hut. The boy lay on a cot with no mattress, sheets, or pillow. He was skin and bones, about the size of a ten-year-old. The cot was placed under a tree that had no leaves. The poor in India are very hospitable, so I agreed to accept some water. Kundan poured the water from a rusty container into a dirty chipped cup. I could see the creepy crawlies in that cup, but the Word says believers will drink poison and not be harmed by it (Mark 16:18). My health was better after that. We took the boy to the hospital for tests. At the end of the day I had the boy admitted into a hospital for heart patients. The doctors who admitted him knew me because their daughters were in my college.

That same night, as I was heating a cup of soup in the microwave, Kundan came running into the dining room. "My son is dying; they have taken all the tubes out." I told him not to worry, because his son was in the best hospital and the doctors had promised me they would do their best. He insisted, "But the doctors have taken out the tubes and said, 'Let him die in peace.'"

I asked Kundan to go ahead on his bicycle and I would follow. A junior nun, named Elizabeth Chatterjee, and I ran into the street and hailed a van. As we got in I noticed six men dressed in white and carrying guns already sitting inside. They were cursing their leader, saying, "We will be late for our appointment to kill this fellow." In English I thanked and blessed the leader for stopping for us. I pretended not to understand Hindi, but I could hear their plans.

At the hospital, Kundan's wife was complaining. Indians worship more than 33 million gods. She was cursing and saying angrily, "If only that nun had not messed up our lives. My son will die because of her. I had him for 17 years and my gods took care of him. He didn't die. My idols kept him alive. But now she has brought him here and he's dying." She and her neighbors stood outside the hospital building yelling and screaming. I patted her on the shoulder and tried to comfort her: I told her, "Your son will not die; he will live."

The power was off in the hospital compound, except for a few dim bulbs in the ER. I pleaded with the doctors to please go back and reattach the tubes. I knew nothing about medical science, but I had the assurance that Ashok would live. The doctors shook their heads, knowing medically it was impossible for Ashok to live. They said, "You're right, you know nothing about medicine. Why do you want him to suffer? He's dying! Let him die in peace. You will just be causing discomfort." I persisted in asking, like the importunate widow in the story in the Gospels (Luke 18:2-5). I also told the doctors that the boy would not die. The rude doctor left the office for the day with his briefcase. The other doctor took his stethoscope and asked me to follow him. He plugged everything back as before and we watched the monitor screen. I realized the boy's situation was really critical.

Greater is the One who is in us than the one who is in the world. (See 1 John 4:4.) Jesus is the Resurrection and the Life. (See John 11:25.) Why trust in tubes and machines? Focus on God, not your situation. I began to thank God and pray in the Spirit for the life of Kundan's son.

Kundan was crying, "Sister, if you pray for my son he will be healed." I said, "No, it's not my hands; it's Jesus who heals. I can't do anything for your son but Jesus can. Kundan, you've tried all your gods…"

"But Sister, if you pray…"

"Jesus is not just one more god. You've got to believe in Him. If you believe in Him, He'll do it for you. Do you believe in Jesus?"

I closed my eyes, lifted my hands and started crying and praying in the Holy Spirit. Suddenly Kundan exclaimed, "Jesus, I believe!" He cried out to God. I don't know how long we prayed, lost in God. It was about 12:00 midnight—God's time not the devil's. The room seemed to shake and a bright light entered (See Acts 16:25-26). Ashok sat up on the edge of the bed, tubes no more in his body. He said, "Daddy, get me my clothes; let's go home. I'm healed." We began praising God. I told him, "Stop being an idol worshiper; put your trust in the one true God." To this day, the son takes no medications and is alive and well, working as a tailor in Lucknow.

Life was going very well until one day I was invited to be on the team for a Charismatic convention being organized by the Redemptorist Fathers in Lucknow. I was a very shy, reserved, and private person, though I had been a famous athlete and had no problem when it came to talking to thousands of people. The Lord used me to speak on truths I had never even heard before. I found my messages were anointed by the Holy Spirit. Why? Because I did not speak in my own strength or abilities. I hungered for God even as I witnessed to others. God wants to use you in your place of work, your school, or at home. The Holy Spirit is going to prompt you. Go, believing that you are meant to be used by God, and you will do great things for the Kingdom.

I was attending a Charismatic convention and I said half to myself and half to God, "I'm not going to go up in front and raise my hands, clapping and dancing. I'm not that kind of person; I'm just going to work on the team with others. I am the type who can cry in my room, but not in front of everyone else." So I was sitting way behind the rest of the team with my arms folded, intending to be an onlooker, an observer.

In no time this preacher, the president of the convention, said to everyone, "Today maybe the Lord is going to use you to give a word of knowledge or a message to someone else. Be that channel, be that vessel, that instrument that God desires to use. Remain open and let God do what He's come to do. Give the glory to God."

I could see people slain in the Spirit, being baptized in the Holy Spirit, and speaking in tongues. I had spoken in tongues in my room, but never in public. All of a sudden the leader said, "Go and stand beside someone and pray with that person." I grumbled in my spirit, "Why did he have to go and say something like that? I have no intentions of budging from here." I was literally feeling in my pockets for the keys to the car to get out of there. I wasn't interested in hanging around anymore in this church.

The next thing I knew, much against my will, I found myself getting up and moving a few pews ahead. I noticed a young man sitting by himself and I went to him and asked if I could pray with him. I stood next to this 17-year-old boy. My hands were no longer stuck to my body. I was crying and praising God. I turned and took the hand of this young man and started praying for him. I didn't know what I was saying, but to my surprise he began to cry. I asked him, "Why are you crying? Have I said anything to offend you?" He said, "No. The very words you just spoke to me were the words spoken by another man before you."

I said, "Which other man? I never saw any other man near you."

"The man in a long white gown," he answered.

I noted that the priests that day were not wearing their white cassocks, so I asked, "What did he look like?"

"He was unusually tall, with golden hair, surrounded by light."

I said, "Did you know that man?"

The boy answered, "No, I'm a Hindu boy; my father is a Hindu priest. I was just walking along the pavement. I heard the music and I was inquisitive, so I came into this gathering. Then He spoke to me and told me His name was Jesus."

"What else did He say to you?"

"The same things you said to me."

"But I don't know what I said to you. Can you tell me?"

"He told me He was going to use me to take His message to people all over the world."

I asked again, "Do you believe in Him?"

"I do," he said, "I do believe in Jesus!"

I thank God that I moved in the Spirit that day and not in the flesh. God uses human vessels in this day and age. God desires to use you. Don't keep it for yourself. Share the glory of God; share God's message. Be the message, not just the messenger. Live the message with your life. On that day I couldn't help but let all the starchiness leave me for good. From that day I was once again a free person in Christ. There I was in the front, refilled again and slain in the Spirit—speaking and singing in tongues and dancing in the Spirit—a Roman Catholic nun with her garb on.

Give the glory to God! Joel 2:28-32 is being fulfilled in our times. God is pouring His Spirit on all flesh in these end times, irrespective of shapes and sizes, colors and denominations, creeds and castes—ALL flesh, not just on a select few. Jesus came for the lost. The Holy Spirit comes to take hold of the lost and win them for Jesus. But He needs you; believe it! God wants to use you.

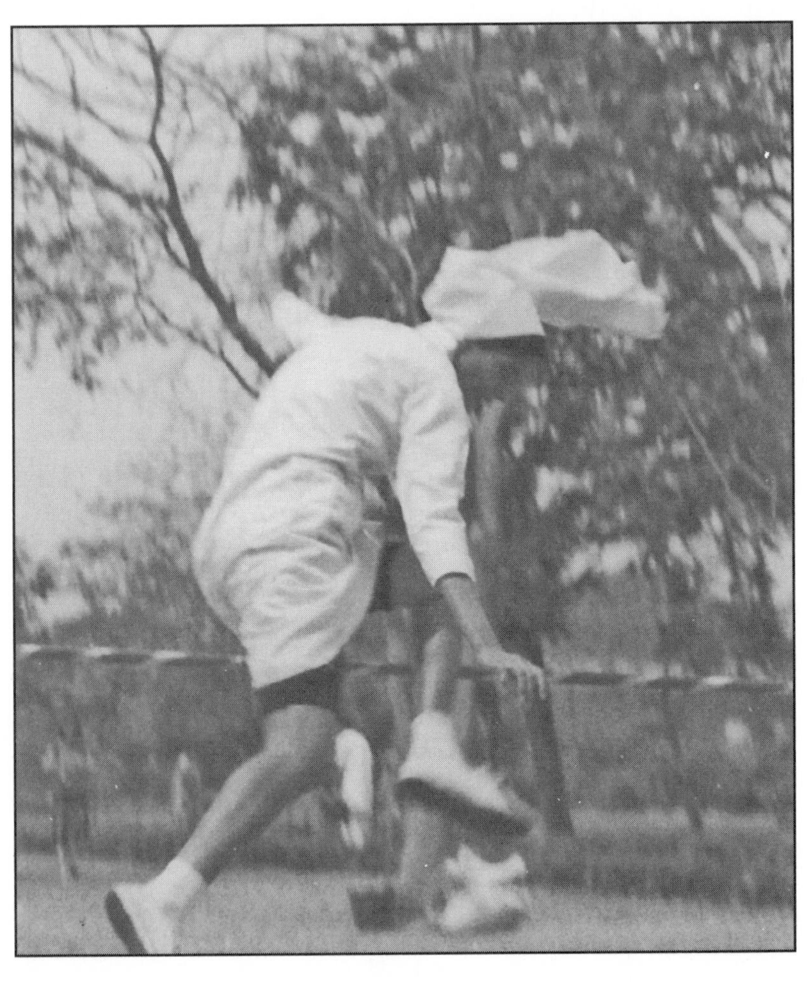

High jumping in nun's garb with the students.

CHAPTER 7

THE VISION TO GO AND PREACH

"So are my ways higher than your ways" (Isa. 55:9).

THROUGHOUT THE YEARS OF 1991 AND EARLY 1992, I BEGAN to see the Holy Spirit work more and more in my life. I received a touch of faith such that I could hardly keep up with what God was doing. He would prompt me to say things to people, sort of like a fortune teller, only I wasn't one in the way the world considers such. I was giving people a word of knowledge or prophecy (1 Cor. 12:8) concerning their circumstances. I said, "Lord, who am I?" But I had to be humble because I had told God to do with me whatever He willed. I was ready to be used of God and I realized He was using me more as I remained open to His leading.

In January of 1991, I first began to see myself standing on platforms around the world. I was no longer dressed as a nun. The first time this vision came to me, that fact seemed strange. Since 1985 the nuns in my congregation had been free to go about in secular clothing. I was one of those nuns, however, who did not believe in changing my garb, for the simple reason that I was a very young nun put in positions that were too high. When I went out to meetings, I didn't want gentlemen asking me out on a date. I needed others to know that I was a committed person, a person who believed in walking with Christ, so I stuck to my religious dress.

At first God began talking to me about this vision only when I was in prayer, then more often, whether I was eating, driving, walking down the corridor, or taking an interview in the college office. It never left me, but I would not believe it.

In the recurring vision, I was standing behind a pulpit with my Bible and preaching to millions—not just hundreds of thousands—millions, literally a sea of people. They all wore different kinds of headgear, colorful clothing, and various garbs. Their faces were different colors; I knew they were Hindus, Muslims, Sikhs, and even Westerners—people of all nationalities and religions. The Holy Spirit was beginning to do things in my life and in the lives of all these people. As I was preaching the Word, it seemed to come up out of my belly and straight out of my mouth. I noticed people being touched by the Spirit, convicted, baptized, or slain in the Spirit. I saw people getting up from wheelchairs and praising God. I noticed the blind seeing, the deaf hearing, the dumb speaking, and lepers getting cleansed.

In my vision, not one person was concentrating on me. They were all lost in Jesus. And then I heard these words very clearly in my spirit. God said, "My child, I will take you to an international Bible college. I will ground you in the Scriptures and I will bring you back to the land of many gods to tell the people of the one true God!" Which group in Asia, which country has the most gods? India worships over 33 million gods; they need to know the one true God. Who will take the message to them?

When I saw this vision and heard God's words I began to panic and I cried, "God I'm so human. I've seen you do innumerable miracles in my life and I know you are at work in my life, but how can this vision be possible?" I was looking at myself as a nun. God was showing me myself as a preacher, as a messenger of the Good News, a minister of the Word. I failed to see it because I kept looking at myself.

It was only when Peter looked at himself in the midst of the wind and the waves that he began to sink into the waters. (See Matt. 14:30.) As long as he had his eyes on Jesus, he could walk on the waters. That's a sign for you and me. We must stop looking at ourselves. We can do nothing on our own, but as we look at God and flow with what He is doing, we will see great and mighty things.

My younger sister, Anita, who continued to live in Mumbai after marriage, was blessed with a son named Shaun. While I was visiting at her home, I could sense that my sister was going through hell on earth with her husband. God started revealing to me so much that Anita had not shared with anyone else. When I checked things out a little, I was surprised. That same day I called my brother Gerald, who happened to be in Delhi, and told him that I was sending mother and child to Delhi.

The next morning I took Anita and Shaun with me to the other side of Mumbai, where I was going to catch up with the pastors of New Life Church. God had been speaking to me about leaving the convent and I had many questions. Cutting across a very broad street in downtown Mumbai, I was carrying Shaun and was dressed as a nun with a veil on my head and the whole garb. I had made it across the street, but Anita had not yet gotten across because of the traffic. It was a bright morning and no one else was on the pavement where I was walking with Shaun. Suddenly an unusually tall man, with a tan complexion and dressed in a dazzling white kurta pyjama (Indian man's outfit), stood right in front of me. He asked, "Whose child is this?"

I thought to myself, "If I say it's my child, he won't believe me since I'm a nun. If I say it's my sister's child, he may not believe because the child is so fair and my sister has a tan complexion." So, like Jesus, answering a question with a question, I responded, "Sir, why are you asking?"

He turned to me and urged, "You take care of this child. He is a gift of God."

My sister joined me and I asked, "Did you see that man?"

"What man?"

"He was here just now; where did he go? He just spoke to me." No way he could have gotten very far, if human.... It was a confirmation from God that I should do everything in my power to rescue my sister and nephew.

The next day they boarded a flight for Delhi. Later Anita got divorced and left India with Shaun. Today she is remarried to a godly man whom she met while at Bible college in London. She and Karim, a Muslim convert and a scientist, have not only Shaun but also Nathan, their own son as well. Karim gave his life to Jesus at the age of seven. Later he pastored a church. Today Karim works as a scientist and they are happily settled in London. Years after that incident, while visiting a Christian bookstore in America, I came across a wooden plaque with the name Shaun, meaning 'gift of God.'

I started having the same vision of me as a preacher over and over; every time I was in prayer it would come back. I had no discernment in those days, though the words kept ringing in my spirit. I was fighting it and saying, "Get behind me, Satan. I don't need to be fooled by something like this." I had never heard of a nun preaching. I struggled with this call for a year and a half.

Even when God would say, "My child, it's me who's calling you," I would resist. Friend, don't try to take God's vision and put it into your mold. I would tell God, "This can't be from you because I don't even own a passport. How can you take me to an international Bible college? I can't leave the country without a passport." God is Spirit and you too have a human spirit. When it is yielded to the Holy Spirit, you will do exploits. The more you decrease and the more the Spirit of God in you increases, you'll be amazed to see what He can do. Believe it or not, God kept confirming this word to me over and over again.

Wanting to discern God's will, I went to an elderly Jesuit priest, Father Rui Cordeiro. Jesuits spend something like 14 years in study, specializing in the discerning of spirits. He was my mentor and confessor while I was a nun. At this time I was principal of the Loreto intermediate college in Lucknow. I was responsible for 60 faculty members and 33 domestic staff. When I told the priest about what I had been seeing and hearing, I didn't know whether to call it a vision or a dream. He sat with his head down, just listening. I said, "Father, I've had this experience. What do you make of it?"

When he lifted his head, he had tears in his eyes. He answered, "Sister, it is Jesus whom you have followed all along. Don't you think this is Jesus calling you? It's the same Jesus who's calling you to follow Him. He wants you to leave the convent. The time has come for you; go and do His will outside now. The Holy Spirit wants to use you in these end times. Get up, leave the convent, and do what He is telling you to do."

Then I started crying too. I felt like young Samuel going to Eli, but I was shocked at his unexpected response. I thought, "This priest is too old. He's lost it." I started praying for his conversion. I went back to my room and cried, desperately calling out to God for a sign, with my Bible lying closed in my lap. I didn't think the priest was discerning rightly for me. He told me to go, but where was I to go? I didn't know where God wanted me or where the Bible college was.

I went to my superior, Sister Monica Alfonso, and said, "If there's any more literature you want to send me from now on, I'm not interested in attending any more seminars or conferences. If there's anything geared to the Scriptures, I'm game for it. Other than that, leave it out of my view."

One night I was crying in my room. We had set times for prayer in the community, but night was the time for my individual prayer, alone. I was crying out, "God, this vision and this dream, if it is from you I'm pleading with you to give me a sign. If it's not from you, I rebuke it in Jesus' name and I ask you to take it away. Please take it away! Give me the freedom to be who I am. You've always heard all my prayers; why not this one?" It was after midnight. The more I cried out, the more I felt I was getting nowhere.

The Mother Superior of our community of nuns, Elizabeth D'Souza, came to my door with a message: "Christine, your sister from England, is on the phone for you." I went downstairs to take the call. Christine knows eight languages and used to be an international businesswoman. She used to sell ships, a big-time business. She also had worked for the United Nations and had been based in Germany. In 1990 the Holy Spirit took hold of her and under Reinhard Bonnke's ministry she was brought back to Christ. She had given up her career and sold everything she owned to come to England to study. God had led her to study with the Elim Pentecostal Church college in London. Today she is a pastor in France.

When I took the phone my sister said, "The Holy Spirit just threw me out of bed and He wants me to tell you that the time has come for you to leave the convent. He's calling you to take His word to the ends of the earth."

None of my family knew a thing about this vision. I pretended that her words made no sense to me. I acted irritated, saying, "What are you talking about? You just said that you were sleeping. That was only a dream. Go back to bed."

Christine cried on the phone. She pleaded for 45 minutes and begged me to listen to the Holy Spirit. Nothing doing! I was as stubborn as a mule and wouldn't budge. I told her it was impossible. "I don't even have a clue about what you are saying. I don't want anyone in my family to influence me to leave the convent." I thought maybe the enemy was using her. I didn't know what kind of a cult she was in or whatever. I didn't even want to know!

I had been trying to take the vision more seriously, even to researching the Bible about it. I felt that if it was from God, it would work out some way. But after Christine called me, I said to God, "I didn't ask you to give my family the sign. I said, 'Give me the sign.'"

A few weeks later, in the middle of the night, I was still crying to God for a sign. The same sister called again, pleading and crying and praying on the phone for 45-60 minutes with the same message for me. I told her, "I have never known of a preaching nun. I don't think this is of the Lord. I'm not going to listen to you. I'm a lecturer; I lecture in colleges. I don't preach. I could even give it to you in writing. If anyone leaves this convent, it will never be me." Hearing all my excuses, she hung up.

I decided to "put out a fleece" like Gideon in Judges 6. I told God, "OK, let the nuns ask me to leave and I'll know." I felt this would never happen in a million years. I was their favorite; they all loved me. I was happy and content being a nun. I acted as though I was carrying the world on my shoulders. Besides that, I was having one of those moments of feeling indispensable. Who could the nuns get to fit into my shoes right now? I prayed, "God, why are you speaking to my sister? Speak directly to me." Again she called with the same words, "Listen, why is God doing this to me? Why can't He just turn your world upside down and show you that He is calling you? I want to convince you that you are no longer meant to be where you are. You have done that well up to now, but if you continue there, you are stepping out of God's perfect plan for you. Stop doing your own will and go. You've committed your whole life to Christ. Walk into the unknown; that is faith."

I thought I had been born again and filled with the Holy Spirit in 1977. I had always been a woman who had faith, but you know, we offer ourselves to God and then gradually, unknowingly, we take back what we have offered. We sneak around the altar and we make it our own. We give the glory to ourselves. It is possible to backslide. So I was in a huff, with the Lord giving me this vision and dream, and my sister nagging me. I actually was saying in my heart, subconsciously, "My will, not yours."

Here was this huge institution and I as a young nun was heading it up. It had about 1,700 students preparing for university. It was one of the most elite colleges in the country. I had everything; I had built a kingdom of my own. Here I was, reigning in all my glory. I started out working for God and ended up working for self. We all make such mistakes. The devil is sneaky and subtle so we don't realize what we are doing.

How could I leave the convent? Most of my family is abroad; out of eight children remaining since my oldest brother had died, six had left India. Only my brother Gerald and I remained in the country. Besides, I did not know where to go or who could advise me. I had many reasonable excuses, valid questions, but God wasn't asking me to try to fulfill His vision through the natural. I was not making room for the supernatural.

A few days later this same sister called again, late at night. London is five hours behind India. This was the fourth time she had called. I was upset with her—ready to give her a piece of my mind—even though the younger one must always respect the older one in the family, or anyone older than you! Before I could speak, Christine said, "This is the last time we are calling you." I said, "Who is 'we'?" She was attached to the Kensington Temple Bible College in London. She replied, "The students are praying and fasting for you. One of them has heard from the Lord. God said that we should leave you alone. He will get your attention and get you out of the convent by May of 1992, albeit much against your will."

So I turned and said, "OK, let the Pope excommunicate me!" I laughed on the phone, much like Sarah laughed when told that she would become pregnant. (See Gen. 18:12.) I told her, "Don't call me again if it's anything to do with this, because it shouldn't worry you."

March came and I was getting upset with God for not talking directly to me. On the 26th, my college closed for a holiday. I decided to go talk to another missionary, a Redemptorist priest who had come to town to conduct a week of missions' services at the cathedral in Lucknow. My family knew him well, though I personally didn't, having left home years earlier. I thought, "He is a stranger; I can share with him. I will go and confide in him, because he's not as old as the other priest. This one might have a little more spiritual sense and can guide me accurately."

While on my way to meet with him, riding my kinetic Honda scooter, I met with a freak accident. I used to be called the 'flying nun,' wearing the nun's garb, my veil, red helmet, and riding a red and white bike. I always got easy access to streets. The police knew me and would always salute when I came by, knowing I was the principal of the college. This time the policeman waved me past other vehicles, so I rode quickly, my veil flying straight back behind me. Suddenly the car in front of me stopped to avoid a man jaywalking across the road. This was the main street in Lucknow. I zoomed right into the back of the car, not seeing what was going on. After hitting the car, I was flung to the other side of the road, landing on and breaking my right shoulder.

As a teenager I used to play basketball during off season. I could shoot a basket and make it from almost any angle. My opponents could not tell where I was going to shoot from next. After the accident, I could not do that anymore.

I was unconscious, so the police took me to the hospital. The nuns told me about it afterwards. I was brought back that evening with my shoulder in a cast, my hand tied to my chest. I could not wear the nun's garb or veil. The nuns draped me with a wrap-around skirt and a blouse sleeve hanging over my right shoulder.

I could not continue fighting God anymore. With the right frame of mind, the scales seemed to fall off my eyes that night. I prayed, "Lord, I've been running away from you and your perfect will for my life. For 13½ years you wanted me in the convent, but the time has come for me to heed the vision you've sent the last year and a half. I'll leave and go preach the Good News. I'm not going to run anymore. God, I'm coming. Tell me where you want me."

The next day I was sitting in my office, seeing everyone work so beautifully. It was a posh college where you have increased standards and so many staff members—three secretaries and four accountants in my office alone. Everything was still moving like clockwork. I said to God, “The sign of a broken shoulder will not do. You want me out of the convent? Give me a better sign than this. You’ve got to show me more clearly that it is you calling me. I’m not leaving.” When you are a well-known person, you have bone specialists coming to your doorstep. You have everyone running at your beck and call. The college was still functioning, I was still at the top, and people thought I was great. I got carried away by the glory they were giving me.

A few days later, when it happened to be a day off for the college, I was in the office catching up with some paperwork. I was in lots of pain. A gentleman walked in with a bouquet of flowers, saying, “Sister, these are for you. Get well soon.”

On a few occasions prior to this, I had noticed this gentleman on our premises talking to people in the next office. I had told them, “Get rid of this man; do not entertain him in our college.” Diana D’Souza, our senior secretary, had told me that all our five phone lines had been disconnected and this man had used his influence to get them all working again. I had replied, “For all you know, this man himself could have disconnected the lines.”

Another time, I had noticed this man in our office trying to get close to the secretaries, who were laypersons not nuns. I had sent for Diana and again instructed her, “Get rid of that man. Don’t have any dealings with him. We don’t need his help in the college.” She said that when there had been riots outside the college, he had protected us by sending police to guard our gates. I insisted, “We don’t need his assistance. We can get this kind of help ourselves.”

A third time, I had been interviewing parents and students who wanted to be accepted into the college, by set appointments only. That man had barged into my office and said, “Sister, can you give me two minutes of your time? I have something very urgent to talk to you about.” He had worn a gray safari suit with a wireless phone sticking out of his pocket. He was trying to look very impressive and serious. I hadn't even asked him to sit down, but he continued on, "Sister, we've just learned that your school admission forms are being printed and sold in the market. If you could give me one of your forms, I can check and bust this whole racket." I said, "Sir, I can guarantee you that that is not possible, because no one has access to our forms but me. I don't need your services." The abrupt manner of this man had put me on my guard.

So on this day when I was alone in the college, this same man walked in with flowers. I had placed papers from drawers on the table to sort through documents, get well cards from the students, and other correspondence. I was obviously in a lot of pain with my shoulder. He said, "I know a very good bone specialist. You must be in a lot of pain, Sister."

I replied rather sharply, "Everything has been taken care of for me!" At that point the phone down the corridor rang and I went to answer it, leaving him in the office. When I finished the call and returned to my office, the man had disappeared.

A few days later, on Good Friday, my superior came knocking on my door, saying that the police commissioner had come to meet with me. Puzzled, I followed her down to the parlor where we received visitors. Police officers stood around. To my surprise, this same man whom the Spirit had been prompting me about now stood with them. His head was shaved and his hands cuffed. I was told they had put him on a truck and paraded him around town as a con-man of high caliber. He had conned the police, posing as Indira Gandhi's personal bodyguard. He had conned several schools and colleges as well as British Airways. He had been trying to get our forms to sell them—acceptance forms with my initials on them. They had brought him to the convent because they had found him forging my signature. When the police had searched his room, he had revolvers in his possession, as well as cards and other documents from my table. He had posed as a friend of mine, claiming he could get a certain policeman's daughter into our college. The girl did not meet Loreto's high standards and had not passed the admission test, so the police had arrested him.

That Good Friday on which the man had been brought in handcuffed, had been my Good Friday too. Though I had always taken so much precaution, that one day I had ignored the promptings of the Holy Spirit, and had gone to answer the phone. After confirming to the police that this man had indeed been in my office with access to my papers, I left the room.

I entered the dark night of my soul. That afternoon as I stood in the huge cathedral for the Good Friday service, I was crying like a child, and not knowing why. The crucifix was 45 feet high. I looked at the figure of Christ and said, "Jesus, I have walked out of your will. Take me. Give me just one more chance to come back to you and I'll vow my life to you. I'll walk in your ways. I do not want to know what's in store for me. I only want you, Jesus. Nothing else matters. I do not want to see the whole picture anymore; I want to be a woman who will walk in faith even when I cannot see." There was no sign of God in view.

I left the service and started vomiting violently. I cried the whole night. I couldn't even keep water down. I felt emotionally confused and mentally disturbed. I had thought I was "Miss Perfect," and now I was a broken woman. I could not even say the word *Jesus*. I thought God's grace had left me! I couldn't express myself to anyone.

As a community of nuns we met four times a day to pray together. Someone would read from the Psalter. I knew the book of Psalms, I knew the Gospels, but not one scripture verse came to my mind. I could not pray. I could not even believe that there was a God. I felt like an atheist who says, "There is no God." Believe it or not, the 'Hound of Heaven' had stopped coming. The Spirit is like the 'Hound of Heaven,' about which Francis Thompson speaks in his poem. He comes and comes, but one day He stops coming. Don't wait for that moment—when God seems to desert us or seems to vomit us out of himself because we are lukewarm. If we are not totally committed to Christ and His ministry we are lost.

On Saturday I sat in my office emotionally broken; I who had counseled so many people. Now I could not even control my own emotions or mental state, much less the situation. The establishment was far too big. I was someone who was a perfectionist, who had everything working like clockwork. If there was a function, I had it planned to the last detail months in advance. I never did things at the last minute. But that day I felt like I could not handle anything. I was crying, something I seldom do unless I am in prayer. I called my younger brother, Gerald, who was vacationing in Goa with his family and my parents for the Easter holidays. I said to him, "Gerald, I need to talk to a member of the family. Can you come?"

Easter Sunday morning at 9:00 he flew into Lucknow. I thank God that I have a family so closely knit that we stand by each other no matter what. He's four years younger than me, but he took hold of the situation: "You need a break. You have been working too hard in your 16-hour workaholic days. I've come to take you home for a three-month holiday. After that you decide what you want. If God is calling you, I'm going to help you. Go wherever God is leading you, but I'm not going to allow you to go until you have taken a break. That is what you need. You have exhausted yourself for nearly 15 years and you have failed to see God's vision for you."

I told him, "It's not a holiday that I need. For 13½ years God wanted me in the convent, ever since I was truly born again and filled with the Holy Spirit. For the last year and a half, though, I have been fighting God and fooling myself. He's been calling me through visions and dreams; and I've not been listening."

"Well, take a break," he insisted. "Come home and relax. Come home and do nothing. After three months, if you wish to be a partner with me in the business, I will give you half of all my earnings to date. You don't have to put in anything." I couldn't believe my ears. Gerald was an international businessman, one of the main agents in India for Pier One Imports to the United States. He exported fashion garments and jewelry. He was very successful. Continuing, he said, "Maria and I need a business partner, a family partner."

But I was adamant, "No, not me! It's not money, not business, not holidays—it's Jesus! I've already made up my mind. I'm following Jesus. I don't care how He wants it; I don't care where He's calling me."

That grace God is giving to you right now, asking you to surrender, don't take it for granted. It's God's grace. If your tears are running, don't take them for granted. He's touching your soul; He's speaking to your spirit, saying, "Child, I'm talking to you. You're the one; I want you. I want to do great and mighty things through you. Don't just look at other people's lives. There are greater things that I want to do through you." You better wake up. Whatever your age, if you are God's child, there is work God wants to do through you as you are yoked with Him.

Don't change what God has put in your spirit, no matter how good something else looks. The enemy will say, "You can send all your dollars to the mission field. You can help Bible colleges and print evangelism literature, even print Bibles." Don't listen to that voice; do what God is calling you to do. No matter how small it looks in your own eyes, you are privileged to be called by God. Get excited that He is calling you.

I went home that same day at 6:00 in the evening. The moment I left the convent and stepped onto the plane, I immediately felt that same peace that I had had within me for 13½ years, after being baptized in the Spirit. That same Holy Spirit came and took root in my life again. I don't want to say that the convent was bad for me. It was the ideal place for me for that season of time, but no more. The time had come for me to step out into the unknown and take hold of that for which God had called me.

My brother took me to his home in Delhi before taking me to my parents, because he knew I just needed to be away from everyone else to recover. I spent two days there, just crying and thanking God for having rescued me again from my own wretchedness and for bringing me back into His perfect will.

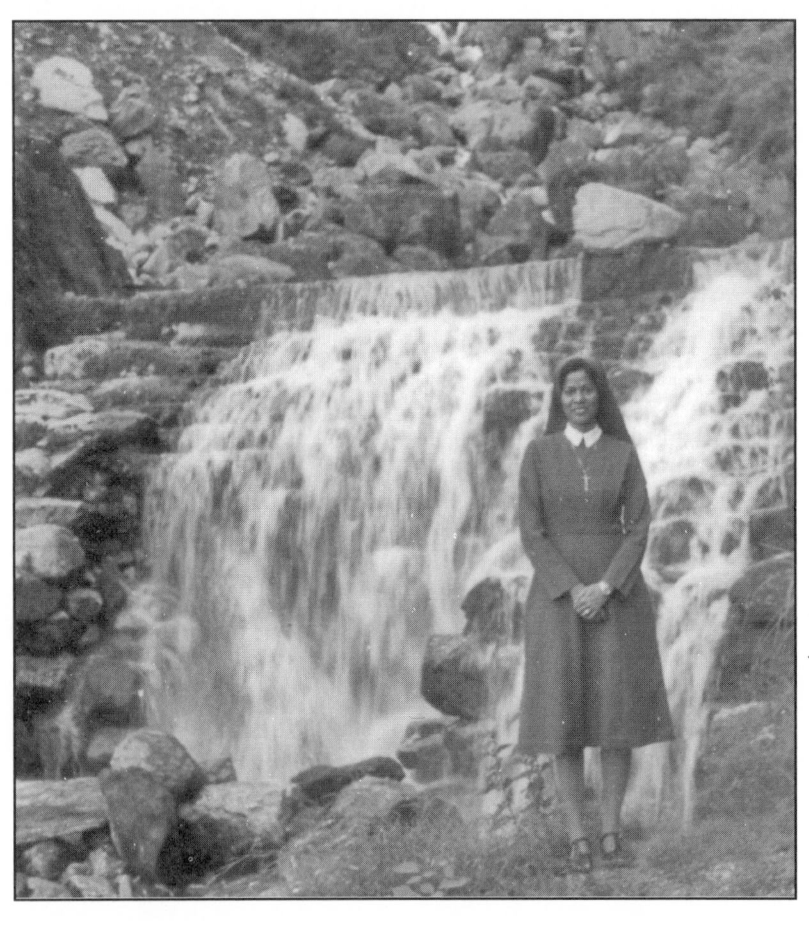

Sister Helen (Theresa) in the hill stations of Shillong.

CHAPTER 8

MY FIRST PASSPORT

"The steps of a good man are ordered by the Lord" (Psa. 37:23, KJV).

MY BROTHER GERALD WANTED ME TO GO HOME WITH him, but I told him I didn't want to stay in Delhi with the maids and staff in his well-to-do home. I needed to get away and hear from God—to be alone—though my right shoulder was broken. I agreed to go to my brother's holiday house in Mumbai. Mom's house was within walking distance. To that point I had never cooked a meal, even for myself! Sports had been my life, so I had never learned to cook. And in the convent we had many cooks and bearers.

I knew I needed to go to Mumbai to get a passport. Previously I had never wanted one, because my family members had gone abroad to study at universities in France, England, Germany, and Switzerland. They had been overseas umpteen times and most of them had settled there; some now in Canada. No one wanted to come back and stay in India. Since God had told me I would go to an international Bible college, He would have to make a way. I prayed, "I know you are a way-maker God. I'm not going to argue; I'm not going to doubt you. Just take me and do with me what you want; I'm ready."

One day I was sitting in the holiday house with my Bible when the Holy Spirit spoke clearly to me, "Go to the passport office." Now that office was in a part of the city quite far away from where I was staying. I would have to take a taxi to midtown. The new passport officer had clamped down on all agencies. Some had been forging passports. It had been announced on

TV, radio, and in the newspapers that the offices were closed and no passports would be issued for the next four months. I knew that, but I obeyed the Spirit and took a taxi to the passport office anyway.

The whole area was cordoned off. I had never been in that area before. There were quite a few policemen in the area guarding thick rope barriers. Frantic enraged people whose passports and tickets were inside the building milled about. Some had missed flights, missed schedules, and had so much money invested in those things. They were ready to strangle those officials inside. I got out of the taxi and with my broken shoulder, walked right in through that entire crowd. It seemed as if the police could not see me. No one stopped me.

I went directly up to the sixth floor, to the end of the corridor, even though I had never been in this building before. I proceeded to knock on the last door, the one the Holy Spirit led me to. Getting no answer, I opened the door myself. A group of high-ranking officials were having a meeting. I walked up to one gentleman and said, "Sir, I'm here for my passport."

He answered, saying, "Madam, for the next four months no passports will be issued from this office. Good morning and thank you." (In other words, "Get lost.") So I put my proverbial tail between my legs and said, "Thank you, Sir." I took the taxi back home and didn't get insulted or feel bad or argue with God. I didn't complain that I had felt like a fool. I said, "Thank you Lord, that I heard from you and I did what you told me."

A few days later I heard the same voice in my spirit telling me to go back to the passport office. I did not argue with God, but just got in a taxi. When I got there it was a similar scene as before. I went up the same flights of stairs, walked to the end of the corridor, knocked on the same door, and spoke to the same gentleman, saying, "Sir, I'm here for a passport." I hadn't filled out any forms, had no documents, nothing! The gentleman I spoke to proceeded to ring the bell on his table and in walked his personal assistant. He asked this man to assist me and help me with procuring my passport. I was even informed by the official that I would not have to come back to that office anymore and that my passport would be at my doorstep in two weeks' time.

Having thanked the official, I followed the personal assistant to his office. He in turn helped me to fill in the forms to apply for my passport. True to the officer's word, I had my passport sent to me in two weeks' time. When we follow the promptings of the Holy Spirit we can never go wrong. Praise God!

People heard about my passport and contacted my brother to get his help with theirs. The huge agencies wanted to know, "How did you get it? We're ready to pay any amount. Get us our passports; get us our visas." Friends, there is a God who has a plan for you. Believe that He is going to see you through all the details.

My sister Christine worked with Kensington Temple in London. Their Bible college was willing to take me. The people there didn't know me, but had been praying for me. It was confirmed to them that God wanted to use me.

A few months later, intending to join the college there and stay with my sister, I went to the British Embassy in Mumbai. I needed a multiple-entry visa to Great Britain, because I also wanted to visit my family in Canada before starting Bible college in London. I was told by the folks at the embassy, "When you get to London just notify the immigration officer at the airport and they will put the multiple-entry visa stamp in your passport." When I got to London and told the lady there what I needed, she was arrogant and rude, saying, "The plane you arrived on is on the tarmac over there; you can go and get on it. Take off to your country and get this work done there and then come back."

I just wanted to please Jesus, so I prayed, "Lord, if you want me to return to Mumbai and go back to the convent, I am willing." Then the power of God came over me. I stood tall and said, "Excuse me ma'am, I'm not here to make money out of your country. If I wanted money I could have stayed in my country. I'm here to study God's Word so I can take it back to my country, to a people who live in darkness, and tell them about the light and eternal life. If you refuse me multiple entry, their blood be on your hands!"

She immediately stood up, took my passport, and stamped in the multiple-entry visa. She shook my hand and said, "You will be our most revered visitor." She gave me her name, in case I ever needed any help. Her whole demeanor had changed.

While I was in London, I got rid of the nun's garb and the ring I had worn since my final vows. I started wearing the secular clothing my brother and sister had provided for me. Then I became very concerned for Christine, thinking my sister had joined some kind of Pentecostal cult. She was so active in the movement, taking care of drug addicts, even entertaining them in her home. I couldn't understand how she could let those street bums use her private personal bathrooms. So I spent a whole day fasting and praying for her. I said, "God, if Christine is in any kind of a cult, get her out of it. If I have gotten out of your perfect will, then take me back to the convent."

The next day I went to Kensington Temple for a prophetic conference with speaker Morris Cerullo, from America. The video was relayed to another building because upwards of 6,000 people were attending. I stood with my sister, brother-in-law, and niece Diana at the back in the main sanctuary. I wore jeans and a blue print blouse. Suddenly, Brother Cerullo stopped and addressed me directly. "I'm speaking to the lady back there in the printed blue blouse; God has a message for you. He says, 'My child, I am pleased with the step you have taken in faith. There will be many who will humiliate and criticize you, but I, your God, will walk with you. I will take you to an international Bible college. I will ground you in the Scriptures and will bring you back to the land of many gods to tell the people of the one true God!"

I realized that the Lord, who had been speaking to me in dreams and visions for one and a half years, was so mindful of me that even in Great Britain He talked directly to me. He confirmed His will with the same words I had heard ringing in my ears for so long. I felt so humbled.

The next day or so, I told my sister that I wanted to go to Canada to visit two of my other sisters and two other brothers before starting my Bible college studies, and that I also wanted to be baptized in water before leaving for Canada. As a child I had been sprinkled by the priest, but I now wanted to be baptized as a believer. So I was baptized by an Assemblies of God pastor in England.

I arrived in Canada to share a two-month holiday with four of my siblings and their families before going back to England to study. They were all staunch Catholics and there was nothing wrong with that, except they were Catholic only in name, not committed to Christ. Some Catholics are committed to Christ and walk with Him. Others are worldly and not really committed to Christ. My siblings had everything. They had 'made it' in life and had success the way the world looks at it. They had not made it on God's scales, however. I was surprised at how God would use them.

Sister Helen (Theresa) with the late Mother Teresa.

CHAPTER 9

EASTERN PENTECOSTAL BIBLE COLLEGE, CANADA

"...a voice behind you, saying, 'This is the way; walk in it'" (Isa. 30:21).

A FEW DAYS LATER I TRAVELED FROM ENGLAND TO CANADA on my first trip to visit my two sisters in Montreal and two brothers in Toronto. Some of them had been settled in Canada for almost two decades. When I arrived in the Toronto airport's immigration area, the officer looked at my passport and she saw the picture of a nun with a veil. She said, "Did you work in India? Do you know Mother Teresa?"

"Yes," I said, "I know her very well. In fact, in my Bible I have a photo of her and me together."

"Can I see it?" she asked. I took it out of my purse and showed it to her. She got so excited she jumped off her seat. She came out of her booth, pulled me to the other side, and called out to all the other immigration officers to come and see the woman who knew Mother Teresa. "We are so honored to have you in our country," she said, and stamped 'multiple entry' in my passport.

I thank God for the good memories I have of Mother Teresa. If her name could get me multiple entries into Canada, then how much more the name of Jesus can see me all through my life's journey!

I remember the time when I was a principal of Loreto Dharamtala in Kolkata and I took some of the children Mother

Teresa cared for into our school. From then on I had her private phone number. When my sister Christine and her daughter Diana arrived from England to visit me in Kolkata, they were in my office and said, "We would love to visit Mother Teresa before we leave." So I dialed Mother Teresa's phone number and she herself picked up the call. When I asked her if it was possible for her to give us some time at her convenience, she said, "Sister Helen, you can come whenever you want. I'm always here for you." That same afternoon the three of us were in her humble little office. She was truly a saint of God.

I recall too that Mother Teresa shied away from the glare of cameras. The Bible says you will know a person by their fruit. (See Matt. 7:20.) She was not one to draw attention to herself. She always gave the glory to God. I know this for a fact. While we were with her, a rich Hindu man came and thanked her for something. He then bent down to get her darshan (blessing), but she said to him, "Son, don't thank me. Go thank Jesus." Mother Teresa was a woman of God. As a child growing up I had read about her and always stood in awe of the work she did among lepers. To this day I have a passion for lepers.

I remember those glorious days, when I was working in the hill stations of Darjeeling and I had taken our final year students, not on an excursion to some sight-seeing place, but to Kalimpong for three days. There Mother Teresa had a home for about 50-60 mentally challenged 'patients.' Just two Missionaries of Charity ran this huge establishment. When we arrived they had a bathroom full of soiled linen, almost to the ceiling, to soak, wash, rinse and squeeze out—all adult clothing. It was a joy for us to relieve them of this.

When I was in Shillong as principal, I recall when the army stepped in with their tents and all they had to assist us in running a one-day fair at the school. The fair was to collect funds for Mother Teresa's school for the blind.

As a principal in Lucknow, I took the staff and outgoing class of students on a three-day trip to visit Mother Teresa's colony for about 300 lepers, their spouses, and children. They were situated on 75 acres of property. We had truckloads of blankets, rations, toys, clothing, and indoor and outdoor games, all donated by the parents of the students. While the staff and workers were unloading the vehicles—as they had to return to the city—we decided to take a walk in this exquisitely kept property. We saw fields of mustard-colored flowers; crops; factories for cleaning grain; and centers for weaving cloth, tailoring clothes, and making sandals. Everything was so well kept!

As we walked on the broad path between the fields on either side, excited that we had come to serve the lepers, suddenly a small dark creature came directly towards us from out of the woods. We were a little anxious; no one spoke.

My stomach went into knots. This was my moment of testing. If I took to my heels, everyone would panic and we would return to Lucknow faster than we had come. It was only the grace of God that kept me going in the direction we had started. I didn't know what to make of this creature. Was it a beast? Or was it a human being?

This creature came and put two of its limbs around the middle of my body and gripped me tightly. Automatically my arms moved toward this creature and held onto it. I looked into its face and it was as if I had seen the crucified Lord. This was no beast; this was a human leper. God at that moment gave me so much love and compassion for this person. Tears ran down my face and I sobbed bitterly. I couldn't tell if the person was male or female. He had no fingers, no toes, no ears, no hair, no teeth. Instead of a nose, just a red hole. But I saw the beauty of what Calvary had done. Jesus too was marred beyond recognition, was despised and rejected, a man of suffering and pain, with no beauty or majesty to attract us to Him. (See Isa. 53.) But now He is risen and interceding at the right hand of God, so that we, the laborers in His vineyard of love, will continue to be His hands outstretched to those in need.

I remember going into one of the male wards there. In one corner, on the shiny cement floor, lay a blind leper in his striped pajamas, an Anglo-Indian ex-athlete. I turned to him and asked, "Sir, what can we do for you today?" He smiled and said, "Please, can I sing for you?" When he started singing "Amazing grace, how sweet the sound...," his voice was angelic. We felt as though we were standing in the very throne room of God. I have never in my life heard that song sung so beautifully. He truly was blind, but he could see the risen Lord of glory with his spiritual eyes. He helped my students and me to see that Lord too.

At the end of three days, we were so much in love with the lepers. We had cried with them, sat on their beds, chatted away, and sung songs. Some of them were geniuses, playing musical instruments with their toes because they had no fingers. They had created their own instruments with tins and strings, strumming them like guitars. It was so wonderful to see women with stumps for hands, sewing clothes for others; men with no fingers making leather sandals, cleaning grain, and assisting each other in various tasks. These city-bred affluent kids of Loreto, who had servants galore at home, did not want to go back to the city. We did a lot of hugging and crying as we bid the lepers good-bye. I remember the parents sending me thank-you cards because their daughters were no longer spoiled brats. They had been touched by the ministry of the lepers to us. They were no longer selfish, but grateful for what God had blessed them with. I wasn't telling the half of it when I told the immigration officer of my friendship with Mother Teresa. I treasure these memories.

In due time I finally got out of the Toronto airport and met my sister Mina and her family, who had come to pick me up. Since the flight had been only from England to Canada, I wasn't too jet-lagged or anything, but I was very quiet and subdued in the car. The family, of course, assumed that I was tired and didn't want to disturb me. I was being very observant of the highways, overpasses, buildings, and sidewalks. They all looked so deserted, compared to India, which is crowded and colorful as you pass any road. I began to wonder, sincerely, if the rapture of the Church had taken place and I was left behind. I saw not a single soul walking on the streets for the longest time. I began to pray, "Jesus, did I step out of your will?"

I'm glad Jesus has delayed His coming. Toronto today is a different story than 1992, partly because so many immigrants are there now. It's still not as crowded as India, where people are all over the place like flies, walking on the sides and in the middle of streets, jaywalking, always moving.

The following day we left for Montreal, where I was to take a break at Mina's home. That weekend we were all together for the first time in a long time—brothers, sisters, nieces, nephews, and in-laws. My sister Mina asked, "Why do you have to go back to England to study? Only Christine is there to help you get started, whereas four of us are here. We can support you."

Now I was convinced of whom I believed in and whom I walked with, so I testified to them, "Mom and Dad don't know this as yet, but I am no longer a Roman Catholic nun. I am a confirmed believer in Jesus Christ. I want nothing less than what God has in store for me. He wants me to be a preacher, a messenger of His Word. That is what He has called me for."

I had been noted for being an educator in India, but God brought me out of that to take His Word to the millions who have not heard of Him. I said, "If I stay here, I will have to go to a Pentecostal Bible college where I can get the training to be a preacher."

Do you know what they did? They took out the yellow pages of the phone book and looked up the word 'Pentecostal.' They put their finger on one phone number, dialed it, and a woman answered in French. I didn't know how to respond in French, so my sister took over to interpret for me. The lady said, "I've heard of a place; it could be somewhere in Ontario. That's where they train people to become pastors and preachers." Now I was in Quebec, so I asked if she had the phone number. She gave it to me.

Immediately I sensed in my spirit that that was the number I had to cling to. You know, God confirms our steps all the time. When you are so much in tune with God, you know that you know that you know! I made a phone call to that number—to a Bible college in Peterborough, Ontario. The voice on the other end was that of Joan Mann, Secretary to the Registrar. I knew this was the place. I asked her for an appointment. We had to drive six hours to get to this place. All I had was my passport, and that showed my photo as a nun. I had still been wearing my garb in India when I had gotten my first passport.

The Registrar behind the desk, John, must have had ample faith or was really in tune with the Holy Spirit, because he believed my story. But he said, "We need more than just the passport. I believe that you were baptized in England by an Assemblies of God pastor. Is there any way you can bring that document?"

I responded boldly, "Listen, I'm going to do my best to get that baptismal certificate, but in case I don't have it when I meet your admissions team next week, I'll come here as I am. You will give me the seat at this college with or without the documents, because I believe this is the place God wants me to be in." When you are so sure of God's will, there's nothing to stop you or to make you doubt it. When I had gotten out of the car that day, I had tapped on the car window and looked back inside at Anna, my Danish sister-in-law, who along with her kids had driven me from Montreal. Sensing the Holy Spirit all over me, I said to her, "Anna, this is the place I've got to be in—nowhere else—not England. This is the college that God wants me to go to."

The following week I was to meet the admissions team. I found out that the pastor who had baptized me in England was on holiday in Africa. There was no way I could get that certificate from him. I didn't have his address, but Christine knew his whereabouts. One minute before I was to enter the college office to meet that team, we drove into the college parking lot and found my brother-in-law Larry (a Canadian from Montreal), already there. He was waving a document which he had received by FAX that morning. He said to my brother Steve and me, "I think you need this paper this morning." It was my baptismal certificate from England.

God makes a way where there seems to be no way! He's always parting the waters, if you believe. But you've got to take that first step of faith if you want God to take the other 99 steps with you. And my God has never failed me to this day. My sister Phil and her husband Gilbert started me off with a check in Canadian dollars for $2,500. Mina and Larry provided all my clothes and many other niceties. Tony and Helen blessed me with a refrigerator and toiletries, as well as my supplements to keep me going. Steve and Anna gave me plenty of bed linens and meals. I literally lacked nothing! My parents even sold their family home to see me through. And within a year and a half, 24 of my family members committed their lives to Christ and were baptized in water, without my going to even one of them and preaching. I just made sure I was doing God's will. You do not have to struggle with God. He has your plan. Just move from where you are to the realm of the divine and God will honor you for that first step that you take in faith.

So, in the autumn of 1992, I entered Eastern Pentecostal Bible College (EPBC) in Ontario, Canada to do a four-year program (though I was able to complete it in less than three due to transfer of previous credits and taking extra summer courses). I felt great joy to be in the center of God's will. He put me there not only for myself, but to bless those around me. I made friends quickly. Near the end of the first year, one of my friends came to my room crying. Her name was Shelly Sackett and she was completing a one-year certificate program at the college. "I have only three days more to get $2,400 for my tuition," she wailed. "If I don't pay it I won't be allowed to take my exams." A 29-year-old Canadian, Shelly was the only Christian in her family. They didn't believe in her conversion. Her boyfriend had left her, thinking she was a fanatic—a Jesus freak. But God had led her to sell her bits of furniture and give up her profession in order to attend Bible college.

I knew her to be a godly, hard-working woman, so I counseled her, "The money is God's problem, not yours. You keep on studying for the exams." After Shelly left my room, I thought about the $1,000 I had in my account. My fees were paid for that semester, but in a week I needed to pay one-third of my $5,000 expenses for the following semester. I asked myself what that money was doing in my account when my sister needed it. I felt the Spirit saying I should give it to her, so I filled out the check and wrote a letter to another friend. "Go to the bank and withdraw these funds," I instructed him. "Give the money as an anonymous donation to Shelly Sackett's tuition bill, but be sure no one knows about this. If you can't do it, I'll get someone else."

The next day about 4:30 p.m., Shelly was crying and running through the corridor to my room, saying, "You won't believe it! Someone put a $1,000 anonymous donation in my account for my fees. But I need $1,400 more in two more days. What will I do?"

How soon we forget God's provision! I wanted to take a baseball bat to her, but instead I told her to go study. The following day she came running through the dorm again. Six ladies had been praying and fasting in a tiny Presbyterian church on the outskirts of Peterborough. The Holy Spirit had given Shelly's name to them and had instructed each to send $100 to her account. So she had received $600 more. "But I need $800 more and there's only one day left," she wailed. This time I wanted to aim a double-barreled shotgun at her. It was time for my devotions so I sent her back to her room.

The third and final day, around 4:30, Shelly was bawling in the corridor again. "You aren't going to believe this! My ex-boyfriend was traveling in his one and only car on the outskirts of a town far from where we are. He heard a voice within his car saying, 'I am Jesus. Go and sell this car right now and put the money in Shelly's account at EPBC.' He had no choice. He sold the car for exactly $800 and wired the money to my account before the office closed today. My bill is paid in full!" (After graduating Shelly went to work in China as an underground missionary.)

That same week, Carl Verge, the president of the college, called me into his office. "I need to apologize to you on behalf of the Board," he said. "We had $1,500 set aside for you as a scholarship, but the accountant forgot to put it into your account."

"But many young couples are struggling to pay their bills. They work all night and find it hard to make ends meet," I protested.

"No, it was the unanimous decision of the Board at their last meeting," he replied. "Since you've come, you've made a big difference in our college. By the way, there was also a grant of $500 credited to your account today." God is a good paymaster! I'm sharing this to increase your faith. As you give in response to the prompting of the Holy Spirit, God will supply your needs.

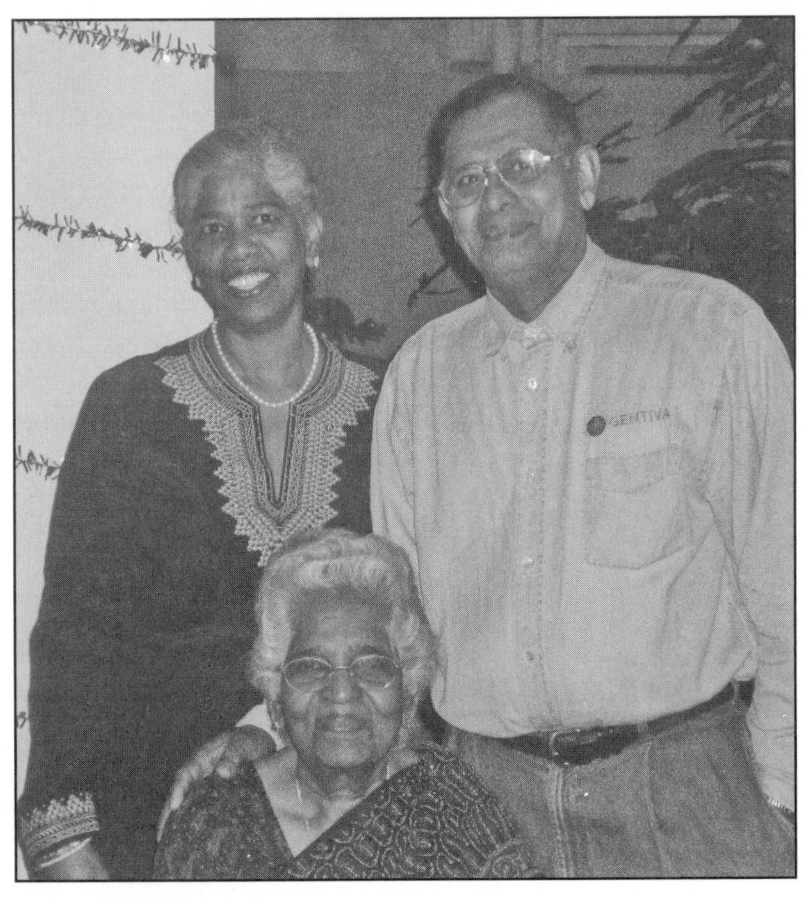

Theresa's older sister Philomena with her husband Gilbert D'Souza on her mom's 80th birthday.

CHAPTER 10

MINISTRY WHILE IN PETERBOROUGH

"That they might be with him and that he might send them out" (Mark 3:14).

WHILE I WAS STUDYING AT THE COLLEGE IN CANADA, David Yonggi Cho came for a missions convention. I happened to be president of the student missions body that year. He counseled me, "Sister Theresa, remember one thing. If your prayer life is not right, nothing is right. If you don't know the heartbeat of the Master, you don't know His agenda and you can't manage His affairs. My ministry is flourishing because I spend three hours every day in private prayer. During that time my wife is not important, my personal assistant is not important. Even if the president of the United States would call, he would not find me. I am with the Director; I am only His manager. I have to get my instructions from Him." Dr. Cho had over 700,000 members in his church at the time, along with thousands of leaders under him, yet he spent three hours a day alone in prayer. Though he was busy and important, he made time to spend with Jesus. Why can't we spend even a half hour praying?

We are ambassadors of Christ, messengers of a great and holy God. At times God has asked me to go into countries I didn't even have visas for. God has made ways for me to get in, and I have preached the Good News and come out. God has a plan, all you have to do is stop walking in the flesh.

I found prayer to be very crucial to my studies. Billy Young, who is senior pastor of one of the largest churches in Toronto, was then pastor of a small church in that city. He would travel to Peterborough two days a week to teach classes at our college, the last class of one day and the first class of the following day. During his lectures we had to be on high alert, knowing that if we missed any of what he said, there was no way we could get him to answer any questions. He always based his exams on his notes. And he spoke very fast as he paced up and down the levels of the 'stadium' classroom. At the end of one lecture Pastor Young read the names of 23 authors that we had to look up for a particular topic. An assignment was due in the tray outside his office before 7:30 the following morning. We had to scan through all 23 to get information for the assignment.

I was lost in God in my devotions that evening. I typically prayed about three hours a night. Towards the end of my time I had a vision of a navy blue hardbound book with gold lettering on the spine. I finished praying and realized it was five minutes to ten. Suddenly remembering the assignment due the next morning, I rushed into my boots, jacket, and gloves, and ran across the street. The library closed at ten and the main door was already shut. The librarian noticed me through the window and asked me to come in anyway. She asked, "How can I help you?" At this point, I did not have my notebook with the names of the 23 authors. All I could see in my mind's eye was that navy blue book with the gold lettering. I told her, "Don't worry; I'll help myself. I kind of know what I want. There's only one book I'm looking for." The Holy Spirit led me through the rows of shelves to a certain place. My hand just went up and took hold of a navy blue book. When I opened the Table of Contents, I found the names of the 23 authors and the topic that Pastor Billy had spoken about. I have learned that when I put God first in giving Him of my time or finances, everything else falls into place.

During my freshman year, I was in charge of a ministry group to the senior citizens' home in Peterborough. The previous team leader had told me that not many people usually showed up for prayer time in that particular home. I told my team, however, "If we believe God for souls, we will get them. And I believe that prayer without action is useless. 'Whatever you ask for in prayer, believe that you have received it, and it will be yours' (Mk. 11:24). So let's go early and just visit and encourage the senior citizens. We'll tell them what we've come for and invite them. It will be up to them to show up or not. Let's put 15 chairs out today, not five."

I had also been informed that the home did not really want any students to come anymore. Several years earlier, our students had been chased out for talking about hell to the seniors. That first evening, all 15 chairs were filled. The next meeting I asked my teammates to make a circle and fill the room with chairs. Every one of them was occupied when our service time came. The ministry started growing and the senior citizens were excited about our coming. They requested us to come even during our spring and summer breaks. I give God the glory for teaching us to trust Him and not to lean on our own understanding.

One morning I walked into class at the college and found Dan, our freshman class representative, sitting alone with his face in his hands. I asked him what the matter was. He replied, "Theresa, I won't be able to take my exams because my fees are not paid."

I said, "God asks us to be anxious about nothing. 'The one who calls you is faithful, and he will do it' (1 Thess. 5:24). Cheer up and give Him glory. He brought you thus far and He won't fail you now!" I promised to pray for him throughout the day, that God would make a way for him.

That same evening, after classes ended, I needed to do laundry. I met one of my dorm friends, Lisa, and asked her to lend me a Canadian dollar coin, which was called a 'loonie.' The machines at the college took one loonie to wash and one to dry. Laundering both whites and colored clothes required four dollars. I had decided to wash only my white clothes and hang them in my room to dry. (I happened to be the only one in the dorm without a roommate.) Lisa said she could give me five dollars or more if I needed it, but I declined and promised to return the loonie to her by the following day. It has always been easier for me to give than to receive anything from anyone.

Still later that night, I got a call from my sister, Mina. She and her husband Larry were nearing Peterborough, intending to spend the night at their friend Rick's farmhouse. They asked me to join them for the night. In no time they arrived at the college to pick me up. It was a cold winter night but we warmed ourselves by the huge log fire in the farmhouse. As Mina and I were chatting away, she opened her purse and took out a pouch filled with 25-cent coins. She told me they were for my phone calls. Next she pulled out another pouch filled with loonies—for my laundry. Lastly she placed in my hand $300, saying, "That's for you, for your personal expenses." My sister had no knowledge that I had run out of money, but God knew. He's always on time!

I was excited the next morning as I ran to look for Dan. I gave him the $250 he needed to pay his last fees, thus enabling him to sit for his exams the next day. I also paid Lisa back the one loonie I had borrowed. I thank God that He has always taught me to share with others what He has lavishly blessed me with.

The remaining money came in handy that night. While eating a meatloaf dinner in the cafeteria, I bit down on a piece of bone and cracked a tooth. I had to pay $50 to have it taken care of in the ER. The cafeteria chef and staff were very fond of me. When they heard about my tooth, they contacted the college authorities. I was almost forced to fill out some forms for their insurance to compensate me for 'damages' of several hundred dollars. God knew I would need to help someone else to make their payments. I was always looking out for someone to help—to meet the needs of others.

While in college, I was elected missions representative and was selected to attend the Urbana conference in Illinois. When it came time to pay for bus fare to travel from Canada to the US,

I had no funds. I went to my mailbox to collect my mail and found a card from an anonymous donor with $300 cash in it. At that point, no one knew that I didn't have the money; only God did.

On another occasion I needed to buy my textbooks at the college. I was in Canada on a student visa, which meant it was illegal for me to work. It was snowing as I got ready to leave my room to go to the library after evening prayer. As I put on my leather jacket, I noticed something in the pocket on the left side. I reached in with my right hand and brought out $300 which I had not earned nor placed in that pocket.

One evening my friends decided to go to Dunkin Donuts for hot chocolate and donuts. It was only a 15-minute walk away. They pleaded with me to join them. Even though I had much studying to do, I yielded to the temptation to have a good time. I loved the snow, but I preferred to look at it through closed windows. This was my first encounter with heavy snowfall.

That short walk seemed to take forever. I felt the cold going through my jacket, boots, and gloves clear into my bones. I was shaking like a leaf by the time we got there. I was telling God that I would not do that again, if I could just get back to school in one piece. Most of the people in the shop were smoking, so my jacket smelled like smoke for days. I'm sure I was totally out of God's will—not like the three Hebrew lads who endured the fiery furnace and came out without even the smell of smoke on their clothing. If we go where we shouldn't, we may carry the smell out with us.

One day the college was expecting a special speaker for chapel, a Russian former general. The auditorium, filled with students, staff, and faculty, echoed with praise and worship. In my spirit I saw a very crowded street in Toronto, though we were in Peterborough. In the midst of the traffic was the car holding the speaker who was to come to speak that day. I sensed that President Carl Verge was tense. I was only a freshman, but being led by the Holy Spirit, I went to the worship leader and asked to use the microphone. He happened to be a music faculty standing on the platform and he gave it to me. God put the words in my mouth and I said, "I have something from the Lord for everyone. Right now the Russian General is held up in a traffic jam in Toronto (two hours away). God's presence is here and God will give him great peace, but we shouldn't be expecting a human being, no matter how great his testimony is. Let's concentrate instead on the King of Kings and Lord of Lords. Let's worship Him!"

The president came and joined me. As soon as I handed the mike back, students rushed to the altar, weeping in repentance. No one gave an invitation; the worship leader continued to sing; faculty and students alike came forward in a real atmosphere of praise and worship. Students were slain in the Spirit. They prayed for each other with tears. We felt holy reverence in the sanctuary that day.

Two hours later no one had left the auditorium. When the Russian General arrived, he said exactly what God had put on my tongue. In the traffic jam he had been anxious, but God had given him peace and had told him that He was in control of everything.

One sunny day, which happened to be a college holiday, I decided to go outside, to a beautiful open space near a wooded area. I took some spiritual books to read and sat down to meditate on a bench that was there. A little creature came and sat between my feet. I had never seen such a creature in my life. I talked to it from time to time as I read and prayed. Eventually the creature got up and went into a hole in a tree not far from the bench. Curious, I followed. I had to lie on the ground to look into the hole, and the creature looked right back at me. I said to it, "Did I hurt you? Why did you leave me? It was nice having you to keep me company. We'll meet again." After some time, I left the creature, as harmless as ever, and went back to the college building. That's when I noticed the college president and a good number of students staring at me. Not one of them opened their mouth to speak. I was known and loved by these folk, so I said to them, "I had such a nice time with the Lord out there. Did you notice, there was a strange animal that came and sat between my feet and it didn't move for at least three hours? I really missed it when it left me."

One person asked if I knew what it was. I said, "No, what was it?"

They said, "It was a skunk!" When one is at peace with God and with self, even enemies are turned into friends.

Pastor Paul Graban, Theresa's mentor at Burlington Assembly of God, Burlington, New Jersey.

CHAPTER 11

FIRST MINISTRY IN THE US

"They will do even greater things" (John 14:12).

HAVING HEARD ME MINISTER ON DIFFERENT OCCASIONS, Glenn and Velma Pagett of Peterborough took a liking to me and often came over to the Bible college to bring me to their home for a meal and a much-needed break from studies. Part of our college training for ministry included doing a three-month internship. I did mine in Covina, California, where Joel Pagett, their son, was the associate pastor and his father-in-law Ron Stevens served as the senior pastor. While there I stayed in the home of Nur and Enid Matthews. Nur was on the Board of the Covina Assemblies of God church. The Matthews had lived in the States for over 25 years by then, but had originally come from India. Nur was a cardiologist and Enid a pediatrician. Nur's family was of Muslim background, whereas Enid's family members were believers from Kolkata. Enid's mom was once the principal of the main AG school in Kolkata. Nur and Enid went out of their way to make me feel at home with them and also made sure they took me to Hawaii for a three-day break before I returned to the Bible college in Canada.

It was while staying with the Matthews that I met Pastor Paul Graban, their spiritual guru, whom they treated medically. Pastor Graban invited me to come and minister at his church in New Jersey without even having heard me preach. I promised him that the first place I would minister after graduation would be at his church. And I kept my word. I was truly touched by the kindness shown to me by this man of God. He came personally along with Susan Esposito to the airport to pick me up and then take me to the Mastoris Diner for a grand meal. Without exaggeration, what was my portion could have fed a whole family in India. I was to minister at the Mother-Daughter Banquet the next morning and then at both services on Mother's Day—Sunday morning and evening.

Pastor Graban had arranged for me to speak at a few other churches in the area and the surrounding states. My intention had been to go back to evangelize in India soon after I had graduated from Bible college. But a week has turned out to be 15 years and counting! God bless the Zahorskys and their pet dogs, who to this day keep welcoming me like a long-lost friend whenever I am back in the States.

By the fall of 1994, the Matthews had relocated to Kingman, Arizona, and the AG church there invited me to preach on a Sunday. I arrived on Friday evening. Enid said, "You've never seen the Grand Canyon. It's only about a three-hour drive from here. Let's go tomorrow. Our housekeeper, Rachel Keller, can drive us."

I said, "No, I'd rather not do that on a Saturday. It's better if I spend time in the Word and prayer for Sunday." They put pressure on me, so I relented, saying, "I'll go only if you agree to put worship tapes on in the car while we travel."

It was a bright sunny morning, the birds chirping on either side of the hills we passed through. As soon as we got to the top of the canyon, Rachel was about to park the car when I said, "I feel we need to go back immediately."

"But Theresa," Enid said, "we're already here."

Knowing I just had to go towards home I said, "If you and Rachel don't want to go back, I'm going to walk home!" I had such urgency in my spirit. God doesn't give you the second step until you do the first. We have to crucify the flesh and give God the glory.

Enid instructed Rachel to turn around and head back. As we started down, a blizzard came up out of the blue. Snow was coming so fast that we couldn't see anything in front of us. As we crept along, we could hear the noises of things falling and people screaming and calling for help from the shoulders of the road. Rachel had taken out the worship tape and hadn't put another one in as she concentrated on driving. All of a sudden the car veered to the right, hit the guardrail, turned 180 degrees, and began to go down the embankment backwards on the opposite side of the road.

I was seated in the middle of the back seat, Enid and Rachel in the front. After the first impact, my head hit the side window and my left leg slid under the driver's seat because of the jerk. I screamed, "Jesus!" Immediately the car came back up the embankment, turned around, and sat on the road itself, in position to continue driving homeward. God says He will give His angels charge over us, to guard us in all our ways (Psa. 91:11). He is always there, omnipresent, from the heights to the depths, from the darkness to the light (Psa. 139:8-12). The next morning, 32 people came to the altars for salvation. My head and foot were bruised, but God won the victory that day. At the name of Jesus, demons flee. Satan will do everything to make you fall; just get up and go on and continue to give God the glory.

When I first started preaching in America I would spend 30 hours of preparation for one message, writing out the manuscript, and praying for the church. I had to hear from God, to receive a fresh anointing. I never used my old notes. When we pour ourselves into ministry, the best is yet to come. You will do greater things than you have seen yourself or anyone else do.

One particular week I had heard a message from the Lord and the Holy Spirit helped me to put it together. By the previous weekend I had it ready for the following Sunday morning. After being out preaching on Wednesday I came home and heard the Spirit of God telling me, "That message won't do." So I started praying and saying, "God, that's such a beautiful message, you know? It's just right, you know, God? The other one I'm hearing is not the one for that church." The Spirit was asking me to preach about homosexuality, which God hates. He loves the person, but He hates the sin. Eight times I was prompted to preach only on that topic.

The next day, whether I heard a song while at the radio station or whether I opened my Bible at random, God gave me nothing but the same theme. I cried out to God, "They're going to stone me. I can't go into that church and preach that message there." In previous years I had preached three-day revival services there; I knew that congregation and most everyone in it.

God said, "Whose will do you want to do?"

I was getting no other message from God, so Saturday night I sat down and worked hard. The scripture verses started flowing as the Lord started revealing things to me. I would look at one scripture passage and the Lord would make me turn to the next one. I didn't have to look at a concordance. In no time I had the whole sermon prepared and I started praising God, worshiping Him.

In the morning I panicked again. My stomach started twisting into knots and somehow we even got delayed on the way to the church. I just prayed, "Lord, you are in control. Maybe it's good that I'm not getting there on time. I don't even want to meet anyone or have anyone speak to me." Sometimes the leader will ask me, "Sister, what's your theme?" And I will tell them straightaway to ask Jesus; ask the Holy Spirit. You don't want to give birth to something that God wants you to deliver at a certain time. You don't want to do it beforehand unless the Lord okays it. I don't like to let people know what I'm called to preach about.

So I didn't want to meet anyone, not even the pastor, whom I knew very well. I just walked in and joined in the praise and worship. I don't like sitting on platforms. I prefer sitting in the pews where no one else can see me praise and worship God. Then I noticed the pastor was not in his usual place—where he usually sat. The attack of the enemy, even in church, was so strong on me: "This message is not from God. It's from your own imagination. You're never going to be invited to minister in this church again, because your papers as an ordained minister are going to be taken away…." All this nonsense was spoken into my mind; it was a real tug-of-war in my spirit.

When it came time to preach, what did I preach? I preached on homosexuality. And the message just flowed out of my belly like wellsprings of living water. All of a sudden, after I had finished preaching, I got a splitting headache. It was as if someone had thrust a dagger into the center of my head. My head was throbbing with pain and I was ready to faint. It felt like a migraine headache that had come from nowhere. I looked for the pastor and couldn't find him. People were running up to the altars, but I felt weak and my knees were knocking. The enemy started to taunt me, "You preached your own message; now look what's happening."

I prayed, "God, please confirm your message with signs and wonders." Just then an old man, leaning against the platform and his walking stick, broke into tongues. His wife, sitting in the pews, gave the interpretation of the message in tongues. It was exactly the same message I had preached—ditto! I felt such a release in my spirit. God's message was identical to the one I had brought.

The presence of the Lord hovered over me again and I walked down off the platform to pray for people. I noticed three men standing at the altars, who caught my attention amidst all the others there. They were like babies, crying their hearts out. After I had finished praying with people, however, I didn't see these three men any more. The altar time had been going on for quite a while.

The pastor's wife came to me, her eyes red from crying. The enemy started attacking me again as she said, "I will be taking you to the restaurant. Pastor will not be joining us yet; he'll come later." The devil said, "Look what you've done. You have messed up things for the pastor. The board members are attacking him in his office."

When the pastor's wife had finished speaking to me, the attack of the enemy started all over again. So I started praying in the Spirit, saying, "Lord, what should I do? I've done my part. I preached what you told me to preach." This was intense spiritual warfare. So I didn't say a word to the pastor's wife, who was a friend of mine, though I hadn't heard from either her or her husband in a long time. I hadn't heard anything about how the church was doing—nothing.

So we got in the car and went to the restaurant. Both of us sat down very quietly. Her eyes were as red as ever and the pastor was nowhere to be seen. All the customers in that place appeared to be Sunday church-goers, so we just made small talk as we waited. Then the pastor came and his eyes were red too. He sat down beside his wife. I could hold my peace no longer, so I turned and asked, "Pastor, can you tell me if what I preached was what God wanted me to say in your church? I've gone through intense spiritual warfare for the last few days. I had another message until Wednesday evening, when the Lord made me change it. On Friday I was struggling again and the Holy Spirit made it very clear to me that the previous message was not the one that I was to preach. I've never encountered something like this in my whole ministry. Pastor, tell me what's wrong. You can rebuke me if you need to."

Then he started bawling like a child there in the restaurant, on Sunday afternoon, when it was filled with people. I didn't know whether to hide under the table or to leave and run. But where could I run? I didn't even have a car to leave on my own. (And besides, you would not want me to drive in North America, because in India we drive on the other side of the street!) So all I did was just sit there and pray silently, "God, you know best. I'm going to just leave the whole thing in your hands. Take over."

Through his tears—and with his wife sobbing too—the pastor spoke, "Sister Theresa, I really don't know how to thank you. God made it very clear to me not to call you on the phone, not to give you any instructions, not to tell you anything, because I know you don't like hearing from a church until you've preached. On Wednesday afternoon I learned that three of my board members were homosexuals. And that night I had to confront them. Sister Theresa, I was ready to hand in my resignation, because they just went all out, making me feel as if I had committed the worst crime, that I had robbed the church. They accused me of being a party-goer, and even of being gay myself! So what could I do?"

This man is a sound preacher, a solid man of God and a man of integrity. When he cried out to God, this is what he heard, "Son, don't hand in your resignation. Don't call Sister Theresa; don't tell her anything. I will use her to preach the Word and the yoke of the enemy will be broken!" Those three men crying at that altar that morning were the three who were homosexuals. They repented at those altars, because the Spirit convicts us "of sin, and of righteousness, and of judgment" (John 16:8, KJV).

These men had asked to see the pastor after the service. They walked into his office and asked him for forgiveness. These three men are still in that church. They are no longer board members, but they are changed men. Why? Because someone dared to believe that God has a message for each church.

God wants to use you too. He wants you to be ready. It's about the treasure hidden in these earthen vessels. We know we are nothing; we're frightened, nervous. So what! When we turn to God in prayer, He strengthens us. He approves of our coming to Him just as we are and crying out—on His lap, on His shoulder, in His arms. We can say, "Father, I am scared to death." And then you hear comforting words from your God.

Theresa's younger brother Gerald, with his wife Maria and children Jenny, Maureen, and Derek on her mom's 80th birthday.

CHAPTER 12

INDIA EVANGELISM OUTREACH

"The Spirit bade me go" (Acts 11:12, KJV).

AFTER GRADUATING FROM BIBLE COLLEGE AND BEING ordained as a minister with the New Jersey District of the Assemblies of God, I used to minister on the radio five days a week as well as preach in various churches. I was associated with the Burlington Assembly of God in New Jersey. Once a year, however, I would travel to India to evangelize for about ten weeks.

On one of my first ministry trips back to India after graduation, I returned to my brother Gerald's home in Bangalore. I found Gerald and his wife Maria looking very exhausted, though it was early in the morning. I asked them what the matter was. They explained that their small son Derek had not slept all night and had kept them up. I said, "OK, give the baby to me and go about your business."

I held my little one-year-old nephew and started singing in tongues to him. Soon he was literally snoring in my arms, so I put him to bed. Just then I heard an eerie sound from outside the house. Not wanting the baby to wake up again, I looked out the window to see where the noise was coming from. I saw two Satan worshipers, dancing and whipping their mostly bare bodies. The man had only a loin cloth and the woman a saffron-colored sari. I thought, "Maybe I should take a photo of this to show to my friends in the US, so they can see what Satan worship looks like on the streets of India." The Holy Spirit convicted me, "You don't have to put that stuff in your camera." So I asked the Lord to forgive me for my thoughts.

Then I became a woman on a mission. I went and stood on my brother's veranda overlooking the street. In no time the street was filled with people coming from their homes to surround this couple. These were highly qualified, educated people wanting to see what the power of the evil one could do. They literally treated the two like gods who had shown up in their midst. The man had on no shirt; he was tattooed all over with a loincloth around his waist. He had long matted hair and wore bells on his ankles. His long whip, tipped with pieces of glass, bone, and metal, would tear his flesh open as he struck himself. The woman had a drum hanging around her neck. With her right hand she beat the drum and with her left she irritated the skin of the drum. The result sounded like silverware scratching crockery, a hideous noise. She wore heavy bells on her ankles too. Both of them danced to the beat of the drum.

The man had one long finger nail, equal to the length of his little finger, on his left hand. On the tip of that nail he balanced a heavy copper plate. He cleverly danced, whipped himself with one hand, and with the other moved the plate in front of the people for money. It never fell from the tip of his nail, despite his jumping and gyrations. He collected enough big bills to fill the dish. All the while I was praying in the Spirit, binding the works of darkness in the area of Gerald's home.

When the Satan worshiper finally looked at me, standing on the ground floor veranda, he had a big smile on his face, expecting money from me too. When he lifted his dish up to me, though my lips were shut, in my spirit I was praying, "Satan, I bind your works in the name of Jesus. I cast you out of this man in Jesus' name. The blood of Jesus is against you, Satan."

Just as I said that, the dish fell and money scattered everywhere. The man curled up in a fetal position on the ground at the woman's feet. He was in intense pain and crying like a baby. He looked at his companion and said in Hindi, "The woman up there has more power than we have. We have to run before they stone us to death. The man could feel his pain because the demonic spirits had left him. He could feel the cuts on his body. They took to their heels without touching the money on the ground. They took their dish and ran. The onlookers were shocked. I went on about my business, praising God for it is "not by might nor by power," but by God's Spirit (Zech 4:6), that we do exploits for Him.

My very first revival meeting back in the country of India was on St. Theresa's Grounds in the city of Kolar Gold Fields, about two and a half hours by car from Bangalore. My name, Theresa, means 'harvester.' The enemy did not want us to bring in a harvest of souls, so he did everything to stop those meetings. The Muslims were against our being there, so while I was preaching, they decided to shut off the electricity. When we walk with Christ, we are not losers. I kept ministering the Word and both I and my interpreter could be heard without mikes. We prayed over the sick and people were delivered. The battle was on!

When we came to the hotel room at 2:00 a.m., having to leave again by 5:00 a.m., there was not a drop of water for a shower. It had been a hot and dusty day with travel and the open-air meeting site. I used the half bottle of drinking water I had to brush my teeth. When I tried to sleep, though my bed looked immaculately white, I felt there were mice nearby. I am terrified of mice and rats. The other pastors were in the same hotel, in different rooms. I was scared to get out of the bed and look under it. Finally I got up and ran over to the door. It was too risky to get out of the room and be alone in the hotel. So I prayed and got the courage to bend down and look under the bed for mice. The floor was clean; no mice there. I moved to get into bed again, thinking maybe it had termites or bedbugs. I quickly lifted the mattress on one end to see what might jump out. I put it down faster than I had lifted it, because a sea of live cockroaches was layered under my mattress. So I sat in a chair and waited for morning to come.

We met at the car at 5:00 a.m. The others hadn't had drinking water either. They were all very tired too. We were ready to leave when we realized someone had stolen the gas from the car. The men pushed the car out of the hotel onto the main street, but no gas station was in sight. A young man on a motorcycle stopped at the car and said he knew a place not far away where someone sold gas in drums. The men managed to push the car there, but the shutters were down at the place. Someone offered to go call the owner from his home. As we waited in the car, a street vendor selling tea and snacks came by. When he saw me, he got excited, saying, "You cannot go without drinking tea. I'm a Muslim who heard you preach last night. We did everything to stop you, but last night you gave me the Living Water. This morning can I offer you some fresh tea? I have become a believer in Jesus Christ and my family too."

I knew that drinking that tea would be like a laxative, with no bathrooms available on the two-and-a-half-hour trip, but I had no choice but to oblige this eager new brother in Christ. After drinking the tea and filling the gas tank of the car, we hit the road. Everyone was quiet for a long time; our stomachs rolling. That was one of the longest trips I've ever made. Everyone was desperate to use a toilet, but there were no bushes to stop at. I had tears in my eyes trying to control myself from answering nature's call. When we finally saw a restaurant, I said to the driver, Pastor Lincoln Soares, "You've got to stop here. I have to go and relieve myself." I went in and said to the cashier, "Here's some money, I just need to use a toilet." He pointed to a dark hole in a corner. It had no lights and stank. I could see the whole thing in my mind's eye. I was glad there were no lights; I didn't want to know. I was only grateful to be relieved. All the others went through the same thing. This was actually the servants' toilet, no toilet paper either. These are some of the joys of ministry. There's never a dull moment when you're working for the Lord.

During another trip to India, I was invited to go to a place called Vijayawada. All I knew was that God had spoken in my spirit and had said very clearly, "Theresa, this time when you go to India, you will be training ministers." I didn't know *how* I was going to do it, because I was a single woman and I didn't have an office or a big team—nothing! And I've never believed in seeking out ministry. I don't even call pastors and ask them if I can come to their church. I didn't even tell people in India that I was coming, but from the day I would arrive until the day I would leave, I would be preaching two or sometimes three times every day. That's how it used to be, because it was the Holy Spirit's agenda.

While still in New Jersey, my schedule allowed me only about one-half hour to pack and leave my room for the airport. I had opened two suitcases on the floor. The Holy Spirit impressed me to pack my best clothes, purses, and shoes.

I hadn't told anyone but my brother that I was coming. I arrived in India and on the same day, a phone call came from a local pastor. It was Lincoln Soares, senior pastor at the Assemblies of God church my brother attended. Gerald was on the board. "I hear your sister has arrived," he said. "Please ask her to join us at the conference being held in the city."

I don't usually feel jet lag the same day I arrive, but I would feel it the following day. I said to my sister-in-law Maria, "All right, I'm not going to get behind the wheel, so you drive." The first few days I don't like to drive because everything is a blur. You get oxcarts and holy cows and people and trucks all coming your way. So she drove and we went to this place. I told her we would sit at the back.

Arriving at the conference hall, we realized we were the only two women in a sea of men. As we sneaked into the back and found two chairs, no one stirred. We saw seven white-skinned men sitting on the platform. I found out later that the team had come from the United States, Germany, and New Zealand. Seven of them had come to put this whole conference together. Then the gentleman at the pulpit, who was the leader of the team, suddenly stopped preaching and pointed straight at me. He said, "That sister who's just come in, it's time for you to come up here and take over. It's all yours from now on." I didn't know these people or anything about the team on the platform; I was a stranger to them. I did know some of the pastors in the gathering, so I walked down the aisle, led of the Spirit. Walking to the front, I sensed no message from the Holy Spirit for this group. I didn't even have a Bible in my hands. I stood below the platform and started speaking the words God put on my tongue like He did for David (2 Sam. 23:2). God's message was simple: "It's time for repentance to begin in the house of the Lord." (See 1 Pet. 4:17.)

I could hardly believe my eyes. The crowd started running to the altars. There was no preaching, just those few words. The altars were flooded. We couldn't and didn't even have to lay hands on people. The Holy Spirit was moving—slaying some in the Spirit and changing them. When you are obedient to the Holy Spirit, that's what He does.

A little-known pastor, Hamilton Tully, who had been invited to the city for the conference, came up to me as I was moving back to my seat. I had never met him. He said, "Sister Theresa, you don't know me, but please can you come and minister in Vijayawada?"

I answered, "If the Holy Spirit told you to ask me, I can't say no. I'll be there." I knew in my spirit I had to say yes.

"But Sister Theresa," he said, "There are no airplanes." I told him that was OK; I would find my way. He asked me if he could send a team along with his wife to pick me up from Bangalore. All I asked him for was the address and the date. I also told him I'd manage on my own.

When I went home and told my mother and brother that I would be ministering in Vijayawada, they were horrified. "Do you realize what you are doing to yourself? That place is known for drug addicts, rowdies, murderers, rapists, and bands of thieves. It's an evil place!" they informed me. Excited in my spirit, I prayed for God to give my family relief and peace in their spirits. My brother wanted to send members of his staff with me. My family didn't travel by local trains. I insisted that I would be fine. In the end, I booked on a local express train from Bangalore to Chennai (Madras), a six-hour trip. Around 10 p.m. I would have to switch to another train. I expected to arrive in Vijayawada about 6:30 in the morning.

I boarded the first train in my jeans and casual shirt and found myself in an all-male compartment. It had air conditioning, but only one empty seat remained, and it was the one beside me. I prayed, "Lord, whoever comes into this seat—man, woman, or child—use me to bring them into the kingdom." A well-dressed Hindu woman in a sari came and sat by me. In good English she introduced herself and asked for my name. She was the principal of a college in Bangalore. She asked what I did. I'm usually very careful about telling people I'm a missionary evangelist. I try never to say that in India, but this time it just came out without my thinking. I told her further that I was going to preach God's Word in a particular town.

Then she probed further, asking what I did in my vocation. I happened to tell her exactly how I win souls to Jesus. I started to tell her my testimony, how God had brought me out of the athletic arena where I had trained and then into the convent for 15 years. I explained that now I travel to remote places of the world, taking the Good News. Before the end of the journey she gave her life to the Lord and prayed the sinners' prayer, tears running down her cheeks. I asked her to go to Pastor Lincoln's church, since she lived in that area. God had answered my prayer.

As I boarded the next train, again I was the only lady. A few minutes before the train left the station, five heavy alcoholics who were stone drunk got in beside me in the sleeper car. It would take the rest of the night to get to my destination. Our small part of the sleeping compartment (called a 'coupe' in India), had three bunks on each side. The lights had been dimmed and they could barely see me sitting stiffly on my berth. They didn't realize I could understand Bengali, though I don't speak it.

I pretended to read Nicky Cruz' book, *The Cross and the Switchblade*, though I couldn't really make out the words in the dim light. Two of the men tried to push me and get close to me. One said to the others, "I wonder where she comes from. Who will have the first go at her to rape her? When the train leaves the station it is very noisy—metal screeching on metal. No one will hear her screams." They were betting on who would be able to rape me first. The toilet, an Indian-style "squatty potty," was located behind me. It consisted of a hole and two places to put your feet while you relieved yourself. The men were planning to gag me and put me in the tiny bathroom. Afterwards they would cut up my body and put the pieces down the hole while the train was moving, so no one could trace me.

"God hath not given us the spirit of fear; but of power, and of love, and of a sound mind" (2 Tim. 1:7, KJV), I quoted to myself. God has given us *dunamis* power. He has angels—"ministering spirits, sent forth to minister" to me (Heb. 1:14). Before getting on the train I had actually finished Nicky Cruz' book, so I had only my study Bible to read. And it was locked in my case; I usually don't bring it out in public. So I kept on pretending to read the same book, sitting on the edge of the bottom bunk. I put my purse beside my right hip as a barrier against the two men who were trying to push toward me. I was praying in the Spirit as the three men on the opposite side teetered toward me in their drunken stupor. The "Spirit himself intercedes for us through wordless groans" (Rom. 8:26).

God's Word was hidden in my heart; I could not open the Bible and search for scriptures. As God told Joshua, if he would meditate on the Word day and night, it would help him to be strong and courageous, and it would not depart from his heart and mind. (See Josh. 1:8-9.) God was bringing scripture passages to my mind: "Give thanks in all circumstances" (1 Thess. 5:18). I prayed, "I give you thanks, Father, that I am the 'apple of your eye' (Psa. 17:8). You know my name, my address, my every move, even the number of hairs on my head. I thank you that no weapon formed against me shall prevail (Isa. 54:17); that you keep in perfect peace, the one whose mind is stayed on thee (Isa. 26:3). You will not let my foot slip (Psa. 18:36); my name is written in the Lamb's Book of Life (Rev. 21:27); you have engraved me on the palms of your hands (Isa. 49:16). Today you will scatter my enemy (Psa. 68:1)." What did Moses tell Israel coming out of Egypt? "Stand still and see the salvation of the Lord," for the enemy you have seen today, you will never see again (Ex. 14:13). In the end Pharaoh's whole army was swallowed up by the sea.

All of a sudden, I felt like a spiritual giant. I literally wanted to roll up my shirt sleeves and take them on. But the Holy Spirit said, "God can do a better cleanup job than you, my child." Give God a chance; believe He'll come through. The battle is the Lord's!

So the whistle blew and the train began to leave the platform. (I knew the sounds because as a teenager I used to jump in and out of moving trains.) I just stayed put. I was not one bit afraid or anxious for my life, just excited to see how God would scatter my enemy. The lights dimmed even more so people could sleep, but I still pretended I was reading. The men were inching closer and closer to me. Above the screech of metal hitting metal, as the wheels of the express train moved faster on the tracks, I heard a voice behind me speaking out loud and clear in good English: "Pastors, we are all scattered for the night. I will give you the seat numbers. You are number 25; you are number 37; you are number 54; you are number 78." I realized this was a group of five men—the same number of men who were in my part of the compartment. As he finished, the person speaking was right beside me. I looked up and saw an unusually tall gentleman, olive complexioned and very well dressed.

I said to him, "Excuse me, I happen to be a minister too." He took my hand and shook it while greeting me. So I continued with holy boldness, "Would you mind, please, asking these men to change their seats for those of yours for the night?"

He shook my hand again and said, "Sister, that's a great idea." He bent down, still towering over me as I was seated, and spoke in some other language to the drunken men. I couldn't understand the words, but like lambs, they quickly picked up their luggage, boxes, and bags, and then like lightening, they moved out of the area. He put the fear of God in them.

My God is a way-maker God. He'll only make a way when we yield to the anointing of the Holy Spirit and do whatever He tells us to do. You don't just tell people to change their seats. They have every right to be where they are. But you say what the Spirit of Truth puts in your mouth, as David did, "The Spirit of the Lord spoke through me; his word was on my tongue" (2 Sam. 23:2).

The tall man was followed by four other gentlemen with white complexions into my section. That night all we did was praise, worship, and talk about giving glory to God; we didn't sleep. They were on their way to hold a meeting further down the line than where I was getting off. I remember giving them bottled water and some basic medicines for headache, diarrhea, and stomachache. I told them not to drink any other kind of water nor eat any lettuce or grapes. I suggested they eat crackers in the villages. I asked them where they had come from and where they were going. They said they had arrived at the Chennai airport and would be getting off at 8:30 a.m., and, further, that I would be getting out at 6:30 a.m. I was very comforted in my spirit; I was not alone. We exchanged business cards and addresses. One pastor was from Indianapolis, another from Virginia. I told them I'd catch up with them within the next couple months in the States.

Later, when I got back to New Jersey, I called the church in Virginia and asked for the senior pastor by name to greet him. The church secretary said, "Excuse me, what's the name again?" I told her and she said, "I've been here 30 years and there's never been a man by that name as senior pastor here." Every place I tried to contact, from the cards of those pastors, I got the same story. Only then did I realize that God had put warring angels around me. When you are on a mission for the King of kings and the Lord of lords, He will make sure the apple of His eye won't go into the hands of the enemy. "Whoever dwells in the shelter of the Most High will rest in the shadow of the Almighty" (Psa. 91:1).

So I arrived in Vijayawada and Pastor Tully met me at the train station. When I got there, I had not even paid one dime down for this conference, a week-long series of meetings. It was being put on by an Australian team, so I thought I was just going to see the pastor's village or something. I didn't have a clue in my mind; God had not given me any clear direction. When the pastor picked me up, he said, "Come, let me take you to show you what is happening, because there is no room in the inn." He meant that there was no place yet in the motel—no time for showering or even to brush my teeth! My bags had to be left in someone else's room and I had to stay in the clothes I had traveled in all night.

He took me to this huge auditorium. Five hundred pastors had been sponsored for the conference by this Australian team. The men were lined up, sitting on one side with the little boys in front of them. The women, in their colorful saris, sat on the other side with the small girls seated on mats in front of them. Pastor Tully led me up to the platform where 15 Australians were seated. There was one chair in the center and he said softly, "There's your seat. That's the Australian pastor preaching. As soon as he's done in a minute or two, it's your turn."

So I prayed, "Well, Holy Spirit, I'm available; you're on!" I didn't even have my Bible. I would be using two interpreters, first in Telugu and then in Tamil. The word that God gave me was to tell them about the baptism of the Holy Spirit, that it's not enough just being born again. There's an infilling, a new charging of your batteries. And you know, many of those pastors were baptized in the Holy Spirit that day.

After the service, I found out that the Australian team had lost their luggage at their hotel. It had been stolen from their room. So I was able to provide the women with a change of clothes, shoes, purses—everything they needed. By the time I left India two and a half months later, I had given everything away that the Spirit had told me to pack in my bags. I left for New Jersey with a pen, a few gifts, and the clothes on my back. I transited through France, stopping to see my sister Christine there. Spread out in my room were lots of new clothes she had bought for me—jackets, slacks, blouses, even underclothes. Listen to the Holy Spirit; do what He directs. The best is yet to come!

During the meetings in Vijayawada, one evening we were all in prayer and the worship had started, when God gave me a word of exhortation. More than 500 local people were there and quite a few people stood on the huge platform. Everything had been highly organized. I went to the worship leader and told him I needed the microphone. It is a bit unusual for an Indian woman to dress in Western clothing while ministering, but that night I had worn a skirt and jacket. The microphone was connected to huge loud speakers facing north, south, east and west within the meeting grounds toward those outside, the lost ones.

Vijayawada is a very Muslim area, but the Spirit was directing me to speak, "Many of you sitting in the pubs, gambling halls, and movie theatres, are eating, drinking, and making merry. Little do you know you are going to hell; you will perish. Repent and believe; only Jesus saves!" Even before I finished speaking, men started coming in from the edges of the grounds and filling the altar areas.

Prayer and worship continued, but I could tell that the Indian ministers were very anxious. They were scared for my life; I had spoken through an interpreter in the local Telugu language over the loud speakers. Here I was, an Indian, a woman, dressed in Western garb with no head covering. They couldn't understand how I had the guts to say what I had said. They thought we might be stoned or the place burned down. The more the crowds pressed in toward the platform, the more worried the ministers became.

Usually I have my eyes closed when I worship the Lord, enjoying the moments of intimacy with Him rather than being distracted by whatever is going on. So I spoke again, instructing the men to sit down because it was time for the main sermon. No more chairs were available, so many sat or squatted on the ground. When I finished preaching, the Word of God, that double-edged sword, had done its work. That night hundreds received salvation, healing, and deliverance. Furthermore, 119 people wanted to be baptized in water the following day in the River Krishna. When the pastor asked me to come and baptize the people, I graciously refused. I had heard that the river was stinking, due to the sewage in it, and people used the shore to relieve themselves as they had no toilets. I'm a clean freak, so I made excuses.

The next day, the final day of the meetings, I was conducting a communion service as well as preaching in the morning and evening. The crowd was passing the grape juice in steel glasses. People sipped out of the cup and passed it on. I was starting to think germs, infection, HIV, disease! I was looking for my purse to at least get a tissue to wipe the cup before drinking from it. Immediately I was convicted by the Holy Spirit, "Yesterday you didn't want to baptize those folks who were risking their lives by taking that step. Today you don't want to drink from the same cup as these people—the cup of blessing." I broke down and wept in repentance, took the cup, and truly became one with the body of believers there. It's a communion service I will never forget.

That afternoon I was looking forward to lunch, since I had fasted quite a bit that week. The women had fixed chicken biryani—a mixture of rice and chicken. Just after I had sat down with a plate of food, seven young Muslim women—medical students—came up to me, saying, "Sister Theresa, we heard about these meetings from other students at the hospital. We managed to come out on the quiet, but we don't think we'll be able to come out again. Before we go back to the college, would you please baptize us in water?" My heart went out to them, because I knew they were risking it all. A Muslim-background woman who accepts Christ becomes an outcast. She loses all rights to property and inheritance, forfeits funding for school, and may even be murdered by her own family members as a matter of 'honor.'

I left my plate of food and told them I would meet them at the River Krishna. I hurried to the hotel, changed clothes, and went to the river. We serve a God of second chances! For me, it was an honor to baptize these seven women with the assistance of Pastor Tully. I forgot the stench and waste. Heaven came down and glory filled my soul. That's all I can remember about that afternoon. If those seven are alive today, I believe that they are on fire for Jesus.

CHAPTER 13

SERVING THROUGH BURLINGTON AG

"Seek first his kingdom and his righteousness, and all these things will be given to you as well" (Matt. 6:33).

IN MAY OF 1995 I CAME TO BURLINGTON ASSEMBLY OF GOD IN New Jersey to speak at their Mother-Daughter Banquet on Saturday morning and both services the following Sunday. Then they booked me for a week of meetings and I ended up on staff, ministering for seven and a half months without a day's break. I was preaching five sermons a week on the radio and traveling extensively as well. I would cry and pray late into the night, preparing about 20 sermons a week sometimes. I wanted to hear from God for each message, each congregation. I got few hours of sleep; my passion was souls. Paul Graban served as my senior pastor.

On Thursday evenings if I was not ministering elsewhere, I was asked by Pastor Graban to lead the church prayer meeting. One Thursday I said to the Lord, "I am not satisfied just giving you 50 percent of what I bring in through the preaching and teaching ministry. From now on I would like to give you the entire 100 percent. But Lord, just in case someone comes up to me and offers me some money saying, 'this is for your personal use,' then I will keep that for my expenses."

I had barely made that vow to the Lord when Dick Gaglio, an Italian gentleman and a member of the Burlington AG who worked in New York, came and knelt down in front of me. He placed a $100-bill in my hand and said, "Sister Theresa, the Lord has asked me to give this to you for your personal use. It is not for the ministry." I couldn't believe my ears. I felt the need during the prayer meeting that night to encourage the people's faith by testifying about what had transpired between me and Jesus and how He had sent Dick to me with the exact words I had prayed.

While I was still sharing the story, two people from the back pews were trying to get my attention by waving to me. Arlene Wilkinson, a close friend and neighbor who drove me places, was the first to talk. Her husband was Mason, a devout believer and member of the Church Board. She said, "Sister Theresa, on my dresser at home I have a check for $100.00 which I have already written and kept to hand over to you. In the memo section I have put *For Personal Use.* When I take you home tonight, I will be handing it to you."

The next gentleman to speak was Earl. He said, "Sister Theresa, my wife Carol who is here beside me is my witness. This evening after we had gotten into the car to come to the prayer meeting, I went back into the house and brought out the $100-bill that the Lord had asked me to give to you. My wife asked me how I knew you were going to be at prayer meeting tonight, because you could be anywhere else in the country. But I told her that the Lord told me that you would be coming to church this evening. Sister Theresa, it is not for the ministry because He specifically told me to give it to you for your personal use." I am learning daily as I walk with Jehovah Jireh, my Provider, that I cannot out give Him! Trust Him to supply all your needs and be anxious for nothing for He cares for you.

When I first started as an evangelist, I did a lot of counseling as well. Though I was single, it seemed like I was called especially to minister to hurting women and to many with shaky marriages. Debra Bercaw, who has been the Burlington AG secretary to the senior pastor, filled up my calendar. One Wednesday night after prayer meeting, I met my friend Ann McKelvor, who had brought 18-year-old Dawn Weiss to church.

Ann said, "Sister Theresa, this young lady needs counseling. Let's go to the local diner." I did not know how to get there and didn't drive, being new to the area. Ann was the only one who knew the way, but we had two cars, and even though Dawn was new to the area too, I was going to ride with Dawn.

I told her, "OK, Dawn, I'll sit with you and direct you." I had confidence because I knew how to depend on the Holy Spirit for direction. When we started, I asked Dawn to turn right, out of the church lot, and then left at the traffic light. Ann was behind us at the light. Several others of the church folk were on the same route in their cars. We turned left at the light and drove for a mile or so. Then I asked Dawn to take the next U-turn to get to the other side of the boulevard. I told her, "The diner will be somewhere on the right." We found it and went inside.

As we sat waiting, 15 to 20 minutes passed. Dawn became anxious because there was no sign of Ann. I advised her, "Don't worry. In the next 15 minutes she'll be here. Right now her car's been hit, but she's being ministered to by Dave and Judy Fulton."

"Sister Theresa, how do you know all that?" Dawn asked.

"God just revealed it to me. A blue car came and hit Ann; she wasn't hurt. The car was meant to hit us. Satan does not like the idea of what God is going to do for you today, Dawn." When Ann arrived Dawn asked her if she had been hit by a blue car and whether Dave and Judy Fulton had ministered to her by the side of the road. Ann confirmed it all. The police officer had arrested the two guys in the car that had hit her. That was the starting point for God to reveal himself to Dawn.

Dawn told me her story. She had been raised in a good Roman Catholic home and had been a perfectly normal teenager. One day she was in her car on the way to visit one of her friends. All of a sudden, outside her car window, she saw a dark cloud with a hideous-looking creature inside it. This demonic creature said to Dawn, "I have your soul." The moment she heard the voice she got scared; she believed this creature. How easily people exchange the truth of God for the lie of the enemy!

In a flash Dawn could not recall where she was going or what her friend's name was. She went to a parking lot and looked for a public phone. All she could remember was her parents' name and phone number. Her mind was messed up from then on. She was attractive, intelligent, and had everything in her favor, but became full of doubts and a spirit of defeat. She told me, "I don't have a face. I don't see my face at all."

"How do you do your makeup or sip coffee?" I asked her.

"I don't know, I can't tell."

So when I prayed with her that evening, she said, "When I'm with you, I have no fears. I feel peace. Can I stay with you?"

"No, you have to go home tonight. You can come tomorrow and meet me at the office." When she came the next day we opened with prayer. I placed a Bible in her hand and asked her to read from the Book of John, where Jesus said, "I am the way and the truth and the life" (14:6) and "I am the good shepherd" (10:14). Satan comes to "steal and kill and destroy," but Christ came to give us abundant life (John 10:10).

She did not even believe that she had hands. "Dawn," I said, "The hands holding the Bible are yours. The eyes reading are yours." I gave her my Bible that day. It took several sessions for Dawn to get free of the lies of the enemy. Only the truth of God's Word set her free. This beautiful woman is serving God today. "He calls his own sheep by name and leads them out" (John 10:3).

On another occasion I was sitting in the same Burlington diner after a late night meeting—about 11:30 p.m. or so. The waitress said, "Sister Theresa, I've not met you, but everyone in this restaurant seems to know you, including the owner. They tell me you can see through people." I just shut my mouth. I didn't want to say anything. There is a waiting period; only when God gives you the word can you speak. So she continued, "Sister Theresa, are you the lady who has that psychic place on the other side of the street? Good one, isn't it?" (A female spiritist lived near the diner.)

Still I kept quiet. My companion, Stella French, an American lady in her 60s, turned around and said, "That's not Sister Theresa's. She is an ordained minister, an evangelist. If she can see through people, it's because the Holy Spirit reveals things to her." The good news is that God has no favorites. He wants to reveal things to you too, to let people know the truth and for the truth to set them free. (See John 8:32.)

"Sister Theresa, can you tell me about myself?" she asked.

"No, I cannot, unless God reveals it to me," I replied. In my spirit I prayed, "Father, this girl is precious to you. She is going to be precious to me. Speak through me life-giving words into her life."

As she started to leave, I told her, "You're not going, stand here." I put my hand on her hand. She was in her late 40s, maybe, but she looked like a teenager in her dress. The Lord just began to bring words out of my mouth, like wellsprings of living water: "This is your third partner. You've not been married to any of them before. Your two daughters are doing the same. The child living with you is not even your own."

She couldn't believe her ears—all these facts about her life, coming out of my mouth. She just knelt there and she gave a yell. Now this is a diner, a restaurant with people in it. She was down on the floor and I just put my hand on her head. I said, "Relax, it's the love of Jesus. He wants to pour into you. You're never going to be the same." I got up from my seat, went to the owner, and reminded her that the woman was off duty.

Then I asked the woman to sit with us and I gave her the Word of God. That woman truly has never been the same! She's still working at the same diner and people have seen the difference. Let people know you have Christ living in you. He's what makes the difference.

Carey Brown, head usher of Burlington Assembly, delivered pharmacy drugs to shut-ins in the New Jersey area. On one of his trips he visited Penny Pappas, who lived all by herself, to give her a new supply. He knocked, but there was no response. The door was ajar, so he put his head in and called, "Miss Pappas, are you there?" Still no response. Her bed was in the first room of the house. She suffered from cancer of the jawbone. Beside her bed on the table were a crucifix and a blade. When Carey came in and stood by her bed, he asked if everything was all right or did she need help.

"I've had enough of sickness in my life. I've decided to end it," Penny offered. She had been a nurse in the army, but life had dealt some tough blows. A few years earlier her daughter, son, and husband had gone out in their sailboat. It capsized and all three drowned. Her in-laws were nasty and took all she had. She had to fend for herself and it had been hard. After scans, tests, and medicines, doctors had let Penny know that there was no more hope for her.

Carey is usually a very shy man. I don't think he had ever prayed for people, one on one. But that day he felt burdened for Penny and asked to pray for her. He knelt by her bedside and prayed. Before he left, he made sure to move the blade out of sight and promised to send his wife Dot and her friend Barbara Williams to care for her needs. A real gentleman, he rushed home to get the two women moving to help Penny. Both of them are prayer warriors. They went to Penny, ministered to her, loved on her, and told her how God was using an ex-nun to preach on the radio five times a week. They urged her to hear God's Word over the radio. They also invited her to go with them the following Wednesday night when I would be preaching at the church.

I don't remember the topic of the message that evening, but I noticed the three women waiting at the altar for me to come and pray with them. My friends Dot and Barbara introduced me to Penny and told me she was scheduled for surgery on her jaw the next morning. Surgeons would try to remove the cancer. "Do you believe that Jesus still heals?" I asked her.

A humble servant of God, Penny answered, "Yes, Sister Theresa, I believe."

"Dave Boudwin, please join us in prayer, agreeing for Penny's healing," I said to the senior associate pastor. He joined us as I anointed Penny with oil and prayed a prayer of faith over her, "Father, I thank you for giving Penny a brand-new jawbone, so that you will get all the glory. I thank you for this in Jesus' name."

Penny was in her 80s, but looked younger. Excitedly she told me that she wanted to come and hear me more often. My friends offered to bring her messages on tape. Early the next morning, Penny went to the hospital for surgery, but this time with a difference. When the attendant asked her to sign the consent form, she refused. She told him she wanted to see her doctor, a Jewish surgeon. The doctor had no choice but to come out and meet with her. She said to him, "Doctor, there'll be no surgery done on me this morning. I've been healed."

He said, "Penny, stop kidding. You've been an army nurse. You know your condition. You've seen the scans and read the reports. The cancer is spreading; we've got to remove it today. Penny, you will look as good as new if you'll let us help you."

"But doctor, I already have a new jawbone."

"Who operated on you?"

"It was the Great Physician, Jesus himself," she declared. He thought she was still pulling a fast one on him. "Doctor, just take one more X-ray of my jawbone, so that you can see it for yourself," she insisted. Again the doctor did as she requested.

After the X-ray, Penny sat waiting for a response. When no one came to meet with her, she pushed right into the doctor's office. She went to his desk where he sat dumbfounded with her X-rays in front of him. He looked up and said, "You're right girl, you have been healed. But who healed you?"

"Didn't I tell you once?" Penny said. "It was Jesus who healed me."

"Oh, you mean 'the man up there?'"

"Yes, He's up there, but He's also with me here in my heart. I'm a new creation, inside and out!" Penny had a photo taken of her with her doctor. She had it printed on a mug and sent it to me. Every time the church doors opened, Penny was the first to get in. She asked Pastor Graban for water baptism and later she was gloriously filled with the Holy Spirit. She was all excited about Jesus and what He had done for her.

As a young evangelist, invited to large churches to preach, I preferred not to know anything about the pastors or congregations. That way I would have no influence from people regarding what I should share and I would get my messages from the Lord. One pastor invited me to share my testimony with his congregation at the 6 p.m. service on a Sunday. I arrived just in time for the service. At 11 p.m. I left the sanctuary, having seen God move. I had to hit the road because I was scheduled to preach in another place the following morning. So I left and never got to know the pastor.

The following year he invited me back to the church to speak both morning and evening services on a Sunday. I was not very happy with the message God asked me to preach there. Half a dozen times I flipped through my Bible trying to find another message. Every time the same message came from the Spirit. Even a song on the radio and a word from a friend confirmed what God was saying to me: "You have robbed God of His tithes and offerings; therefore you are under a curse" (see Mal. 3:8-9). I thought that was a word for a senior pastor to bring, not an evangelist.

The more I struggled, the harder I found it to hear from God. I will only speak what God wants me to speak, so I was up most of the night working on the message. I had been to Bible college, but I didn't know the passages on this topic very well. How little I knew of God's Word, yet He was willing to use me! I kept hearing this word on 'paneled houses' in my spirit. Little did I realize that it was from Haggai. Even after putting the message together, there was a tug-of-war in my spirit, right up to the time I got to the church. The sound of drums and loud music jarred my spirit. It seemed like the cackle of geese when the people sang. My spirit was grieving, though I knew nothing at all about this church.

I turned to the senior pastor, who stood beside me on the platform, and said, "Pastor, it's time for me to preach."

He was a humble, godly, elderly man. He said, "Sister Theresa, our Sunday morning congregation does not know you. Can I introduce you?"

"No," I said, "there's no need of an introduction. They don't need to know who I am. I have a message from the Lord for them and it's burning in my bones."

"OK, Sister," he said. "Go ahead." He then moved down and sat in one of the front pews.

For 45 minutes, a strong word of rebuke came from my mouth—a challenge to the congregation. "You have robbed God of His tithes and offerings and have left His house in ruins. You've built your own paneled houses and allowed His house to rot and rust." When I was done ministering the Word I told them that no one should come to the altars, but instead, I went on to say, "'Your iniquities have separated you from your God; your sins have hidden his face from you, so that he will not hear' (Isa. 59:2). Go home and come back this evening with God's tithes and offerings. Put IOUs in the offering if you do not have it now. Be sure to pay God. When you have done that, you will see God move mightily in this place tonight." I noticed that the pastor was crying bitterly and the woman beside him wept too.

Between the two services the church had Sunday school classes. One senior associate came to me and asked me if I would take over his Sunday school class in the main sanctuary. I've always been very careful to guard the anointing and not do anything other than what God wants me to do in a place. I told him, "God did not send me here to teach your Sunday school class; you can do it yourself." He started weeping and I could sense God's anointing all over him.

Not knowing that the lady I met was the senior pastor's wife, I asked her if there was any place I could go and hide myself until the next service. "I don't need anyone to come and bring me in for the next service. I'll come when it is time," I told her. She led me to a little room where I could lock myself in and be alone with God. Later I joined the senior pastor on the platform for the second service.

Again the music and drums jarred my spirit. Again I turned to the pastor and told him it was time to preach. I went to the pulpit and for the next 45 minutes preached just as in the first service. I was told later that I had preached the exact same words I had brought forth in the first service. I told the people not to come forward, but first to repent, change, and give back to God what was His. Only then would He hear their prayers.

I decided that I wasn't going to lunch, so I excused myself and told the pastor I would return in time for the evening service. I did not want to be influenced by anyone from the congregation about anything to do with that church. I knew God had a message for them and I knew what it was. That night the sanctuary was packed with people. In fact people were standing outside the doors because there was no more room inside. They were bringing in the sick in wheelchairs and cars kept coming into the parking lot.

I ministered a much milder message, bringing comforting words from God. Afterwards God brought a mighty move of the Spirit, healings, and deliverances. At one stage the altars got so packed that the people had to stand in the aisles to pray. I went toward one young lady, who was crying bitterly and leaning on the shoulder of a gentleman. My eyes were open and I started moving in the flesh. I thought, "This girl is too young. He's old enough to be her father." When I got to them, I put one hand on each of them. Speaking in the Spirit I said, "Stop crying; start listening. God's not deaf. He's heard your cry. Start receiving." When I said this, the man fell to the ground. God led me to anoint him with oil and I prayed, "Right now you are receiving brand new kidneys." I found out later that he was one of the pastors of the church and she was his daughter. Both his kidneys had been failing; the doctors in New York had given up on him. Little did I realize he was the same man who had come to me about teaching his Sunday school class that morning. That pastor is still alive today with those new kidneys.

While I was ministering at the same altars, I began to sense in my spirit that I should go to a man who was wearing a long-sleeved shirt with orange stripes on it. I wondered if he was a clown. The Lord reveals the second step only after we follow the first, so I had to depend on the Holy Spirit to lead me to this particular person. As I started praying in the Spirit, I was moved from one end of the sanctuary to the other. Down below, a man was curled up on the floor and was wearing a white shirt with orange stripes. I put my hand on his back and gave him a word of knowledge. The Lord revealed to him through me the following message, "Son, you don't have to be in two minds anymore. Stay on at the prison as a corrections officer. I know you have a burden to take this gospel to the 10/40 Window. The time will come. My timing is perfect."

After the church had cleared, I went for a meal with the senior pastor and his wife. He told me God had burdened him, even given him a vision, about building a new sanctuary. People in the church were affluent, but not tithers. They had already broken ground on the other side of the present sanctuary. The foundation was laid and the steel beams put up, but they had rusted for four years because of lack of funds to continue. Within six months of my message, the new sanctuary was up and finished. The next District Council meetings for that denomination were held in that new building.

The following year at a different church, when I had finished ministering at the altars one night, praying for people, a man came running down the center aisle waving a video at me. "Sister Theresa, I've been to the 10/40 Window. Here it is. You remember that day when you gave me that message from the Lord? I stayed where I was and God opened the right door at the right time and put the right people with me. God paid for everything and I was able to minister extensively over there. I'm here to tell you that you did hear from God for me." (I must admit I cannot remember what I tell people most of the time unless they refresh my memory.)

One Saturday I was sitting in my room preparing for the Sunday services and praying, "Lord, don't let the enemy touch one soul that you want in that church tomorrow." It is "'not by might nor by power, but by my Spirit,' says the Lord Almighty" (Zech. 4:8). It is God who gives His Word and the anointing to bring it forth.

As I sat there, suddenly I received a vision of four dress suits in a row. I said, "Get behind me, Satan. I'm not even interested in shopping." In the best of times, I'm not a shopper. Men, you would be very happy if you took me shopping. The thing is, I like to know what I want and where it is. I look at clearance racks, nothing more. I pick it up, pay, and get out. That's my way of shopping. It has to be $9.99. I cannot bear window shopping. Believe it or not, I think it's the athlete in me. I've got to keep moving; there's so much to do. My sisters and sisters-in-law tell me, "We've got to go shopping with you, because you get the best deals in no time."

I say, "No, I don't just go shopping. I go when I'm pushed by the Holy Spirit. I have to know that I need something. You know what? Most of the times I don't even have to go; it's brought to me."

So when I saw those four suits, I wondered why the Lord was giving me such a vision. The suits looked really exquisite, well made, and just perfect for the fall season just ahead. I was trying to put this picture out of my mind, though I felt the Lord was prompting me to go shopping. I said, "Lord, you know better. I don't go shopping on a Saturday, because I'm waiting on you. I've got your message in my spirit. I've put it together, but I'm just going to pray and fast today."

Just then the phone rang. Of all people, the lady who called me was a member of the church who just couldn't stop talking. There have even been times when I've heard her voice and I've just let the message go on the answering machine. When you are in prayer, you don't want someone to take you out of that time. So when this young lady called me she said, "Sister Theresa, I've taken the day off, because the Lord told me to take you shopping."

I responded somewhat impatiently, "Wait a minute. Don't you know that on Saturdays I don't go shopping?"

"Yes, I know that," she continued, "but when the Lord tells you, you know you've got to do it. So come on! Girl, I'm coming to your place in an hour's time."

"No, give me an hour first. I need to pray about this."

"No, you don't have to pray about it. The Lord has told me to take you shopping. There's no praying about things the Lord has already spoken."

So I said, "Give me an hour."

In one hour's time she was at the door, honking her horn. As soon as I got to the car I said, "Listen, put on a worship tape, OK? Then I'll enter your car, because we're not chatting and we're not talking in the car. We're going to worship the Lord all the way."

She responded, "I'm ready to do anything, but I'm supposed to take you shopping." She took me to the Burlington Coat Factory, which was just about ten minutes' drive away from where I live. We went inside and the very suit that I had seen in the vision was there, marked down from $250 to about $30 or so. You won't believe it. Not just one suit was there, but in no time three suits I had seen were there.

Then I said, "Lord, this is getting too much. I've never bought three suits at a time." They were just the ones I had seen, but there had been four in the vision.

As I started to leave the store my friend said, "No, I don't think you're done. You've got to have one more suit, don't you?"

I said, "No, this is enough for the whole year. You know what I do. No one knows what I have worn in the other state where I have ministered, so who cares? I just carry three or four outfits and rotate them. You know it's not about clothes; it's about the kingdom of God. I like things that don't need ironing and don't get creased when you pack them in a suitcase. Anyway, God knows best."

She wouldn't budge from that store, saying, "I've got to do some shopping, so you'd better just go look for the fourth suit."

I was almost at the door, but something would not let me go out. I tried to go through the door, but I seemed to be pulled back. So I decided I had better wait for her on the inside after all. Just then I was drawn to a rack where everything was marked down to $9.99 and below. I said to myself, "No, I don't need those fashionable dresses, because I'm a preacher. I need something that's decent enough and modest...." But suddenly, something made me turn that rack and in between all those beautiful flowing dresses I spotted the fourth suit I had seen in the vision—the red and black one. I took it out and couldn't believe my eyes. It was $250 marked down to $9.99!

I just couldn't believe it. I'm not greedy over clothes or anything, so I went looking for the manager to tell them they had made a mistake. The manager said, "Girl, if I were you, I'd run out with it. I don't know why you're even bothering to ask why it's marked down."

I said, "I think one of your sales representatives must have made a mistake. This suit should not go for $9.99."

She asked, "What's your size?" I told her I was a size 8. She said, "You know what? This is size 8. You'd better take it and run."

"No," I insisted, "I don't see why you should be marking this down." I was arguing with her because I didn't feel right about buying it. So she asked to take a look at the suit. She found that a button was missing. That's why it was marked down. "So for one button missing, you mark it down that much? No, I'll take it only if it fits me."

I went into the fitting room and met an older lady that I had been trying to evangelize some time back. I said, "Mary, I can't believe it. This suit is marked down to $9.99."

She replied, "Girl, if I were you, I wouldn't wait. I wouldn't even come to the fitting room."

So I said, "No, there's a button missing, that's all. But I still think, really, someone has not done things right here."

"Go try it on, girl." So while I went to try it on, Mary went to get me the button. See how gracious God is? This was a unique button, but she went in somewhere and got the exact button from a container of ones that had been picked up off the floor. That's our God! Even before you ask Him, it's there. He answers even the prayers we are not thinking of. He is Jehovah Jireh, our Provider. He provides health, strength, abilities, freedom in the Spirit, boldness, and confidence—all there for the asking. He says, "You have not because you ask not" (James 4:2, KJV).

On another occasion I needed a white skirt. I wanted one with lining, so I need not wear a slip, and I asked God for it to be wrinkle-free fabric and to cost only $9.99. Later I saw it in a vision and knew that it was at a J. C. Penney's store. On a Tuesday morning I went to teach my Bible study. My friend Stella French was there waiting, so I asked her why she was not at work. She said, "I came to take you shopping. God spoke to me and told me to take the day off, take you to lunch and go shopping."

I told her I had no time to talk and would see her after the Bible study. I went to the office to collect the mail. After the study, we had lunch first and then Stella asked where I wanted to shop. I said, "I'm not really a shopper, but I have a skirt waiting for me at Penney's which I need to pick up." We walked into the store and headed for the women's section. On a rack was the exact skirt I had asked God for, at the exact price. The Holy Spirit walks with us. The Shepherd of Israel who never slumbers or sleeps knows the desire of your heart and meets it. Stella took it and would not let me pay for it, saying, "This has to be God."

On our way out of the store I saw some white sandals on a table. My sandals in India had split in two from walking on hot tar roads. I had no time to take them to a cobbler; he couldn't have fixed them anyway. I looked at the price of this pair and put them down quickly, shocked. They cost over $40, which

I thought was too expensive. Do you know what that much money could do in India? "Let me get them for you," Stella offered. Just then God showed me the exact same pair for $2 in a thrift store, on the left side, second shelf. I told Stella we weren't buying the sandals. "But don't you need them?" she asked. She even went on to say that she wanted to put shoes on the feet that take the gospel.

"Yes, God knows I need them, but He has a better deal for me. Come and let me tell you. Right now, the identical pair of sandals is waiting for me in a thrift store. As we walk in they will be on the left side, second shelf from the top, for two dollars." Now Stella is a classy Italian lady and hadn't been in a thrift store in her life, but there's always a first time.

She said, "Sister Theresa, I've never been in a thrift store. Do you know which one it is?"

"No, you can take me to any one that you know of."

"On my way to work every morning I pass by one."

"OK, take me to that one." Stella would not wait in the car. She had to see this. I found the sandals exactly as God had shown me, for $2. She wouldn't let me pay for them either. Start walking with Jesus. Become a friend of God. He will grant you the least desires of your heart. If we can just lean on Him, not our own understanding, He will direct our paths. (See Prov. 3:5-7.) "Seek first his kingdom and his righteousness, and all these things will be given to you as well" (Matt. 6:33).

One year, Evangelist R. W. Shambach set up a tent on the Burlington church grounds for evangelistic meetings. I shared his passion for souls and was seated in the front at a Friday night meeting. At one point he said, "I would like to have a larger tent, so I could win more souls. I'm going to distribute these pledge cards. If you could help me, I would be so grateful."

I thought, "Whatever he has as the highest figure on that card, I'd like to pledge that amount." My pastor, Paul Graban, had generously given me the liberty to travel to other churches to evangelize, paying for my meals, travel, and accommodations as part of their staff. Since leaving the convent I had not taken one cent of offerings for myself. It all went for missions. I was scheduled to preach that upcoming weekend at the Word of Life Church in Springfield, Virginia—three services on Sunday plus speaking to the students of their academy on Monday morning. When I received Shambach's blue pledge card in my hand, I saw that the highest figure was $1,000. I was not disturbed, but rather relieved, because I had exactly that amount in the bank. I wrote out a check and dropped it in the offering the next morning before leaving for Virginia.

The couple driving me to Virginia was Eleanor and Pete, our church treasurer and board member. She also handled my banking. Monday afternoon, after Pastor Wendel Cover had taken us to lunch, he put an envelope into my hand. I thanked him and later handed it to Eleanor, asking her to put it into the account. She opened it and said, "Take a look." I told her it was for God's glory and for missions and to just deposit it. She insisted that I needed to look at it. The church offering was for $3,000. I had given Evangelist Shambach just $1,000. You really cannot out give God!

God has constantly used the humblest people to bless me with my day-to-day needs. Stella French, a widow, went back to work in order to support us on the mission field. Brother Lonnie and Sister Leria Scott for several years supplied me with a monthly stock of Amway supplements as well as toothpaste. Just when the Scotts became bedridden and disabled, God laid it on Lou and Kathy Houston's hearts to bless both David and me with supplements on a six-month basis. This couple knew nothing of the Scotts having supplied these items to us. I never missed a day of taking my supplements for my God is mindful of me.

Retirees Annemarie and Desmond Jackson are another neat couple that God used. Annemarie went back to driving the school bus route and working at the mall in order to keep us harvesters going in India. Kay Mosley, Dorothy D'Mauro,

Carol Tillinghast and Kathy Keane have been and still are God's charioteers to take me to my appointments. God knows that He does not want me to be driving if I've got to be preaching. I am in prayer and the study of the Word until I finish my preaching appointments. Secondly, you would not want this Indian to bring the traffic in America to a complete halt. While in India, I drive on the other side of the street and my steering wheel too is on the other side of the car. And finally, I truly don't know what I'd do without my "prayer warriors" in the different states God has used me to minister in. I especially want to mention the New Jersey, Missouri, California, and Arkansas ones here.

CHAPTER 14

ANGELIC VISITATIONS

"Are not all angels ministering spirits sent to serve those who will inherit salvation?" (Heb. 1:14).

TRAVELING PRESENTED OTHER CHALLENGES AT TIMES. ONE time I left a country and planned to return a few days later to minister at a convention. While out of the country, I was supposed to get a stamp in my passport from the embassy of the country I was returning to. I thought it would be no problem, but after contacting two different embassies, I discovered that I could get an appointment only after 15 days. I knew God wanted me to preach at that convention. I had a return ticket by air. My friends offered to drive me across the border, but I didn't feel that was the answer. They said, "OK, if God wants you to go by air, and you aren't permitted to leave without that stamp, we'll wait for you here."

I told them, "No, that won't be necessary. My God is a way-maker God."

I went to the airport, got my boarding pass with my passport and ticket, and was proceeding to the immigration check. At the entrance to the immigration hall stood a tall, tan-complexioned gentleman with a white uniform and a big smile on his face. He put out his hand and I started to give him my boarding pass and passport, knowing that I did not have the required stamp in it. Instead of taking the passport, he motioned me to go ahead. With a smile he said, "Sister, you go right in."

I went on to the immigration area, where the booths were. There were no officers and no one in line—in fact no one in sight. I peeped into two of the booths on either side and walked on through as the man had instructed. In the boarding area I called my friends' home from a pay phone (no cell phones in those days). I left a message telling them, "God has seen me through."

On another occasion my friend Kay Mosley from New Jersey had booked an air ticket for me from Philadelphia to California. The evening I was leaving she came from work, picked me up, and took me to the Newark airport. We were chatting all the way. After parking, we headed to the counter to get my boarding pass. I handed the attendant my ticket and remarked that he had the same name as my older brother, Tony. I could read his name on his ID badge. This Tony turned to me and said, "I don't think you'll make it on time for this flight."

"But," I started to protest, "I've got an hour before the flight leaves."

He explained, "Ma'am this flight leaves from Philly and you are at the Newark airport."

Just then "the Spirit of the Lord spoke through me" (2 Sam. 23:2). I opened my mouth and said, "Look into your computer right now. There's a plane on the tarmac. Get me on it. I already owe the airline $100 and here it is. My luggage is here; my friend Kay is here. Tell me which gate to go to."

"Ma'am, that plane leaves in two minutes."

"That's OK, make sure I get onto that plane. I'll get my connecting flight to Orange County, California, where Joan Longobardo will be waiting for me." He gave me the gate number and I said, "God bless you, Tony. I'll be praying for you."

With tears in his eyes he told me, "I can do with all the prayers I can get. My wife just divorced me."

"My friend here will minister to you," I called out as I started running with my carry-on bag and purse. Pretty soon I was huffing and puffing as I looked ahead at the entire corridor. Behind me not a soul was in sight. "God, you're not going to let me down now, are you?"

Out of nowhere appeared an unusually tall gentleman driving a cart right up beside me. He had a smile on his face as he said, "Sister, give me your bag and your hand." He put me in the cart and like lightning we were at the gate. The door of the plane was just starting to close as I ducked inside. I stood in front of a flight attendant who was asking if I was OK. I told her all I needed was something to drink. I got to my seat and she brought me a glass of orange juice. For the next few minutes I just laughed and laughed. The joy of the Lord is our strength! I had messed up big time by going to the wrong airport, but my God doesn't mess up. I got to my connecting flight and made it to Orange County; my luggage made it too.

On another ministry trip, this time from O'Hare, Chicago, to Little Rock, I went to get a boarding pass for my next flight. I handed my thick passport to the ticketing agent who looked through it three times. The man's last name was Fernandes, the same as my mother's maiden name. He was mean and said, "I'll see to it that you do not get onto this flight." He seemed jealous as he flipped the pages and saw all the places I had been.

"Can you please get me the supervisor?" I asked.

"They're on break right now."

"My flight is about to leave; can you please give me my boarding pass?"

"Didn't you hear what I told you?" he snarled.

Led of the Holy Spirit I went and knocked on the door beside him. This was Saturday evening, with no other flights available. I was to preach in the Beebe, Arkansas, Assemblies of God church the next day. The supervisor who came out was an African American lady, kind and godly. I had tears in my eyes as I said, "Ma'am, my flight is about to leave and I do not yet have my boarding pass. I was told to collect it here, but this man's giving me a tough time. She went to a computer and gave me my boarding pass. She called someone on her wireless phone and said, "Stop that plane that has just left the gate. There's one more passenger."

I started running with my carry-on bag. An agent met me at the stairs, took my bag in his hand, and started running to catch the already moving airplane. The plane stopped, opened the door, put down its steps, and allowed me to board. Praise God, that I was able to make it to Pastor Glenn Dorsey's church for ministry. The God of miracles never ceases to amaze me.

Lisa and Brett, the daughter and son-in-law of Pastor Dorsey, got married in August 1998. They started trying to conceive in late 1999. After a year without conception, Lisa went to her gynecologist for help. The lady didn't have much to offer, so she changed doctors. The next doctor did a few tests and found nothing wrong. So, the next step was to have Brett tested. Lisa received the results over the phone at work. She works at an Outpatient Surgery Center and many there do not see through eyes of faith, but they see logic and medicine as their only hope.

When the doctor told Lisa the news, she was devastated. He said that Brett had a very low sperm count, poor motility, which is poor movement of the sperm, and only two percent of the sperm were normal. The doctor said he had talked to the top fertility specialists in the state, and they had said there was no way she could conceive. She then cried her eyes out, and all of a sudden God spoke to her clearly.

God told Lisa to take her hands off and let Him do the work. She had tried so hard to be in control and to figure out a way to fix it. God spoke to her and Brett individually and told them they would have a child. They both knew it would happen; they just didn't know how and when. The day she received the bad news from the doctor, she also received a letter from her cousin that boosted her faith.

In the letter, her cousin talked about how she was a miracle baby because her mother didn't have fallopian tubes. Her cousin had later had three miracle babies herself. The letter couldn't have come at a better time. The next day when she went to work, her coworkers couldn't believe how happy she was, knowing the news she had received the day before. She knew God wanted her to proclaim her faith before He would do anything.

Lisa asked her coworkers to gather in the lounge because she wanted to tell them why she was so happy. A variety of denominations were represented—from Baptist to Mormon. She read them the letter her cousin had sent and told them that when God would give them this conception, He would get all the credit. That was February 2002. As time went on her coworkers and other people would ask her if she was going to adopt. She would tell them they didn't feel that adoption was for them. They knew God was going to give them a child.

In October 2004, while ministering at Lisa's church and not knowing then that she was the senior pastor's daughter, by the grace of God I prophesied over Lisa and said, "You have been attacked from every side, but the Lord wants you to spread your wings and try one more time to fly and not look at your circumstances. The Lord wants to put a fire in you that will last. You have said you're not asking the Lord anymore. Will you believe one more time? There has been gossip, but you are a fruitful bough. You will hold the blessing in your arms to show them."

When I told Lisa that she was not asking the Lord anymore, she knew it was God, because she had spoken those words only to her husband in their bedroom one night. She meant that if God would give them a child, that would be great, but she wasn't going to ask Him anymore. Six months later, in May 2005, she became pregnant. She went back to work, gathered all her coworkers together, and told them the news.

They were so excited. When she went for her first ultrasound, they found cysts on both of her ovaries. One was the size of a tennis ball. The doctor said if they continued to grow he may possibly have to do surgery during her pregnancy or maybe after the baby was born. They prayed and God did another miracle. When she went back for the next examination, both cysts were gone.

On January 24, 2006, Kallie Elizabeth Vandiver was born. On May 11, 2009, Kaden Brett Vandiver was born. It took six long years to conceive Kallie, but God's timing is perfect. He stretched their faith and made it easier for them to believe for another child, or anything else for that matter. Kaden only took six months to conceive, and he is an awesome blessing. Lisa and Brett continue to give all the glory to God.

One sunny Saturday morning Eleanor came to drive me to a breakfast meeting for women at the Metuchen, New Jersey Assembly of God. I asked her if she had eaten anything and she told me she had eaten some oatmeal. I got in the car in the front seat beside her. A worship tape was playing and my Bible lay on my lap. All of a sudden, while we were going down the highway, I noticed Eleanor was driving in the passing lane and then zooming in and out of both lanes. Her hands were on the steering wheel, but her eyes were tightly closed. I tapped Eleanor on the shoulder and asked if she was all right. I didn't get a response. She seemed to be unconscious.

I realized we were in intense spiritual warfare. I knew that the place we were heading to had a good number of Hindu women who were planning to attend that day. The church operated an academy which had a number of Indian students, and they had invited their mothers to come that morning. A large Hindu temple was located near the church.

So I called out to the Lord, "God, you've got to send your warring angels to take over." All of a sudden, brighter than the daylight, two large angelic beings came and settled down on the front fenders of the car. Great peace came over me. All I could see was the outline of their wingspan and the shape of their bodies, not their faces. I turned to Eleanor and patted her on the shoulder, saying, "You can sleep all you want, girl. God's in control!" We reached Metuchen Assembly safely that morning and we had a great breakfast meeting. When I told the folks what had happened to us on the way, the senior pastor and his wife, Don and Cynthia McFarren, were not surprised. They said that every preacher who tried to come to their church had experienced intense attack.

CHAPTER 15

DIVINE APPOINTMENTS

"The Spirit of the Lord is upon me" (Luke 4:18).

PASTOR JOHN BEDZYK OF ELMIRA, NEW YORK, CONTACTED Pastor Graban saying, "Please ask Sister Theresa if she will come, because the Lord spoke to me and asked me to get her to my church. But ask her not to wear any makeup or jewelry." My response when Pastor Graban approached me was, "Please tell that pastor that if he wants me in his church, he takes the chicken with the dressing—no offense please."

After a few days I started praying. I had my own teeth, good hair and skin, and wore minimal jewelry. I decided to go; God had given me a word. The invitation was to speak at a Friday banquet for senior citizens, Sunday morning and evening services, and a TV program airing before that Sunday. The church was packed with people on Sunday. They had heard that an ex-nun would be speaking, who had nothing to say against the Catholic Church.

We are not here to point fingers at any denomination. I thank God for placing me in the Roman Catholic Church for such a time as that, so that I could be trained in prayer and spiritual disciplines. Later on when I left the convent, I used to pray six hours at a stretch every night. Without prayer and without the Word, I couldn't stand in front of anyone. God takes what I offer Him, uses it and anoints it for His glory. If I don't have His Word, what will He anoint? At times I was preaching 12-21 messages a week without reusing any of my notes. I want to hear from God for the people He sends me to. Don't get your sermons out of your books or your filing cabinets and say, "Thus saith the Lord" when you come to church. You didn't spend five minutes in prayer to be able to serve fresh manna to the people. Let us speak as His mouthpiece, walk in humility and love and feed His people.

That Sunday evening in New York, some other churches closed and joined with the Assemblies of God service. For ten days, we had church! If you want something from God, Joshua told his people, "Consecrate yourselves, for tomorrow the Lord will do amazing things among you" (Josh. 3:5). I need to be consecrated; you need to be consecrated. We are a "chosen people, a royal priesthood, a holy nation, God's special possession" (2 Pet. 2:9), a people set apart through God's authority. We are busy binding and loosing and cursing and rebuking instead of walking in His authority. Don't waste time doing things God did not ask you to do.

While the revival continued, the church did not have to pay for advertising. The TV Director came to me in a restaurant and asked me for an interview. I replied, "I will, but not here. Come to my church." He did! You have authority. Start using your authority as a child of God. We move in the power and anointing of Elijah, of John the Baptist. These men ministered as God spoke through them. You want to see power? Learn to wait on God; learn to hear from God. He is in charge, not you or me.

Another time I was invited to minister at a church and the pastor had advertised in the town that I would be coming. God had used me mightily in the past and revival had broken out in places I had spoken. This was a huge church with high-tech security all over the place. The pastor was of German background. I was ushered into the sitting area of the senior pastor's office—fit for a king. My friend Susan and I were directed toward a seating area. She sat in a comfortable easy chair and I sat on one end of a sofa. A glass table sat in front of us. The associate pastor walked in and icily said that he was horrified to see Susan sitting on the chair that was meant for the senior pastor. We knew nothing of this, of course, since the lady who had brought us in didn't instruct us, except to invite us to make ourselves at home. The associate asked Susan to please move out of that chair.

We were now on our guard. He turned to me and said, "Here's the lapel mike." He placed it on the glass table. "There's the bathroom; you can go in there. Give yourself two minutes and be back here so I can give you instructions." He walked out of the room and came back after a few moments. He saw the lapel mike still on the table and asked, "Why didn't you do what I told you to?"

"I have no problem fastening a lapel mike on right here in your presence," I told him. He looked shocked. He then told me that I would have just 30 minutes in the first service. As soon as the 30 minutes was up, I was to introduce him and he would take over at the pulpit and give people further instructions. He told me to say, "Now the senior associate pastor will give you instructions as to how you are to come up for the altar call."

I very graciously agreed on the outside, but not on the inside. I could sense in my spirit that with all these rules and regulations, the Holy Spirit was being quenched in this place. I prayed, "Lord, forgive me. I don't want to be rebellious. I just want to stay yielded to whatever you want to do in this place today. Be glorified!"

When I was done ministering the Word, I stopped on the half-hour mark and introduced the senior associate pastor and moved away from the pulpit. I went to my place, stood with my eyes closed and hands lifted, and started crying out to God in my spirit for the Holy Spirit to break loose in that place. I don't think I heard the instructions being given as the associate organized the people; I started moving in the Spirit. The senior pastor, associates, and board members were all at the altars, lined up in regimental rows like an army. God led me first to pray for the senior pastor of that congregation and then the senior associate and down the line. Board members, altar workers, counselors, ushers, everyone went down one by one like ninepins. They were falling under God's power, which is somewhat unusual in my ministry. And they could not get up. Then God led me to pray for the rest of the congregation. Not a soul had moved from that church. All the people were down front.

The second service went on without any hindrance. One of the women altar workers handed me a little baby to pray over. I anointed her with oil, prayed, and handed her back. I stretched out my hands and touched the tall American father and his wife on their backs and prayed. Both of them fell down. The woman lay calmly, but the man struggled to get up. I told him to stay calm and let God minister to him. Then out of my mouth came the words, "Go home and get rid of your idols and images, then your baby will live." I moved on to pray for others.

The Holy Spirit truly was in charge that time. It was 3:30 p.m. when we left the sanctuary that afternoon. The senior pastor's wife came to me and said, "This was like Azusa Street today. I wish we could have more of this more often." I could see she truly was a woman of God and wanted Him to move in the church.

A few Sundays later I was ministering in the evening at another church in the same state. People from several churches had joined; in fact about three-fourths of the crowd was from other churches. The worship leader had not shown up. The senior pastor tried to take over, but could not hold a note. Finally he said, "Sister Theresa, come and preach."

The message was like a fire in my bones ready to explode. When I finished preaching, people rushed up to the altars for prayer. I don't have a set format for who I will pray for; I allow the Holy Spirit to lead me. At times He can direct me to someone seated far back in the pews. That evening a little baby was crying at the altar. I went toward the sound of the baby, who was lying in a baby carrier, with her parents kneeling on either side. God led me to anoint the baby's feet with oil—she had no socks on—and she started smiling immediately. Then, led of the Spirit, both my hands moved to the parents who cried bitterly while I prayed. I found myself saying, "Go home and get rid of your images and your baby will live."

The man stood up with tears in his eyes, "Sister Theresa, last time when you gave us this message, we went home and got rid of all our idols and images from our Roman Catholic background. The doctor has given our daughter only a couple more months to live." At this stage the wife stood up as well and said the same thing. They were desperate for the survival of this little one. They had tried everything and nothing had worked.

I was not hearing anything more from the Lord for them, but neither did I feel led to move away from them. I was praying in the Spirit. All of a sudden, the man said to his wife, "Honey, in your Jerusalem Bible you have a picture of the Virgin Mary that you have been praying to. That is what Sister Theresa is talking about." Then I moved on from them.

A few weeks later they met me again in one of the churches where I was speaking. They brought their little daughter, who had been given a clean bill of health. This time they were worshiping the one true God, not the 'mediatrix.'

Sometime later I was invited back to the hi-tech church. The pastor had advertised on TV and radio and in the newspaper. Several other churches had cancelled their Sunday night services to join this one. It was a similar situation to begin with; I was once again against introducing the senior associate pastor to take over. He had not learned from his first knockout encounter, however. When I went to my seat this time, I prayed, "Lord, please do not hold this against the people. Your Word will not return back empty (Isa. 55:11), even though this leadership is so organized and rigid. People are here, who have tried everything and found that nothing has worked for them. Reveal yourself to them today."

As usual I was oblivious to the instructions of the senior associate. I was having my own session with the Lord. Then I opened my eyes and noticed the ushers and the senior associate were still giving instructions. "Everyone will stand at least three feet away from the platform, and stay where you are placed." He had also announced that I would start praying from the left side, but I hadn't heard that part. So when I went down to pray, I began from the opposite side. The very first person happened to be a leper in a wheelchair—in America! I took his hands in mine and started praying in the Holy Spirit. To me it was like a kindred spirit, because I have a passion for lepers. I knew God was going to do by His Spirit what He wanted to in that place. Words of knowledge started flowing out of me, healings, deliverances, and other miracles came.

Late into the night, when I had come to the last row of people who needed prayer, the Lord gave me a revelation. My eyes were closed, but I could see in the spirit realm a woman with vipers in every ringlet and curl of her long blond hairdo of cascading curls. I told her, "You were sent here by the enemy to disrupt the service. You are a Satan worshiper. Your power is nothing compared to the power of God in this place today." She fell to the floor in an instant, shaking like a leaf and crying to the Lord in repentance. She accepted Jesus as her Lord and Savior. She came from darkness into God's own light.

Towards the end of that line stood a young man, tall and good-looking. He wore a circular silver earring on his left ear. I placed my right hand on his left shoulder and found myself speaking a strong rebuke over him. The Lord revealed to me that this young man had been working as a youth leader in this church and influencing the youth with drugs. Immediately he fell to the ground, broken and crying. That night, having done enough 'floor time,' he got up a changed man.

One Sunday morning as I was ministering in another church, a man who appeared to be the pastor's right-hand man started moving with me. He stood behind each person I prayed for at the altar. I did not feel too comfortable with his presence, but did not say anything. I prayed for several people and finally only a few were left at the altars. I turned to the man, who did not ask for prayer for himself. He pointed toward a woman seated in the third row of pews and said, "Sister Theresa, that's my wife. She has never been in church before; this is her first time. She is very stubborn. Can you please pray for her?" At that point, instead of moving toward his wife, I turned to the man and looked him in the face as God gave me a word of knowledge. "Sir, you're a corrections officer at the local prison and you yourself have been peddling drugs to the inmates. It's you who are stubborn and need to change, not your wife." I didn't even pray for him, but moved on.

I was invited to preach a Mother's Day service at a church I had been to once before. The message God gave me had to do with wolves wearing sheep's clothing. It did not seem appropriate and I didn't want to do it, but God would not give me another message. I prepared, cried, and prayed over it. God always wins!

When I went to the church that Sunday morning a half hour early, I asked the friend who had driven me there, Kay Mosley, to circle around the church so that we could pray in the car until the time for the service. I had not heard from the senior pastor and his wife, and I knew in my spirit that I could not mingle with anyone until the Word had been preached. Some board members waited at the entrance and led me to their 'green room.' They held their hands out for us to join in prayer, but God led me to put my hands behind my back and close my eyes. The senior pastor had been there 50 years, but that Sunday he and his wife were nowhere to be seen.

One of the board members sat where the senior pastor usually sat on the platform. I kept standing during the worship, trusting God to lead me, keeping my eyes closed, and remaining in tune with the Spirit. Instead of the senior pastor's wife at the organ, the wife of a board member was playing. When it came time to preach, I let the Holy Spirit use me and I preached the message God had laid on my heart, "Wolves in Sheep's Clothing." The congregation cheered and clapped when I finished. That was a confirmation for me that I had heard from God. One of the board members took over and concluded the service.

When they asked me out to lunch, I declined. I told them I would return in time to minister in the evening service. I did not want to have anything to do with anyone in that church or be influenced by anyone until I was done for the day. Usually only about one-third of the morning crowd shows up for the evening service. That Mother's Day was unique. I don't know where they got their crowd from.

After the service I spoke to one of the board members who was an Indian physician. I learned that he did not know the whereabouts of the senior pastor or his wife. The Holy Spirit prompted me to question him as to why he had not stood by his senior pastor. I do believe most Indians in the US are loyal and faithful to their senior pastors. They are raised to respect those in authority, especially those with an anointing.

Soon after I left and got into the car, I called the senior pastor and his wife. We decided to meet at a diner in the next town. That night I was horrified to hear what had happened. I was told the board members had approached the senior pastor and said, "It's time you went on leave and took a good holiday. We'll see to things in your absence." So he went on vacation for two weeks, though he was not used to leaving his church with anyone. From previous times I had been in this church, I could tell that he and his wife were well loved.

When they returned from their holiday, a letter was waiting, informing him that he was no longer needed as senior pastor of the church. The board gave him 30 days to vacate the parsonage. The letter said the board would handle things from then on. With God's help, this pastor had founded and built this church from nothing. He had poured his life into it. Like the mother in Solomon's court who did not want her child cut in two (1 Kings 3:16-28), the pastor did not want a church split. Two board members were opposing him. One wanted his wife to be the church musician. The other wanted the district superintendent's son to be the pastor and himself to be the associate.

The senior pastor had no pension, no savings at all. He had sowed everything back into the ministry. He and his wife had nowhere to go. God had spoken to him very clearly not to phone me. God had told him I would come and speak a very timely word to the congregation. He really could not go to his district superintendent either, because the superintendent wanted this fast-growing church for his son.

My calling is to be an evangelist. I'm grateful that, much against my will at times, I am still able to be used by God to speak into people's lives and situations. God doesn't always bring a word of encouragement. At times the exhortation may be a hard message that the Holy Spirit uses to convict people. Be faithful to your calling and to the voice of the Spirit.

I did try helping this pastor and wife with contacts I knew who could support them during this difficult time in their lives. I'm not sure how God worked everything out, but I'm sure that He did.

While evangelizing for some time in a particular country, I met a pastor of a large church who also served as chaplain at one of the country's main prisons. He wanted me to speak to the hardened criminals. These people even took new names when they entered the prison, to protect them from the other inmates. The pastor reminded me to take my travel documents to show as identification (ID) proof at the prison office. I preached at his church on Sunday morning and later traveled to speak at the prison on Sunday evening.

That Sunday morning, due to my vanity, I changed my purse to match my shoes. After church we traveled one hour by car to reach the national prison. As we neared the entrance, the pastor asked for my passport. I suddenly realized that I had left it by mistake in the other purse. I did have my ministerial license and business card, but he said, "I don't think they will let you in today. It's too far to go back; they are sticklers for exact times too."

The pastor and his wife got very anxious. The musicians, who had come in other vehicles, met at the prison entrance. All of them were nervous and agitated too. But I knew I had a message from God for the prisoners, so I felt great peace and calm in my spirit. I had to get away from those nervous wrecks to maintain my peace. The pastor had told me that even though he was a national, the prison authorities had twice before refused him entrance to minister, even though all his documents were presented intact.

I moved away from the group and started walking up and down, praising God, giving thanks, and praying in the Spirit. I was called to a window where we had to meet the prison official to check our documents. I put out the two cards—my ministerial license and business card. As he wrote my name down I looked at his name tag and said, "Sir, you have a Portuguese name. Somewhere way back, we must have come from the same Portuguese background." So he was chatting with me. Finally he instructed, "You will wait 30 minutes for the prison chaplain; he will check your documents and let you in."

The prison chaplain happened to be a Muslim. When the pastor heard that our documents were to be checked again, he got even more nervous. The pastor turned around and said, "The prison chaplain has never learned to smile. I don't think we'll be going in today." Some 30 minutes later we heard a loud voice calling from another window. One by one the team showed their documents and received keys to the lockers for their personal belongings. The top of each one's right hand was stamped with a seal and they were asked to wait at one side.

"Your passport please," the chaplain said in a gruff voice. I handed him my ministerial license and business card with the photo on it. He turned around and rudely stated, "These will not do here; they may do in heaven!" The pastor's wife was in tears, about to faint. No one moved or whispered a word.

"Sir," I said, "You're absolutely right. I'm here with a message burning in my bones to tell the prisoners that there is a real place called heaven where there are no electrical fences. If you will not let me give them that message, eternity is at stake."

The man had his head down. Then he raised it, looked in my eyes, and said, "Let's go." Those Christians thought he was going to lock us up, but he came out and told us to follow him. He put no stamp on my hand, nor did he take my purse. The team followed nervously through the prison to an upstairs room where 48 hard-core prisoners waited. Even up to the point that we were led into the room, those with me were breathless and scared to death of what might happen next. Two other services had been planned on either side of the hall—one for Jews, the other for Muslims. He said, "I'll be back." He went out and came back, sitting right in front. He was all ears and heart while I ministered.

When I gave the altar call, 45 of the 48 men raised their hands and stepped forward to receive Jesus into their hearts. The Muslim chaplain had slipped away to be with his own group. I have learned never to doubt God, but just to trust Him. Even when I make big blunders, He is a way-maker God and I can depend on Him. The weaker and more humble the vessel, the more glory He gets! He said, "My power is made perfect in weakness" (2 Cor. 12:9).

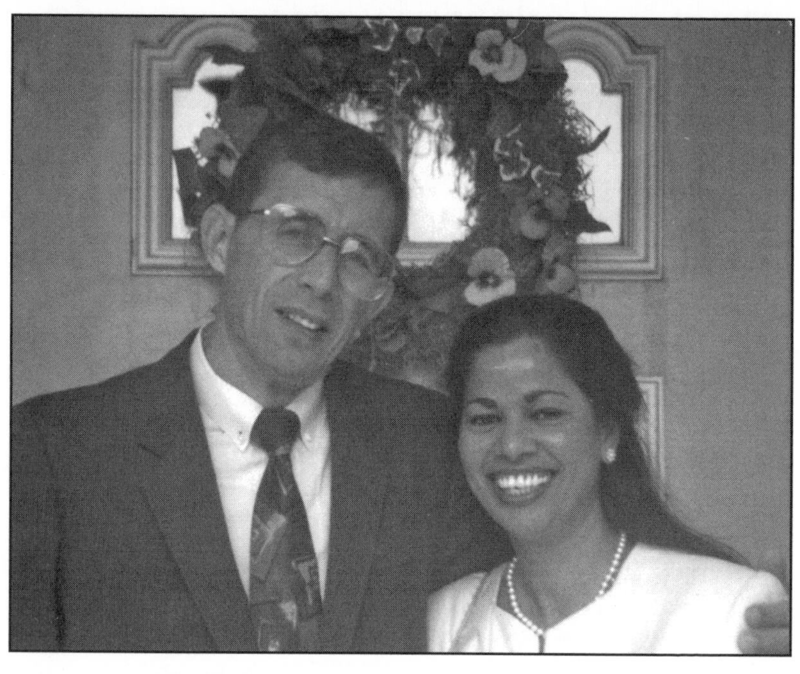

Photo in front of Joe and Joyce Zahorsky's home in Burlington eight months before David and Theresa wed.

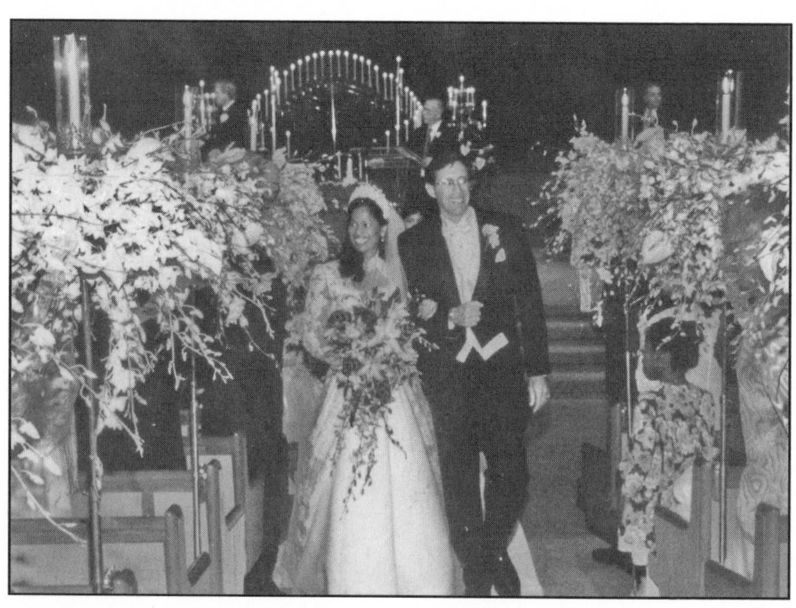

October 17, 1998 wedding at Burlington Assembly with 1,000 white orchid stems lining the center aisle.

CHAPTER 16

MARRIAGE

"If we live in the Spirit, let us also walk in the Spirit" (Gal. 5:25).

I BELIEVED I WAS PERFECTLY HAPPY; MOVING IN GOD'S WILL through open doors and seeing His miracles in the lives of people He brought my way. My ministry centered around the Burlington Assembly of God Church, in New Jersey, but every year I returned to India for evangelizing. Debra Bercaw would keep in touch with me from time to time. My brother's home in Bangalore always served as the base of my travels for those two and a half months.

One day Debra received a call from a man on his way to India who wanted to contact me. Always tight-lipped, she reluctantly gave him my location, where I would be working, and my phone number in India. This Canadian gentleman had been ministering in Jamaica for five years and was on his way to teach at Bethel Sparks Bible College in Coimbatore, Tamil Nadu, India. The Indian Pentecostal Assemblies, an indigenous group of about 400 churches then, had started the school. He had agreed to raise his support and come to teach for them.

Later I found out what had led up to that phone call. This man, David Greenhough, had been waiting to meet the senior pastor in Reno, Nevada. While waiting outside the pastor's office, he picked up a copy of the *Pentecostal Evangel* to read. When he opened the *Evangel* to the first article, the Holy Spirit fell on him. The article was about me and included a back view of me praying for people at a gathering. The Holy Spirit said to David, "This woman will be your wife."

When David had given his life to Jesus, he had heard God say to him that his wife would come from India, so David had decided not to date anyone.

David proceeded to call the New Jersey District AG office, since the *Evangel* article had given that as my affiliation. Ed Spinoza, one of the district officials, answered the phone and gave David glowing reports of how God had been using my ministry. Ed also had suggested that he call the Burlington church office for more specific information.

I had stopped in Europe briefly on my way to India. David wasted no time in sending a packet of papers to me in care of my brother's address. It got there even before I arrived. I opened it to find documentation of all of his biodata, from copies of his baptismal certificate to his degree from World Evangelism Bible College and Seminary in Baton Rouge, Louisiana, and commendations from some of his former professors. Included were references from leaders in Jamaica, in case I wanted to contact them. In his letter he said he was on his way to India to work in Coimbatore and would like to meet me.

My brother was incredulous, "Do you always get mail like that from men?"

I answered, "No, of course not. And I'm not interested."

I left Bangalore and traveled to New Delhi to minister as the evening speaker in a series of special meetings for the pastors and students of the area. A team from Missouri, headed by Evangelist David Grant, was taking care of the daytime sessions. I spent the days in fasting and prayer. Every evening it was clear that God was weaving together all the messages.

Revival broke out at the Bible college in Delhi so the principal and his wife, Robert and Pat Jeyaraj, extended the meetings to 60 days without a break. Many accepted Christ as Savior every night, and the crowds kept increasing. I sat and worshiped in the front row each night as the singing ascended to the Lord. At times I could feel the breeze of the Holy Spirit moving my hair. I knew the Spirit was hovering over us; I was so aware of His presence and I wanted no distractions, so I could hear from God and not anyone else.

One evening as the worship team was leading, God told me that the man in the third row behind me was demon possessed, and if I did not move and act, that spirit would take control. I went to the platform and took the mike from the worship leader's hand. The man began dancing like a cobra and hissing. People around him were getting scared and moving away. I told them, "Leave him alone. Don't try to cast out the demon; just continue to praise God. Get lost in the worship of God. As we worship, the power that is in him will go out of him and leave the service."

As the people returned to their worship, the man fell to the floor. I asked them to carry him out and minister to him. He accepted Christ that night. The following night many of his family and relatives came and gave their lives to the Lord. God showed himself through many signs and wonders in those meetings—remembered by the people to this day.

After those two months, I returned to my brother's home in Bangalore. He told me that a Reverend David Greenhough had called twice, asking for me. From Reno, David had gone to his parents' home in British Columbia for the balance of the Christmas holidays. He was waiting there until he was to leave for India.

I told Gerald that I didn't know who he was and to forget it. At 2:00 a.m. that night I finally got to bed. At 4:00 a.m. the phone rang and woke me up. It was David, but I didn't recognize the name. He said, "Did you get my package?"

"No, what package?" I answered. Then I remembered, "It's not here. What are you calling about?"

"I want to come to India," he said.

"All right, maybe I can help. But I'm leaving for France. I'll be in the US soon." He asked for my travel dates and said he would postpone his trip to India for a few days to meet me in person. We agreed to meet on a particular Saturday and he asked me if I was free to have lunch that day. I agreed, "Okay, the offices will be closed, I'll do lunch with you. You can pick me up at noon and we'll go to the diner. But could I ask why you are coming to India with your family in May and June? It's so hot here then."

Then he told me he was single. I was shocked. I had given him my cell phone number, my number in the US, my address ... and I had never gone with a guy alone since my salvation. I knew that Joyce and Joe, who had graciously welcomed me into their home since 1995, would be at home with me; I wouldn't be alone. But I was suddenly quiet on the phone.

"Are you there?" he asked.

"Yes," I was jolted wide awake by now. "I don't usually give my phone numbers to males, but since I've given my word, I will meet you as agreed." I still was thinking he just wanted advice on what medications to take, names of contacts in India, and information like that.

So I returned to the States and when that Saturday came, David arrived at 11:00 a.m. instead of 12:00 noon. I was still in my jogging suit, not expecting him so early. "You're too early," I told him. I stayed in the upstairs of the home of Joe and Joyce Zahorsky, but Joyce was working at the bookstore that morning and Joe had gone out to the post office, saying he would be back soon. I didn't want David in the house with me, but I reluctantly invited him to sit down while I ran upstairs to get changed.

We quickly went to the Prince Diner on Route 31. Still I was not clued in. I was giving him information on what clothing to take, the weather in India, and how to be careful with salads and water. I avoided any personal connection with him. I just wanted to get out of the diner and back home. He needed directions to go to Lancaster, Pennsylvania, so I went with him to the church office. There we met Pastor Ron Graban, who got talking to David and gave him directions. Suddenly David said, "Oh, Theresa, we forgot to pray together."

"No, no, I don't want to," I replied nervously.

"Okay, I'll take you home and we can pray together there." So we went.

"All right, you pray," I insisted. I did not want to risk speaking my heart to God in front of this man. I didn't want to be seen with a man. I had never had a man act like that before. So he prayed.

David went to India and sent letters to me about how he was getting along at the Bible college—five letters—but I did not respond. So he called my brother Gerald and asked, "Doesn't your sister answer letters?"

He told David, "No, that sister doesn't."

"How old is your sister?" David asked.

"How old are you?" my brother replied. When he received the answer, he added, "Okay, she's younger than you." David asked if I was coming back to India soon and Gerald told him that I would not be coming that year. I was going only as far as Europe and then back to the States.

In the next letter David revealed to me about the *Pentecostal Evangel* article and how the Lord had told him I was to be his wife. He wanted to know if I would marry him. He even said that he had heard from my brother that I was coming to France and if need be he would pay for my trip from there on to India, if I would come for a week so we could get to know each other.

I was livid! I took the six letters and showed them to my senior pastor, Paul Graban. He said to me, "Theresa, you're the counselor for our church. What would you do with these?"

I said, "I would just leave them alone. If this is of the Lord, it'll happen."

I received three more letters. I was so upset, I tore up all nine letters and vowed to myself not to give him any more contact information. About five months later I was invited to preach for 40 days in California, so I would be away from New Jersey.

I traveled to California, but one morning I could not pray. The heavens were brass. I had my Bible on my lap and I heard God saying, "You need to contact Reverend David Greenhough."

"No way," I told God. "I would never do that." I wondered if the voice indeed was that of God or that of the enemy as it came again.

So I prayed, "Lord, if this is you, I'm putting out a fleece. He has not called me on the phone all this time. If this is your voice, let him phone me." I thought that was impossible, since David did not know where I was.

Then my friend Joe Zahorsky phoned from New Jersey, "Calls came for you yesterday and today from a Reverend David Greenhough in India." I replied, "I wish you hadn't told me this." God had specifically told David to phone at that time.

Again I prayed, "OK, Lord, one more fleece. I have no contact information for David. I know he's the president of his own ministry in Baton Rouge. I can get the information, but I don't want to. Lord, let the phone number come to me."

I left California to go back to New Jersey. I walked into my room and Debra had put mail from the previous weeks on my table. As I glanced at it I saw David's newsletter, with the phone number highlighted in neon yellow! I hadn't even taken off my jacket or shoes.

I went to the phone and dialed the number in India. "Okay, Reverend David Greenhough, what do you want?"

"I put it all in my last letter to you," he said.

"Tell me what you have been calling about, because it costs me two dollars a minute on this phone."

He then said, "I'm still hoping your answer will be 'yes' to my proposal."

Then I blurted out, "My answer is no! For all I know you could be a conman. I was in the convent for 15 years. What were you doing all that time?"

"That's why I sent you all that detailed information on myself, if you wanted to check," he patiently replied. I told him that I had discarded it in India.

"No problem," he said. "I'll FAX you all the information again, tomorrow."

The FAX messages started coming. Upset again, I took them to my pastor. "Sister Theresa, do you want us to check on this guy for you?" he asked.

"No, if I'm supposed to be marrying him, I'll check on him myself." I proceeded to make $800-worth of phone calls. I called every number on the list that David had given me, plus the police and courthouse in his hometown. All gave glowing reports. Rod Bitterman, who had been David's pastor in Vancouver, said of David, "He's a godly man, cares for the elderly, and is always available to serve. I have never seen him with a woman alone; he's focused, but I'm not sure about his social skills."

Professor Mervin Harter, who had taught David, described him as a humble godly man, a straight-A student throughout his studies. Bishop Herro Blair, the Jamaican bishop who had housed David at his ministry headquarters in Kingston, reported, "I would take him back any day. People love him. He's committed, humble, dedicated, down-to-earth, and godly."

The more I called, the more I felt like a worm. "This man is a saint!" I thought. I decided to call India to ask Pastor Robert Jeyaraj to help me out. He answered the phone, saying, "If you had called one minute later, you would not have gotten me."

I said, "Robert, there's a man, a Reverend David Greenhough, working at Bethel Sparks Bible College in Coimbatore. Would you check him out for me? I gave him your name before he left." Robert replied, "Right now I have a meeting with a Reverend Greenhough, who is seated in my office." Robert called me back the following day, saying, "Girl, I don't know what you're waiting for. That man is so humble, a born missionary, ready to rough it out. Do you know whom I'd compare him to? Mother Teresa of Kolkata...." He rattled on and on.

So, okay, no more questions. I had to concede that this was the person God had been speaking to me about for some months. The day before I had left Bangalore, I had stood beside my mom, who was cooking. The Holy Spirit had come upon both of us. My mother had spoken to me very seriously, "Child, the Lord has a man after God's own heart in mind for you. You need to keep your mind open."

I had told her, "Mom, pray I will always do God's will." Usually if anyone suggested such a thing, I would tell them that that chapter of my life was closed. All I desired now was souls. My prayer was, "Lord, give me souls or I perish." But this time I kept my own counsel.

After finishing the ministry in France, I was at the airport leaving for New Jersey. My sister Christine was hugging me and the Holy Spirit fell on us there. She said, "The Lord has a man in mind for you, a man after God's own heart."

I just answered my sister, "Pray that I will always be open to God's will."

After arriving back in New Jersey, I was meeting with my senior pastor Paul Graban, his son Pastor Ron, and the senior associate, Pastor David Boudwin. We had been discussing the radio ministry and they wanted to know if I could do five broadcasts a week instead of the two I was presently doing. We often had to tape all the messages when I traveled out of state for ministry. Suddenly Pastor Graban stood up and spoke to Ron and David, "Sister Theresa will be married to a man after God's own heart. Pray that she will keep her mind open." This was the third time the same words had been repeated to me on three different continents. I responded to them in the same way, asking them to pray.

Up to this time, I would have said, "No, don't even go there." At the altar services, I always prayed for both men and women. One time a man just put my hand on his head. I told him, "No, God told me very clearly not to even pray for you. You have lust in your eyes." Another man just proposed, saying God had told him I would be his bride. I replied, "No, if He tells me I will keep you informed!"

Soon after returning to the States I had gone to Tuscarora, Pennsylvania to speak for the Pennsylvania-New York women's conference. The chapel was filled with women the first night. God had given me a burden for these women and their marriages. During the message I asked those whose marriages were hurting to please stand up so we could pray for them. About half the women got to their feet and my heart was moved with compassion. Suddenly Reverend Ruth Farina, the organizer of the conference, stood up and said, "One moment please, right now God wants to minister to Sister Theresa. God has a man in mind for her, a man after God's own heart. And we need to pray that she'll keep her mind open."

I was dumbfounded—*a fourth message from God*! I wished the ground would open up and swallow me. Instead I meekly told the women to just pray I would always be open to God's will.

At about 11 o'clock, when we were done at the altars, an elderly woman came crying to me. "Sister Theresa, while you were ministering I had a vision. I saw the rings leave your hand and a solitaire take their place." The rings I was wearing had a story of their own. When I had first gone to Montreal, after having left the convent, I was working for my sister Mina in the fashion/jewelry business. When I would travel by Metro from my sister Phil's place to Mina's, I would have one man following me every morning on the way to the subway, asking me for a date. At the subway, another guy would get in with me. At the bus stop a third man would keep step behind me.

One day it was Phil's birthday and I went to the grocery store. I asked the store owner, "Do you have any fresh strawberries today?"

A voice answered from the other end of the store. It was a Greek-looking guy, "Oh, I'll be your strawberry today." Later I found out that he had been coming to my sister's office to inquire about me. I called Gerald, back home in India, who advised me to get a wedding band.

So after I joined the Bible college, one day at the mall I bought one for half price. I had gotten a ring with a blue sapphire stone from my mom, too, so I wore the two rings together to protect me from these and other fellows. So I told the woman, "Pray I'll always be in God's will." I was like a stubborn mule, thick-headed.

Then a young lady came crying to me. The Holy Spirit was moving her to say, "I don't know if this will make any sense, but I must tell you that from the time I met my husband-to-be until we were married, we had only three weeks together. Yet we have a very beautiful married life. Be prepared for something like that." It made no sense to me; I was not thinking of marriage. I gave her the same answer I had given the others.

A couple of days later after I had talked with Robert Jeyaraj on the phone, I called my mom. She had come from Canada to Bangalore to visit my brother Gerald. She told me that David Greenhough was there visiting too. Surprised, I asked her what she thought of this guy. She said, "You better be nice to him, I've already accepted him as my son-in-law."

Later I called my brother's home and David answered the phone. "Just make yourself at home," I told him. That was the first time I had spoken to him cordially, and he took it as a 'yes' to his proposal.

While in Malaysia and Singapore for ministry in February of the following year, David got a special $500 ticket to the U.S. and back. He asked if he could come to New Jersey for a week. I agreed, so he came.

There was only one house between the one I was staying in with Joe and Joyce Zahorsky, and the one where David was staying with Bob and Hilda Beckett. Pastor Graban had arranged this since Bob was a board member. That week, wherever I was ministering—in New York, Pennsylvania, Ohio, and New Jersey—pastors had made arrangements for separate living quarters each night for David and me.

One morning just before we were supposed to be leaving for New York, I said, "David, I've been asking you for your laundry. While you're going to get your jacket, bring your laundry too. Here's a bag for it. I'll leave it with mine, so Joyce can get it done." Joyce did my laundry every Monday. She would tell me that God had called me to spend time in prayer and the Word, so I should let her do the washing, vacuuming, and keeping the house. She saw to all my needs and kept my room—and has continued to do so even till now. May God reward Joe and Joyce richly!

When David returned with his laundry in the bag, he had two shirts, two pairs of pants, hankies, vests, and so on. They were white no more, "typical missionary clothes," I thought. I rolled up the bag and put it all in with my garbage. Then I asked David to please carry the garbage out and put it in the larger bin outside the house. He had no idea what was in the trash bag.

While on the road to New York, I tried to spot a Big and Tall store. So we stopped for lunch at a diner right next to such a store. I suggested to David, "Why don't we go in there and look for some shirts for you?"

He said, "No, I have had six shirts for the past ten years and it's all I need. I have two in India, one at Bob's, one I'm wearing, and two in the wash."

I looked at him and confessed, "David, you have only four shirts now. You know the garbage you took out this morning? Your laundry went in there." He did not get upset; he's a very patient man. We both had a good laugh. So we bought one shirt. He said one was enough, because they were too expensive. He was getting to know this woman God had chosen for him.

As the young woman had said to me, through the Spirit, we had only three weeks together before our marriage—this week and two weeks just before the wedding day. He brought the rings he had purchased in Singapore when he came the second time, more than seven months later.

As the date for the wedding was getting closer, my friends were asking what they could do for me. My preaching schedule in America kept me busy speaking two or three times every day. For those seven and a half months, I had not a day's opening on my calendar. After the wedding we would fly overseas. So I told my friends, "Just pray I will be on time to say, 'I do.'"

One day I was praying in my room in New Jersey, preparing my sermons, and interceding for the church. I suddenly had a vision of an exquisite-looking wedding gown, with beadwork, lace, and beautiful fabric. I saw every little detail of the gown. My friend, Donna Gibilisco, owned a bridal store. I called her on the phone and asked if it was possible for her to put anything like this together for my wedding gown. She started crying and told me that very gown was already in her showroom, "When could you come and try it on?" she asked. I told her I didn't have time then. She answered, "I'll bring it to your room the next time you are in New Jersey." It fit like a glove! So I asked how much the gown cost. Her 'cost price' was so high, I almost had a stroke. I was leaving for India the week of the wedding, so I told her I could not take the gown. I asked her if there was anything in her shop I could rent. She said, "No, this is the gown Jesus wants you to wear. It will be a wedding gift from Jay and me."

On another occasion, I received a vision of the entire sanctuary decorated for the wedding. I saw the long-stemmed orchids, the candle stands along the aisle and on the platform. I saw the bridesmaids and flower girls on the steps coming down both sides from the balcony—my four nieces and my sister Mina Duprey from Canada as Matron of Honor. They had golden skirts and ivory brocade tops, descending so gracefully.

So when my sister Mina flew in to ask if I needed help, she wanted to know what my colors were. I told her, "Gold and ivory." Philomena, my older sister, is good at fashion garments. So I said to Mina, "Tell Phil to go with Gilbert (her husband) to a fabric store. As they walk in the material will hit them in the eye."

"Do you know the name of the store?" she replied.

"No, just tell them to go and they'll see it," I said confidently. They did go and found exactly what I had seen in the vision. A woman from their church sewed all the gowns free of charge. They were perfectly beautiful.

Some days later when I was blessing someone else's wedding, my friend Penny Simcox came up to me and asked what my favorite flower was. She owned a huge flower shop. So I told her I loved orchids. She asked, "What color?"

I said, "White." Penny stood there crying.

She went on, "Sister Theresa, please can I do your wedding? God has been telling me that I would be called to do a white orchid wedding. I've been telling everyone in the store about it. I've checked the Internet as well as magazines for ideas." So I told her to go for it. In the end, Penny and the eight pastoral staff at my church paid for 1,000 long white orchid stems for the center aisle and platform.

A few days after meeting Penny I went to see Charlie and Peggy Day, owners of Minuteman Press, to choose my invitations, thank you cards, and so on. They helped me to choose the best they had and to place the order. When I tried to pay for everything, they told me to put my checkbook away. This was their wedding gift to me.

When I went to order the three-tiered wedding cake, with the help of the owners of the bakery I selected the best they had. At that point the owners, whom I did not know, told me not to worry about the payment, "It has already been taken care of." To this day I do not know who paid for the cake. I wanted the best, because God doesn't want second best for His friends!

One Saturday my friend Dorothy D'Mauro took me to a tuxedo place in Pennsylvania, across the Burlington-Bristol Bridge. I had to select tuxedos for David, the groomsmen from Canada, and those out of state. Afterwards the owner of the store, who had been helping us to choose the best, said, "For David, everything is free—for the groomsmen, fifty percent off." She outfitted four of the ministers from the church, the candle lighters, and ushers, for half off the regular price as well.

Usually people spend a fortune on photographs and the like. Well, Joe Zahorsky took all the pictures himself and his sister Donna arranged for the video for our wedding. Tom and Susan Kaye housed David's parents and made them feel at home with them. Dave and Diana Boudwin organized the wedding rehearsal and made sure that the actual ceremony went like clockwork with no problems. The Houstons and Keanes came over to where I lived and hung wall paper as well as fixing up the whole place. The Burlington AG church folk literally went out of their way to make our wedding day a memorable one for all our friends and family.

Seven hundred guests came from far and wide to witness my October 17, 1998 wedding to David. Family members came from Canada and France. My large family is fun-loving, full of pranks, and mischievous. All of them were staying at the Day's Inn in Burlington. David and his brother Ted came over to visit with my family, but Larry Duprey, my brother-in-law from Montreal; David Thabot, Christine's husband from France; Tony, my older brother from Canada; and Steve, my younger brother from Toronto; all sat there with a solemn look on their faces. They said to David and Ted, "We've called you here to ask how much dowry you're willing to pay to get Theresa's hand in marriage. We paid big bucks to get one of these D'Souza girls." David and Ted were stunned, speechless. Just then I walked in, realized what was happening, and rescued them. I told David this was only the beginning of what he would encounter marrying one of the D'Souzas.

David and I decided to write our own marriage vows and surprise each other. This is what the Lord inspired us to write:

Dear David,

It is not by chance that our paths have crossed,
This meeting was ordained before creation began,
God chose us for Himself and for each other.

David, it is with heartfelt gratitude and appreciation for you,
As the Ephesians Five Man of God,
That I make this vow in the presence of our
Families, Friends, and the Ministers of God's Household.

David, this 17th day of October 1998,
I vow to remain faithful and true to you for life.

I desire to:
Love you as my lawful husband,

Lift you up in prayer and sacrifice,
Strengthen you in times of sorrow and pain,
Walk with you through your valleys and peak experiences,
Affirm you in your dreams and desires,
Appreciate you in your own uniqueness,
Bless your name in the presence of all, and
Share with you the best that God has gifted me with.

I truly love you, David, and am blessed to know that God kept you for me.
May God who began this good work in us bring it to completion into eternity.
Amen.

Dear Theresa,

By the will of God and by the will of my heart,
I take you, Theresa,
To be the companion of my life and the object of my love.

Apart from my affection for Christ,
My desire is for you and you alone.
I pledge myself to you with a devotion that shall increase,
As we walk together in the path the Lord has prepared for us.
Through moments of affliction and times of trial,
Through days of rejoicing and seasons of triumph,
Through any circumstance that may happen across our path,
My devotion is for you, Theresa.

With faithfulness and tenderness,
I promise to live with you, to love you, to cherish you,
And be with you all the days of this life.

Beyond this, Theresa, our partnership is forever,
For by the grace of God you will abide in my heart for eternity.

These words are spoken in the name of our Lord and Saviour Jesus Christ.
Amen.

We didn't want anyone knowing where we would spend our wedding night. I asked Debra to make the arrangements and not to tell David, saying, "My brothers will get him to tell them and then they will give us a hard time." Debra put the information in a sealed brown envelope, together with our luggage, in Bob Beckett's new white car. No one knew what vehicle we would be traveling in.

My brother Steve, a conniver full of mischief, went up to Pastor Graban and said, "Pastor, it's a custom among us Indians to decorate the bridal chamber. We have not done anything as yet. Please can you tell us where they're going to stay?" Pastor Graban fell for it and told them.

The reception was a hot gourmet meal including ham and Italian sweets, served buffet style, with plenty for everyone. Susan Esposito, Dick Gaglio, Judy Fulton, and a host of helpers worked tirelessly to make sure that the more than 700 wedding guests were treated like royalty. The reception hall was professionally decorated by the Gibiliscos and Wargos. Brass Indian elephants, rugs, and other artifacts were provided by an aunt of Caroll Tillinghast, who used to be a missionary in India. She had all these in her home. Gold and white heart-shaped balloons filled the ceiling. Many took off work and labored late into the night for the special day of a match that was made in heaven. Everyone enjoyed a great time of celebration.

So while the reception was going on we didn't notice that some of the immediate family members were missing. John Keane and Steve Endicott, the church pranksters and friends of mine, had planned all this the previous day. These two, together with my brother-in-law Larry and my brother

Steve; my sister-in-law Helen and her mom Mary; my niece Roshini from Ohio; Jan and Bob Reed, friends from California; and a few others left the reception and went to do up the wedding chamber, their style.

They arrived at the Marriott with huge floral decorations, tool boxes, bags of colorful plastic Easter eggs, crepe paper streamers, snack food, and plates. They told the staff, "The bridal party is on the way; may we have the room opened please?" So the staff let them in.

Some hours later, after the farewells and send-off, we arrived at the Marriott. As soon as I walked into the room, I was stunned. I told David, "My family has been here. Why don't you go and check behind the bathroom door to see if Steve is there, I'll check behind the drapes for Mina." Stuffed toys covered the sofas, the huge flower arrangements in the middle and bright Easter eggs all over the floor. A brightly-printed canopy was over the bed and trays of food on the tables.

Just as I was reading a note saying, "We got you, didn't we?!" I heard a huge splash in the bathroom. A basin hung from the door and David looked like a drenched scarecrow in his tuxedo. I doubled up laughing. Then I shooed him aside saying, "I've not used the toilet all evening; let me go in for a pee break." When I opened the lid, I realized there was Saran Wrap stretched tightly over the toilet. They had even wrapped the toilet paper with gray duct tape. There was none we could use, so I got Kleenex from my purse. Exhausted, David got in the shower, but all the towels had been covered in white toothpaste, so he couldn't even dry off.

Then the phone rang. When I answered it, the receiver stuck to my ear—more toothpaste. My sister Christine was calling, using a phony Sri Lankan accent. When we tried going to bed, we found it short-sheeted. More plastic Easter egg shells had been placed in the pillow cases. An alarm went off within half an hour; we couldn't find it. The alarm in the bedside clock radio went off next, at highest volume, wild as ever. Eventually David yanked it from the wall.

The next day, Sunday, all the family joined us in church. As we walked in, I said to Jan, "You won't believe what my family did to us last night." She smiled and said, "I was in on it too!" Thus began the next chapter of my life. Now David has loosened up a whole lot and I have become the more serious one.

David's parents, Harry and Mary Greenhough in Victoria, British Columbia, Canada.

David with young Joshua, formerly one of our boarders.

CHAPTER 17

PIONEERING IN INDIA

"I have placed before you an open door that no one can shut" (Rev. 3:8).

WE LEFT FOR INDIA AS FULL-TIME MISSIONARIES THE SAME week we got married. We began working in Coimbatore helping at the Bethel Sparks Bible College with the Prakasams' orphanage complex and lecturing at two other Bible schools run by the same organization. We stayed there for a year.

Having felt the urgency of rescuing the lost and Christ's soon return, we did not feel the need to itinerate and go around looking for funds in America. We knew that God, who called us, would be faithful to provide. We were aware that if we had the 'vision' for souls, then He would be the "Provision." Before I had married David, I had told him about my decision to give 100 percent of any offerings I received for preaching or teaching back into missions. He had responded, "I will help you keep that vow." Our first donor was Angie Arnao, an 83-year-old widow. She was very excited to hand me the $200.00 that she had managed to collect from yard sales and making preserves and selling them. She said, "Sister Theresa, this is for the 'Babbies' of India."

The next time I returned to the States, I went looking for Angie to tell her how we had used the money she had put into our care. Not finding Angie, who had been a regular churchgoer, I approached Pastor Dave to check on her. He said, "Sister Theresa, Angie is bedridden with pneumonia as she went without heat all winter." I could not believe my ears. And this old saint of God made sure to send us missionaries to feed the street kids of India! I can hear God saying to Angie, now that she is gone home to be with the Lord, "Well done, good and faithful servant! What you did to the least of these, you did unto Me!"

When I had gotten married in 1998 and had left with David for India, our accountant in Louisiana had informed us that we had received a check in the mail for $25,000. She couldn't decipher who had sent it. We asked her not to put it into our account, but to try to find out who had sent it.

A police officer friend from Burlington, New Jersey, was able to trace the check to Steve and Heidi Reed. Heidi had heard me speak once in New Jersey. Her husband, an African American, had served on the board of a Methodist church that was closing down. The board had decided to send part of the money received from the closure of the church for our orphanage in India. We let them know that we had not yet started an orphanage, though we had a vision for it. At that time we had started running only a free medical clinic and a small church service. They replied that the money should be considered seed money for the future orphanage, so we received it with joy. You cannot out give God! "As you sow, so shall you reap" (Gal. 6:7, KJV). In 1997 I had decided not to travel to India from the US, but to send the funds instead to Matthew Barnett's Dream Center in Los Angeles. I had sent $1,500 to the Dream Center and within a year God had sent us $25,000.

A month after my wedding my father passed away. When we got word he was failing, we left the Reinhard Bonnke meetings in South India, and flew back to Bangalore to be with the family. He had been paralyzed after a stroke, so had been in a wheelchair or bed for the previous seven years. He had lost the use of his right side, lost his ability to speak and much of his eyesight. My mom or brother Gerald had to diaper and care for his every need. While joining in praise and worship at his funeral, my spiritual eyes were opened. I saw him standing tall and straight in a silver gray suit, with not even a cane! He was praising God with a radiant glow on his face. I was very grateful to God for this vision of my dad in heaven.

For the first year we traveled great distances every weekend for ministry. David and I used public buses (together with the chickens, goats, and babies), trains, and local auto rickshaws (small three-wheeled vehicles powered by a motor and able to carry two or three passengers comfortably). At times, in the buses, the driver never took his hand off the horn. I suffered from the stench, dust, and diesel fumes. I would carry a plastic bag in one hand, to puke into, and a bottle of water in the other, to keep from getting dehydrated. The only time I was not sick was when I was ministering under the anointing. I was passionate, saying to God, "Give me souls or I die."

I was a stickler for cleanliness. I carried disinfectants in my luggage to clean the hotel shower and toilet before using them. I also brought toilet paper, which was never provided. Antacids and diarrhea medicines were our companions. But we were excited about what God was doing through two ordinary people. Everyone invited us to come back again.

In the early days we did a lot of tag-team preaching. David would teach from the Word and I would follow him with illustrations. At times I would wait for my turn and would complain to God that David was using all the verses I had planned to use. But when my turn came, the Word of God would just flow. Paul said, "Do not be anxious about anything" (Phil. 4:6). I learned to trust God.

One Sunday we were ministering in two different churches in Madurai. I spoke at the first service in one particular church, while David preached at another. At the end of my service I happened to announce that that evening we would be ministering in the power of the Holy Spirit and teaching the people how to receive the Holy Spirit. David and I never discussed the topics or themes God had laid on our hearts. We each did our individual study without comparing notes. When I left that church to go elsewhere for ministry, David arrived. Towards the end of his service, he said the exact same things I had said to the congregation regarding the evening service.

Though I seldom take my camera when I travel, that evening I didn't want to leave it in the hotel. I had it in my purse. After I finished preaching at the evening service, I left David to handle the altar call. I stood on the platform praying in the Spirit, always in awe at what God would do in each service. The men and boys sat on mats on the floor on one side of the church; women and girls on the other. David asked the people to face each other with an opening in the center for him to go up and down, lay hands on them, and pray for them. So they stood in rows and prayed. Matthew 7:7-8 says, "Ask and it will be given to you; seek and you will find; knock and the door will be opened to you." It means to keep on asking! Ask God for the baptism in the Holy Spirit. Several little Hindu-background girls from a local church's orphanage, who were present in the service, suddenly started receiving the baptism. The Lord prompted me to get my camera out and take shots of their little faces turned heavenward. They were weeping in the Spirit and speaking in heavenly languages. "Unless you change and become like little children, you will never enter the kingdom of heaven" (Matt. 18:3). It is the "pure in heart" (Matt. 5:8), who see and receive.

When we had first started our ministry in India, the Lord had prompted us to start a free medical clinic for the poor. Friends from Delaware had sent us two whole boxes of medicines whereas Steve and Donna Phillips from Baton Rouge had sent in 37 homeschooling videos. While I was involved in ministry in Australia I got word that these things had arrived. My brother Gerald phoned me, saying, "The Foreign Customs Office has sent you a notice. They want you to go to the court and get the sanctions to bring these drugs into the country." I asked my brother to relax, as I would see to things on my return.

When I got back, I didn't go to the court but to the authorities of the Foreign Customs Office. "I'm involved in charitable work," I told the man. "I'm not robbing anyone; I'm not earning anything to give you a bribe. What are you asking for?"

They said, "These things have come addressed to you."

"I don't even know what all is in those boxes," I replied. "All I know is that I've got a notice to appear before the court, and I'm not doing that. I know there are some used videos and medicines inside, sent by our friends because we're doing good work among the poor in Bangalore City. If you are expecting a bribe from me, you are getting nothing, Sir. And if you keep those boxes, remember that on judgment day you're going to stand before my God and give Him an account of what you did with what came into your hands for the poor."

I just walked out after that. My brother, standing beside me, was as nervous as ever. His knees were shaking as he said, "You should not have spoken like that to that officer."

"Don't even go there," I told him. I just pressed the elevator button and we went down.

My brother went on, "You know, they could put you behind bars."

I said, "There's someone who knows how to get me out from behind bars too." You have to know whose you are; who dwells within you. That's all that matters. Just make sure you stay humble in your own eyes. And at the right time, God will put the words in your mouth.

A few weeks later I happened to be at the airport in Bangalore standing in line at the immigration check. A gentleman dressed in a white uniform moved from one side of the hall to the other, across our line. All the while he kept staring at me and I at him. I just could not recall where exactly I had seen or met this man.

When I passed through Immigration, I had to get my passport stamped at the customs table—a routine to be followed by everyone before proceeding through the security area. I searched my mind once again, wondering where I had met this gentleman who was working at the customs table doing a very ordinary job of stamping passports. Finally I turned to the gentleman and said, "Sir, I have seen you somewhere, but I just don't know where."

All he said was, "Woman, will I ever forget?" It still didn't ring a bell. I moved on and after some time I got onto the plane, still intrigued about this man's words to me.

Sometime later I flew back to America for some meetings and David stayed in India. He called me after some days and said, "Believe it or not, those boxes are at the local post office. Now they want to know whether they should deliver them or if we are coming to collect them." It was only then that I realized who the man at the customs table was. He had been the top official at the Foreign Customs Office who was now demoted. When you walk with the Master's agenda, you follow His direction and leave the results with Him.

At the free medical clinic we offered basic check-ups and medicines. We had hired a doctor, a nurse, and a pharmacist to work with us three days a week from 1:00-5:00 p.m. Once a month we set up medical camps in the slums. The day before the camp we would distribute about 1,000 handbills door-to-door, printed on pink and yellow paper in the local languages. The colorful paper would remind even the uneducated poor that a medical camp and free medicines were going to be available. The goal was to evangelize, so we would conduct the medical camp next to a church or on church premises. When we would leave them, those interested could be discipled through that church.

For the camp we would hire more doctors and medical personnel. As the years went on, we took our teaching staff and boarding staff with us. We never stayed in an area past 6:00 p.m., when drunks would be coming home. I was very careful to hear what the Holy Spirit was saying in each situation. Our group would see 150-300 patients a day and then refer them to a free clinic in the area, where they could get ongoing care. We gave out gospel tracts in several languages. Teams ministered to people while they waited in line.

On one of my ministry trips to the US, I was invited to speak at Beebe, Arkansas, where Glenn Dorsey served as pastor. He said, "Sister Theresa, I know you do not make a plea for money, but our board has unanimously decided to put aside $5,000 for a personal need you have. These funds are not to be used for ministry."

I couldn't think of any such expensive personal need, and replied, "Pastor, I do not take funds that a church gives for myself. I have vowed to give 100 percent to missions."

"Sister Theresa," he responded, "I'm also a pastor and I also hear from God." So I had to seal my lips for the moment. I did not want to get distracted from the message coming up. I usually don't like to discuss anything until I'm done preaching in a church."

But the pastor came back to me, "Sister Theresa, do you have a car in India?"

"No, but in God's time He will provide," I said.

"How do you think, girl, that God provides? He uses people!" the pastor said with a smile.

In India I worked with street kids. You don't find street kids in nicely paved neighborhoods, but in back streets with the garbage dumps and no room for a car. Thieves would steal parts off cars and force the owners to buy them back. And I really preferred to walk the streets to meet kids who were scavenging garbage for their breakfast—a mango peel or stale piece of bread. Most of the kids' parents were day workers. Bosses would come with their trucks to take workers to some distant construction site or development project, where they would work for the day and come back at night. The children had to fend for themselves. Oftentimes three or four families shared one small hut. Many children had to sleep outside with the rats and stray dogs in the streets. These are the kind of kids we opened our free school to.

How could I be moving in a car when my ministry is working on the streets, one-on-one? I refused to accept the $5,000.

Pastor Dorsey came to me again the following day. "How much would it cost you for a car? Why don't you go into the office and phone David and ask him?"

"Pastor Glenn," I protested. "We really are not interested."

He said, "Stubborn, aren't you?"

I didn't want to be bothered about a car. I had to purchase vegetables, medicate sores, bathe the kids, shampoo and clean their heads of lice, look for clothes, and teach lessons from scratch. Kids would smoke a 'bidi,' an Indian cigarette; or they would sniff a Xerox liquid from a small vial to get high. Most were street smart, stealing clothes from lines to keep warm, sleeping under someone's truck or under a water tank on a public roof. They would run out before anyone else awoke. They feared and ran from the gangs that would abuse them and the policemen who might jail them. Their parents, if alive, were often drunks, beggars, and garbage sorters who used their kids to get money to buy alcohol or to gamble with. Most of the children could not even hold a pencil properly.

Glenn and Gladys Dorsey took me to the Little Rock airport. As they were seeing me off, Pastor Dorsey said, "Sister Theresa, you have two more days in the US. While you are in New Jersey, please contact David and ask him what it would cost for you to get a car. I will take it to the board and we will make sure that whatever else is needed, you will get it to buy a car."

I returned to India and forgot about the conversation, but Pastor Dorsey had heard from God and persisted. So in the year 2000, his church sent us $11,000. What we needed for the car and aluminum partitions for the clinic and office doors was exactly that amount. The little white car, a five-seat Hyundai Santro, was soon being used to bring in 15 little Muslim children, 5-to-7-year-olds, from the slum opposite a railway station to school every day.

There were about 350 little squatter huts near the Bangalore Cantonment Railway Station with not one single faucet for water. Twice a week a government water tanker came and representatives from all 350 families showed up to push and jostle their way to get their container in for water. No one had electricity; some did not have even a kerosene lamp. They looked forward to the white Santro car coming to pick them up each day. Another teacher would travel with me so I put ten excited kids with her in the back and five in front with me—standing, sitting on laps, and generally squeezed together.

It was like a picnic for them each day. We taught them nursery rhymes, ABCs, action songs, Bible verses, and lessons in English, Kannada, and math. We bathed each one every day, pouring water on them, soaping and scrubbing them. The older ones stood in their underwear to be bathed. Then they got fresh clothes every day. We served them rice, lentils, veggies, and fruit for lunch. After lunch we spread mats on the cement outdoors for the kids to take a nap for an hour. At home they slept on dirt floors or outside their little huts. We had indoor and outdoor games for them, and a heavy snack in the evening before they left. For most it was the last meal of the day. As soon as they got into the car, they would sing Christian choruses all the way home. As a rule we never admitted anyone who was going to another school or had both parents alive, unless they were physically challenged in some way. We gave everything free of charge.

In India traffic keeps to the left and the driver is on the right side of the car. I sat beside David in the front seat, but all the while I used to keep my hand on the hand brake. We live in a country steeped in idolatry; behind every idol is a demon spirit. If you are not prayed up, the demons may attack. But praise the Lord; we know that greater is He that is within us than he that is in the world! (See 1 John 4:4). Dinnur Main Road is a main street of R.T. Nagar, Bangalore near to our home. While David was driving, the Holy Spirit prompted me to tell him, "David, see that man walking on the pavement in the distance?" He had on a full-sleeved beige-colored shirt and looked absolutely normal and healthy from the back view. "When you get near that man, get ready to put your brakes on. He's going to jump right in front of the car." And that's exactly what happened. I thank God that His Spirit never leaves us nor forsakes us.

One of the doctors who worked at our free medical clinic, Dr. Gerard, owned a plot of land 60 kilometers from where our school was. He asked me if we could take a team to the village close to his plot of land. We agreed to go there one Saturday with our staff, youth, doctors, and nurses. We would hold a medical camp and sports day for this very poor Hindu village of Dodbalapur in Karnataka.

The last seven miles of approach to the village was nothing but dirt tracks. They had no electricity and not a single store in sight to buy anything. The village also had no medical facilities, no dispensary or clinic, no government school or classroom. The nearest school was seven miles away. They had to depend on the rains to fill their open wells, which provided their drinking water. It was a very poor farming community with only a few goats and some weak-looking cows.

The morning we arrived, someone pointed out that my right rear tire was flat. We were already in the village, but a half hour late, so I ignored it and got busy starting the medical camp for the day. We had arranged for tents for the free medical clinic for adults. In a nearby shed we would meet 250 or so kids to do a Sunday school program with them. They were excited to sing the action songs we taught them. After that we planned to distribute new toys, so each child could get one, and a bag of snacks for each one. That evening we had a sports event for all ages—young and old, male and female. As the sun was setting, it was time to say good-bye to these people.

I had asked the doctors, youth, and other staff to go ahead and stop by a lake where we would have a meal. Three female doctors and a female pharmacist were planning to ride with me. All of a sudden I remembered that I had had a flat tire. I didn't know how to change one; I had never done it before. What was I going to do? No one in the village even owned a bicycle tube.

The heads of the village were all seated under a tree not far from the car. With the help of my interpreter, I asked the village leaders if there was anyone among them who could change a car tire. They looked very confused. I thought they didn't understand me at first, so I repeated the question. They turned to my interpreter, "Why does she need her car tire changed all over again?"

When I looked at the tire, I realized it was not flat anymore. I turned to them and asked, "Who is the man that fixed my tire? I need to pay him." They seemed confused again.

"Why does she need to pay someone who was with her all the time?" they questioned.

I answered, "In my car when I arrived this morning were just these same ladies you see here."

They exclaimed, "No, there was a gentleman who got out of the car when you did."

"What did the man look like?"

"He was very tall and fair skinned," they said. I am married to David, a Canadian, who is tall and fair, but he had not been with me. He had stayed back in Bangalore.

So I quizzed them further, "What was he wearing?"

"He wore a loose white gown from his shoulders to his feet. His hair was golden and he had a big smile on his face. He kept looking at us. Then he moved to the car tire. Nothing was in his hands, but he lifted the car on one side and touched the tire. All the while he kept looking at us with a smile."

All through the day, when I had seen how excited the children and the women were, I had been a little disappointed that we had not been able to reach the men of the village and warm their hearts with the love of Jesus. When I realized what had happened, and who had assisted me with the tire, I took the opportunity to tell them about Jesus. With the help of my interpreter, I said to them, "Once upon a time, I too was like you. I worshiped idols. I carried statues and images, and burned candles and incense sticks to the idol gods. I garlanded them and went on pilgrimages to shrines. I prayed long hours on my knees. But ever since I had an encounter with the living God, He carries me!"

"I've learned that an idol cannot do anything for me. I have to do everything for it. But once I gave my life to Jesus, He does everything for me. He has never let me down." Tears welled up in their eyes. Then I asked my interpreter, Claudia Nair, our pharmacist, to give them the salvation message in the Kannada language. Dr. Gerard was a Christian and after we left he continued to minister in that village. We sowed the seed and he watered the plant that sprang up.

In those early years, my knees used to knock when I would think about the heathen world around us, the politicians, and the government authorities. I wanted no one to know what kind of work we were doing. Providing free medical service and medicines was no problem. Taking care of 130 children who used to sleep on the streets and eat from the garbage dumps; that was no problem either. The government is not going to attack you for doing social work or charitable efforts. But the moment they would know you're evangelizing, that would be another story. They think we convert people, but of course it's the Holy Spirit that brings conviction and draws them to Jesus. We just tell them the plain truth about the love of God and that Jesus died for them. But I was nervous anyway.

One day I realized that I was actually scared to start a church. I knew someone would have to pastor the church and God had not told us to call anyone else to pastor. My husband was not called to do it, so I knew it would have to be me. The moment I heard that from the Spirit, I started praying and fasting. I didn't do it alone, however. God gave me the names of several women who would pray and fast with me. At that stage we had just three of us who were born again in the group. The rest were all Hindus who were halfway out of idolatry, including the alcoholics whom God was delivering. When we started the prayer and fasting, we were very few. I called the women and told them what the Spirit had shown me and said, "The Lord wants us to pray and fast. I'm going to start the fasting on Sundays. Every Sunday I will fast from morning till night. I'll eat something only at night after the evening service, if I'm ministering somewhere. But I need someone for each of the other days." They responded and after that I received so much confidence and boldness inside of me. I was not scared anymore.

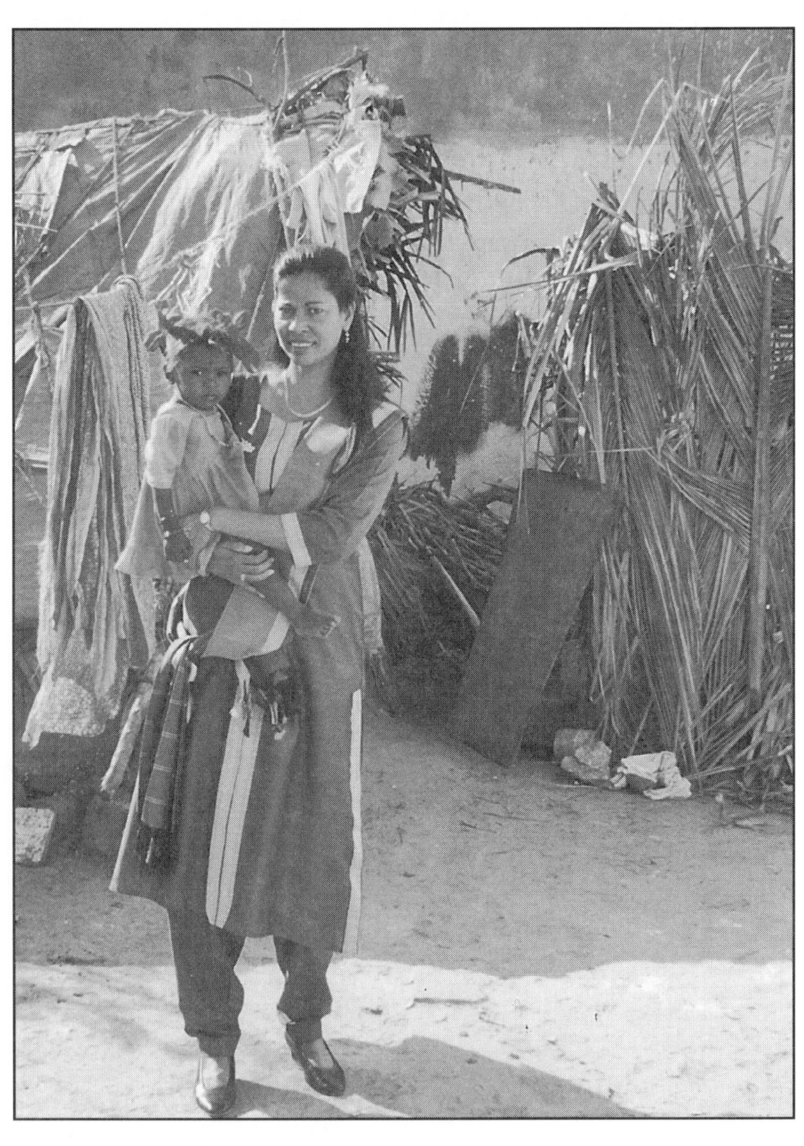

Theresa with Karthika, who was found at home after being left there alone. *(See her story on page 221.)*

CHAPTER 18

MIRACLES AT THE FREE MEDICAL CLINIC

"Not by might nor by power, but by my Spirit" (Zech. 4:6).

THE YEAR FOLLOWING THE ESTABLISHING OF THE FREE medical clinic, 15 seriously addicted alcoholics had been set free. We had had no choice but to obey the Lord and start a church for the poor who wanted to get out of idolatry. My mom, Eliza D'Souza, was now a Canadian citizen, but she still had great compassion for the lost and the poor. She was visiting us. We were able to minister to these folks because she was educated in the local language (Kannada), whereas I had to use an interpreter. Through her these 15 men and women joined our church. Mom was my first interpreter.

The church started in a shed in my brother's garden. At one point I went back to the US to preach. In the early years I went back three times a year for one month each time. In my absence, my brother took over the ministry of the Word. He too has a passion for souls and loves the Lord. Mom, an asthmatic, found it hard to preach. Gerald called me while I was in the States and said that 12 people were ready for baptism. I told him to go ahead and baptize them. God gave him creativity. With the help of his elderly Hindu gardener, Gerald dug a trench in one corner of his garden. He put a tarp in and filled the trench with water. At midnight, so as not to attract the attention of unsaved neighbors, he baptized those 12 converts. By morning the water was drained and the trench was filled in, with a coconut tree planted in the middle. Today that tree is over 50 feet tall.

The following year we started a free school for the street children of Bangalore. We gave them free education in English, meals, clothes, and medicines. And we gave them the love of God along with the gospel. My schedule was packed each day—one hour in prayer, one hour walking and visiting the street kids early in the morning or late in the evening, running home to get breakfast, and then tending to the school from 8 a.m. till 8 p.m. During that time I used to bathe 14 kids at a stretch. We also continued the free medical clinic and went into the slums for medical camps once a month.

It was one of those days. I was seated on the floor with five of the smallest children around me who were too tiny to feed themselves. We had to get ready to leave for a medical camp. I prayed, "Lord, I just put the last of the rice we had into the pot to feed these kids. I have money but no time to go and buy rice for tomorrow to feed all these kids and staff. You know I will be coming home very late from the free medical camp; then I will have to see to the boarders...."

I had barely finished speaking to God when my Hindu neighbor, Ranjani, called out to me over the next-door wall, "Theresa, I have 25 kilos of rice here with me. Please can you come and take it or send someone for it?"

Talk about God answering prayer. In a couple of days, when that rice had finished, I still had not gotten the time to buy our ration of rice. I taught all day long, trained other teachers, counseled parents through interpreters, and purchased all the medicines we used for our camps and clinics. We had so much to do, but never enough time to do it. God was always mindful of our needs; I can truly say I never worried about things.

My brother Gerald called and said, "Mr. Das, who has just purchased the property on the right side of your free school told me he has a sack (100 kg.) of rice that he wants to donate to you." He was going to start his *puja* (a ritual of prayer and thanksgiving, including giving to the poor, to dedicate his property to his gods), because he had been able to get a good deal on that property. Talk about the wealth of the wicked stored up for the righteous! (See Prov. 13:22.) I must admit, to date we have lacked nothing. We've never run short of anything we needed for the ministry—never even had to wait for it. God is truly Jehovah Jireh; He provides all the time.

When we first started the free school, the water that we got from the little well was not suitable for drinking. So I wanted the government to supply us with corporation water fit for drinking. The guys in the government office expected a huge bribe out of us because of the name Gateway International (which they thought had something to do with Gateway computers). They soon realized they were not getting a cent out of us. We would not stain God's ministry by offering a bribe to anyone and to this day we have not. Our God goes before us and opens doors no one can shut. (See Rev. 3:8.)

My neighbor Ranjani came back to me again and she offered to supply us with the needed drinking water daily—from her tank—for our entire project. She was getting corporation water. She did this for a full seven years until we got ours without paying any bribes.

Meanwhile the church grew and we moved onto the next street into the one and only classroom, where we would have a Sunday morning service for former idol worshipers. The Sunday evening service was designated for the youth. Tuesday afternoon at 2:45 we would close the free school and have a Bible study. Most of the folks were illiterate. Their kids were the first generation of their families to be educated. Ninety-eight percent of them could not even sign their own names. They gave thumb prints to register their children in the free school.

In order to be taken in by us, they had to be absolutely destitute. That was the focus of our mission. These children were beggars and garbage sorters; their parents prostitutes, drunks, ex-cons, and thieves. Their future was to be sold as child laborers or trained into prostitution or thievery to support their parents' drug and gambling addictions. On Friday evenings I told stories, like Jesus did. I used stories from the Bible. Then we invited the sick to come forward for prayer in a healing service. The only ones who could read the Bible were our own immediate school staff.

In the early days of the free school, I used to walk the streets with an interpreter every morning after prayer meeting. I didn't know even a single word of Kannada, Tamil, or Telugu—the languages spoken in the region. I spoke Hindi, Marathi, Konkani, and English. We would round up the kids who were busy sorting garbage or begging on the streets. Some of them had just run away from their homes. We sought the permission of parents, if there were any, or the local police, before registering the kids in our school. We soon had 150 children in the program.

One morning I was playing with the kids before assembly time. We tossed colorful beach balls in the air and they were all excited to play with me. A fruit vendor with his cart stopped just outside the school gate and began yelling and screaming at us. I could tell he was very angry, though I couldn't understand his words.

I called a staff member and asked what exactly he was angry about. She said, "Don't even think about going near him. He's so violent, and he's using abusive language. He's very upset with you." She was pretty scared.

One staff was willing to come outside the gate with me. I had to meet with him and try to calm him down. I tapped him on the shoulder and asked, "Brother, can you tell me what you are so upset about?"

"I'm angry because you took away all the children from our slum into your school. Now there's no one left to play with my daughter at home." I told him I would not want even one child left in that particular slum in the daytime, without parents. Wicked people roamed about, who would do bad things to the children.

"Please bring her to us and I will admit her into our program," I invited.

His face was downcast; tears beginning to fill his eyes and spill down his cheeks. "I don't think you would want my child," he said.

"Why not?"

"Because she was born dumb."

I explained, "All the more reason for me to have that child in our school." The father looked shocked at my response. "Sir, if you will bring her tomorrow morning, one of our staff will help you fill in your address and other information on the entry form. If you bring her every morning, since we know you come home late in the evening, we will make sure that your child is brought home when your wife is there."

The next day he brought eight-year-old Anjudha, riding on the fruit cart. He lovingly carried her in his arms and placed her in mine. He was a very relieved man. I took Anjudha in to my mom and explained the situation. I asked her to take over this child's case.

My 70-year-old mom had this girl with her on the floor of the only little passage to our school. I was leading the others in praise and worship in the classroom. While everyone was lost in worship to the Lord, I walked between the rows of kids and happened to look out the classroom window into the passageway where Mom and Anjudha sat. Mom could read and write Kannada fluently. She was to teach this girl the Kannada alphabet. Instead she decided to lead the child to Jesus. She had her left arm around Anjudha's shoulders. Looking straight into her eyes, Mom spoke to her in Kannada and said, "Say 'Jesus.'" I witnessed what took place in that moment. Anjudha looked straight into Mom's face, and with the joy of the Lord welling up in her, said, "Jesus!" That was the first word this eight-year-old's tongue had ever spoken.

To this day, ten years later, whenever I see this fruit vendor on the streets, he is all excited. His daughter is now a young lady and is able to communicate with him in his language. It's not just education or baths, meals, and medicines; but it is giving the fullness of all God has for them when we move in tune with the Holy Spirit.

One Tuesday afternoon, our Bible study group was meeting in the passage outside the classroom—a space about six feet wide and 15 feet long. I sat on a low plastic stool with my interpreter beside me. I was about to begin when a woman I did not know came in. I found out she was Shanti, the Hindu niece of our cook Sagama. Shanti told us how she and her five-year-old daughter, Bindu, had been walking on the street that morning to go visit Sagama's family. All of a sudden Bindu went missing. Shanti had frantically looked for her everywhere in that Muslim crowd that was celebrating a major festival. She had searched all morning and into the afternoon, but could not locate Bindu anywhere. She knew Sagama had gotten a job at Gateway Free School, so she had come looking for comfort. Beating her chest and crying loudly, she sounded and looked like a crazy woman. Her hair was all disheveled and she was talking in Telugu. I couldn't understand a word, but the staff told me what she was saying.

The clock on the wall read 3:00 p.m.—time for Bible study to begin. I turned to Shanti and said through an interpreter, "Sit down right now. There's no time for crying; it is time to hear God's Word. Wait until I'm done sharing God's Word and anointing everyone here with oil and praying for them. When we have concluded this service, Bindu will be standing outside the black gate on my left. God will have sent His angels to place her there."

I proceeded to speak and actually forgot all about little Bindu. I believe His Word will not go back to Him empty, but will accomplish the purpose for which it was sent. (See Isa. 55:10-11.) As I said "Amen" to the concluding prayer, I heard the black gate rattling. Three small children stood there, Lakshmi and Manju on either side of another little one wearing shorts and a shirt and having a bald head. I turned around and looked over the wall. "What is it kids?" I asked.

"Auntie, Bindu's here!" So when the folks heard the name Bindu, they all stood up. It was Shanti's daughter, who had gotten lost that morning. Mother and daughter cried many tears and shared hugs in their reunion. Her mother asked Bindu where she had been all morning. When she described the place, everyone was surprised that such a little one could have returned such a distance. It had to be angels! Today Shanti and her entire household are believers because of what God did for them.

Three or four times a week we would send our staff to witness in pairs with two or three kids, so they would learn to evangelize. A staff member and I would go into different neighborhoods and start ministries in areas where we were known—where the kids who came to our school lived. Very often in India, neighbors love to come and see what is going on. That's how people would join our services. While our staff were witnessing in one area, someone happened to tell them about a paralyzed man who needed help. He was Hindu by birth and totally bedridden, afraid even to sit down without help. Over time his faith increased as we visited him or the family would bring him in an auto-rickshaw to the Tuesday afternoon Bible study. He could not stand on his own; he was tall and heavy-set. Because he could read Tamil, we gave him a Bible. He was very interested in Scripture. We wrote down the faith-building verses he should read. As he read and heard the Word of God, he believed and accepted Christ. He's no longer an idol worshiper, but a believer attending an AG church, totally healed by the power of God. His name now is Ananias and his wife is Miriam.

We had begun the school with about 50 street kids. We fed them cookies and fruit in the morning and rice with lentils and vegetables at lunch. A nearby store supplied an Indian sweet made from milk, sugar, and Indian butter. This finished off the lunch. In the evening we gave them a heavy snack of *sooji* (grits) with milk and sugar or Indian cereal called *ragi* with brown sugar. Later in the evening they got additional fruit or cookies.

Sagama, who had recently been converted from idolatry and delivered from severe alcoholism, cooked the meals for the school kids. She went to the little well at the back of the school shed to draw a pail of water out with our rope and pulley system. The metal lid on top of the well kept the kids and dirt out when the well wasn't being used. One day around 10 a.m., Sagama came running into the classroom where I was teaching, like she had seen a ghost. Speechless, she gestured that she had seen a huge snake resting on the lid of the well. It was a cobra.

I left her in the room with my mom and all the children with instructions not to allow anyone out into the compound. I told Mom I was going to look for Gerald, who was good at killing cobras. He was not scared of them. We would say he had a special "anointing" for the task. I had to scale two compound walls to look for Gerald on the next street. When we came back together, we looked but couldn't find the cobra. We came around to the front of the school and saw Mom. "What are you doing out here? I asked you to stay inside," I scolded.

"The cobra came up here. I commanded it in Jesus' name to leave and never come back," Mom said. "You won't be seeing another one here." To this day, we have not seen another one.

One night as David and I were coming back from a series of preaching appointments, we came through a heavy rain storm. I turned to David and said, "This afternoon while I was teaching, a coconut fell from our neighbor's tree and broke a hole in the asbestos of our little roof. Let's pray that this rain storm doesn't drop anything more on the roof and that no snakes get in through the hole." The streets were overgrown with weeds and there were lots of snakes in the general area.

Every morning I would meet about 25 older women and kids for an hour of prayer with our staff. After that we had breakfast, and then prepared for school with 150 kids. That morning when I walked down the street from home, the whole area was strewn with fallen branches. The place was a mess. But as I walked into our little compound, it looked like not a leaf had moved out of place. Not a drop of rain had come in the gaping one-foot hole in the roof. Everywhere else was mud, slush, and water flowing down the street, but it was as dry as ever inside our compound. God had heard our prayer. We kept functioning out of a little shed, despite the fact we continued to grow.

When we first started the school, each morning we had to go and bring the children to our site. If not, they might wander to the garbage heaps for food or get sold into child labor for the rest of the day. A good number of their parents sorted garbage for a living. The kids were sent to beg coins for their parents' bad habits. One morning I had taken a fifth grader by the name of Geetha Venkatesh to a slum as my interpreter and to help me round up the kids who were registered with us for school. Some lived in tents, some in lean-to shacks with thatched and patched roofs that the water came through. Sometimes the kids had no choice but to sleep on muddied dirt floors. The whole area had not one faucet or one latrine. People had no way to clean up after relieving themselves.

Our kids got excited when they saw me coming. I grabbed clothes from their huts and started putting on their shirts for them and combing their hair. They hadn't eaten anything since waking, so they were looking forward to school. These street wanderers had no sense of day or time. After rounding up eight or nine children, I came to Manju Srinivas' little hut where her father was turning and swinging his head like a cobra and banging it on the cement floor in front of the hut. People were warning me not to go near, but I was worried about his wife. I wanted to get her out of there. Some women told us that Manju's dad had beaten her mother with bamboos all night. He was blaming her for the death of their seven-year-old daughter. Manju was ten years old and had a baby brother at home. Instead of bringing the daughter to our free medical clinic, the father had taken her from temple to temple and dedicated her to demons.

He had performed all kinds of rituals and nothing had worked. Ultimately she had died.

The opening to his little hut was about three feet high and 18 inches wide. He was bare-bodied except for a loin cloth around his waist. Seated at the opening, he was totally demon possessed. His wife sat weeping and wailing inside, the baby in her arms. Geetha was not afraid, because she saw that I wasn't. The hut had no light in it; we could only look inside on either side of the man's shoulders. I knew he could be dangerous; I also know the Word of God. "No weapon formed against you will prevail" (Isa. 54:17). Greater is He that is in me than He that is in the world. (See 1 Jn. 4:4.)

I asked the mother to come out so we could help her and the baby. She could rest at the school and we could protect her from this man. But like a typical, poor, uneducated Indian wife, she did not want to leave her husband, though he had physically abused her all night. I managed to get her to give me the baby. As soon as I took him in my arms, I heard in my spirit, "Run!"

I said to Geetha, "Run to Basama's home and get her and her four brothers to quickly join us. Meet me round the corner; don't wait and don't look around. Tell them to come running, dressed or not." I turned to the children with me and told them to run away from there too. I must admit that I didn't know what would happen next, but I had to be obedient to what the Holy Spirit had spoken to me.

Basama, age 12, and her brothers came running. No sooner had we taken to our heels, the demon-possessed man sprang to his feet. He took a huge branch from a coconut palm tree and started swinging it violently. He thrashed both men and women within his reach; no one could control him. By then we were about 100 yards away from him. We never stopped running until we reached the school and locked the gate. Thank God, the children were safe in our little school. Sadly, later that year, 12-year-old Basama was given by her uneducated parents in marriage to a relative. She had to leave for her husband's village.

Being a Canadian citizen, my mom was spending six months of the year in India and the other six months divided between England, France, and Canada, visiting other members of the family. On one of those trips, before she left India she told Gerald, "This year I want you to do something for me. Use my funds to put roofs on six poor people's homes, even before the monsoons break." Gerald, being a very devoted son, would do anything for Mom. She went back to Canada and within three months of her doing what she had felt led to do for the poor, six of her own children moved into their own homes—three in Canada, one in France, one in England, and David and myself in India. I can tell you only my story. My husband and I had been living in my sister Anita's fully furnished apartment in Bangalore. When David's parents learned about it, they purchased the apartment from Anita and gave it to us free of charge. We had not even asked God for it. He's a truly amazing God!

Friday evenings I usually held a healing service in our one and only classroom—our sanctuary. All the people sat on the floor, and the interpreter and I sat on low plastic stools. We had finished the prayer and worship; I was about to start bringing the Word. A woman walked in the front door and put a small piece of paper on my lap. Written on the paper were the words, "Gateway Free School." She moved to the back of the room with another woman and an 18-year-old girl. They all sat on the floor mats too. We had never met these three persons before.

I continued preaching God's Word. At the end, everyone stood, and I called the 18-year-old girl to the front. All the while I had been ministering the Word, her eyes kept rolling in their sockets, continuously. Praise the Lord, I was not distracted. Only when I do the first thing the Holy Spirit prompts me to do, is the next step revealed to me. As she came up to the front, the Spirit revealed to me that a demon of dumbness was holding on to her vocal cords. Her name was Ammu Kutty. I turned to the congregation—mainly children, women, and old folks, and asked, "Children, how do demons flee?"

In one voice they responded, "Auntie, when we praise and worship the Lord, then demons flee."

"OK, let's all worship the Lord," I said. We sang one chorus in English and Kannada, "In the Name of Jesus," and then one in English and Tamil, "There Is Power in the Blood." I said to Sister Pushpa, my interpreter, "Today you will not interpret into Kannada, but into Tamil for this young lady." I prayed a simple prayer, taking authority over the spirit of dumbness and telling it to leave then and there and never to return to this young lady again. I reminded it that the blood of Christ was against it.

Even before Pushpa could interpret the 'amen' as I concluded my prayer, Ammu Kutty shouted loudly, "Amen!" Everyone started cheering and praising the Lord even more. The two women with her had already come to stand beside her while we were praising and worshiping God. One of them, by the name of Rukmani, was a Roman Catholic neighbor of Ammu Kutty. The other was her stepmother, an idol worshiper. They told us that Ammu had been unable to speak from the age of six. Her drunken father had been a womanizer who had caused his first wife to commit suicide. He had three daughters; Ammu being the eldest. She had been raised by her grandmother. One day the grandmother happened to yell at her for some reason. Ever since that day, she had not spoken and had behaved very weirdly.

On the streets in our area this girl used to be considered a mad woman—a mentally challenged person. Kids would throw stones at her. She was so possessed by this demon that she would walk up to stores, open the candy jars, and get the candy in her hands to steal it. The owners knew she could not pay, so they would slap her. That Friday they had brought her to our free medical clinic. Dr. Gerard and Claudia, the pharmacist, had realized that she did not need medicine, so they had given her this slip of paper with our school name on it. They told her attendants to take her to the school at 6:30 p.m. and I would give her the "medicine." As soon as Ammu had said the 'amen,' she began mouthing the words of the songs we were singing in praise of our Lord. The next day she joined the nursery section of our school to learn English. From then on Ammu Kutty always wanted to lead the praise and worship.

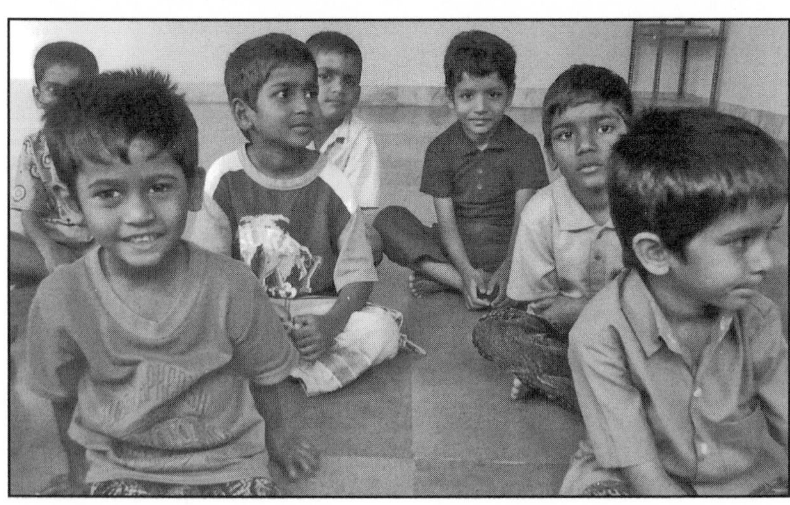

Gateway Residence housing the Children's Home, Free School, and sanctuary.

CHAPTER 19

GATEWAY BOARDING SCHOOL

"Train up a child in the way he should go" (Prov. 22:6, KJV).

AS I WALKED THE STREETS OF BANGALORE, SEEING AND smelling the open sewage drains and human excrement everywhere, all I thought of was souls. I'm actually a hygiene freak, but when you are moving in the Holy Spirit, you don't even notice all the filth. I saw some of the street kids picking orange peels out of the garbage bins, sometimes two or three kids fighting over some tidbit. My heart was breaking! How can we sleep in our beds when these children are out on the streets? When I couldn't sleep I prayed in the Spirit. I wanted to reach more children; 130 in one year's time was not enough. Whatever we do to the least of these, we do as unto the Lord. (See Matt. 25:40.)

When God called us to work in Bangalore, I didn't know any of the three languages spoken in our area. One morning at the school assembly, I noticed that our little three-year-old, Karthika, was missing. I asked the children from the area neighboring hers if they had seen or heard anything of her that morning. They said they hadn't. She usually came to school on her own. Like the shepherd who left the 99 to search for the lost one, I left my flock of about 150 to take to the streets looking for Karthika. My sister Christine was visiting from Paris and decided to join me. When I entered the slum where Karthika lived, no one was in sight. All the adults had left for daily wage jobs. I stooped and looked into her dark hut, where she was softly whimpering all by herself.

Four families shared that tiny hut at night. I crawled inside and brought her into the sunshine. She had only a small panty on. No Mommy had been in sight when she woke up, to care for her basic needs. We picked her up, dressed her, and combed her hair. She was so frightened at having been left alone; she clung to me and I hugged her tightly. That's what Jesus would have done—and what we are called to do to the least of these. We took our little one back to school and she was all smiles. Christine was so touched with the rescue that she took a photo of Karthika and me with her camera.

I often stayed up till midnight marking the children's exercise books. Then I got up early for a prayer meeting every morning from 6:00 to 7:00. Sometimes I had not had any sleep, but I would be up by 5:00—ankles swollen, head swimming, feet tired from walking in the streets in the dirt and heat. Our school had no air conditioning, no phone lines. I had to bathe the little ones, and sometimes they would vomit or have "loose motions" (diarrhea). Our kids did not use diapers, so there was never a dull moment! We did it all for the Lord.

One day I had been showering a good number of the kids in our little wash area and didn't realize that the gate had been left open. A Hindu gentleman by the name of Hari Narayan walked into the compound with the intention of checking us out. We were to purchase property from him—two and a half acres. I had been bargaining for a good deal, and had told him we needed to use it for the poorest of the poor and the ones society had rejected. I had told him that we were doing similar work in the heart of Bangalore with street kids. He knew I was the president of Gateway International, but before he signed the deal with us he was curious to see what we were really doing.

The 30-by-40-foot property that we had was small; barely big enough for our 12-by-20-foot little hollow block classroom/ church building and a 6-by-10-foot storage area for grain and rice, bed linens and ration boxes, behind which we hid our

Bibles. The roof had seven holes that leaked whenever it rained. Sometimes we had to stand and teach in water. We even used the passageway for classroom space. The kitchen was 5-by-6 feet, the same size as the bathroom for 150 kids and staff. We squeezed 80 to 120 people into the building on a given Sunday.

We wanted to purchase the additional land from this particular owner, but it was made very clear to us that we needed to take a stash of cash with us to be given to the registration officer as a bribe (black money)—which is not documented and for which you do not get a receipt. It's a good sum, not just $50 or $100, which you have to pay for that person's signature on your documents. That's the way things move in India. But God has called us to be people of integrity, in spite of the situation. He doesn't want us to compromise with the heathen world and its ways. He says He's a way-maker God and we've got to dare to believe that He will come through for us.

The previous day, I had decided to go to the 'Registrar,' that is, the government official who works on the registration of property. I wanted to meet the official, and find out exactly what it was that she wanted us to bring, what documents, what files, etc. I wanted to check to see if everything was in order. So she checked the file and gave me the official amount we'd have to bring in. I told her, "I've already got that in on-demand drafts." She didn't mention the bribe and I didn't either.

Ammu Kutty had seen Hari Narayan walk in through our school gate. From the day she had gotten delivered from the evil spirit of dumbness, she had been able to talk normally. People who had known her before would ask, "What brought about the change in you?" She would answer, "Jesus healed me at Gateway Church." She knew we did not allow strangers to come in, because children could be kidnapped. She went straight up to the man and literally slapped him on his cheek to get his attention. He had been looking into the shower area for some time without my knowing, watching me soaping and rinsing the kids' hair. This could have been the 14th child I had bathed in a row! My apron was drenched.

None of the kids had water in their homes. If we didn't provide soap and water and teach them to scrub themselves, they wouldn't bathe for weeks. Ammu turned and said to the man, "Sister Theresa has not been doing this only today. She does this every day for the children." Out of the mouth of a newborn child of God, He gave us favor.

The next day I had to go and register our new property. So I called the lawyer's office to let him know I was coming and to ask if his colleague was ready to go with me to the registration office. He told me, "Theresa, I hope you've got the bribe ready."

I replied, "Don't even talk to me about bribes." This lawyer is supposed to be a Catholic gentleman who knows the Word of God. I'm not talking against Catholics. It doesn't matter whether you are a born-again, tongues-speaking Pentecostal, when you compromise and give in to the ways of the world you lose your anointing. You can be a Baptist, Methodist, Presbyterian, a Charismatic—whatever. But you cannot afford to compromise. You've got to dare to believe that when you stand for the truth, the truth will set you free.

The lawyer asked me to bring some thousands of rupees for the bribe. I said to him very clearly, "Sir, don't even talk to be about it, because I don't even have that kind of money and I'm not going to look for it either." I was raging at this stage. I sat in the car and I was angry in my spirit. When I realized that, I put on a worship tape and started praising God. I didn't want that anger to hit at me.

We went into the registration office and there were a lot of other lawyers and VIPs waiting to meet with the Registrar. I put my file on the table and everything was moving like clockwork for us, because God was giving us favor. Then the Registrar said to me, "Madam, you have to go to that table and give your thumb impression and your signature on those documents there."

Just then the Hindu gentleman who was selling us the property whispered to me, "I hope you brought the bribe."

I said, "What are you talking about? I don't know about bribes; I don't do bribes."

He said, "No, it won't work, because in this office last month I paid 10,000 rupees (i.e. about $220) over here for one single document that I needed."

I told him, "That's your problem; it's not mine." Then very humbly I added, "I don't do it, sir. We don't have that kind of money."

I went to the table to give my thumbprint and the female Registrar, who is used to taking bribes, called one of her officers. One of my staff, Claudia Nair, was sitting at that same table and overheard what the Registrar told her officer. "You see that lady over there? (She looked toward me.) I don't want any of you taking any bribes from her, because she is doing good work. And if you do so, you'll fall dead."

Nothing is impossible for God. He wants you to continue to believe. He opened doors for us to buy the land for 20 percent less than its actual value. So in the year 2000 we were able to purchase those two and a half acres for a minimal price. Today it is valued ten times as much as we paid for it. To God be the glory! This is our site, Lord willing, for ministering to lepers, widows, and senior citizens in the future.

For the first eight years in India, besides helping nine other organizations financially, we would help towards the building of one structure each year. We would look for people with genuine need, regardless of denomination. God never led us to build for ourselves during that time. God had laid it on our hearts to help provide buildings for other ministries that were doing genuine work for the poor. For eight years God asked us to keep operating on my family-owned property. They had not charged us a dime to use the site.

In the ninth year my oldest sister Christine offered me her land just down the street from where we had been working. She and her husband David Thabot also had a passion for these poor kids and had come out every year from France to spend time with them. Like a fairy godmother, her suitcases were always filled with storybooks, chocolates, toys, and other treats for the children. I handed the land over to the Gateway International Trust. So we prepared to build there for our own orphan kids and other boarding students.

When we started building in 2005, some kids used to be beggars in our area. We had both boys and girls. I asked my brother Gerald and my husband David if we could buy bunk beds for the kids in the school. Gerald owned a penthouse in the same apartment building where David and I lived, so he let us use it for our temporary boarding for these street kids. Gerald said he didn't think we could buy such beds, but we might be able to get them made. I said, "I don't have time to stand by carpenters and supervise them while they go for their tea break and potty break. In the long run, it would drive me crazy to watch their undisciplined work habits."

I did not give up, however. I believed if God wanted this, He is Jehovah Jireh. He knows what I need to take care of His kids. The next day at six a.m. prayer, I suggested to the children and elderly folks, "Let us ask Jesus to provide us with bunk beds right now. We need two pairs to begin with." I quoted, "My God will meet all your needs according to the riches of his glory in Christ Jesus" (Phil. 4:19). After seeing to the kids' breakfast, I went home to do my household chores. We lived just behind the free school on the next street.

Just as I arrived, our phone rang. It was Gary Marcyes of Colorado Springs, who happened to be a missionary in Bangalore with his wife Tina and five children. He said, "I hear you need bunk beds." I was astonished, because no one knew but our little group taking this to the Lord in prayer that morning.

"Yes," I said, "I just need two pairs."

He went on, "We have 22 pairs, custom-made, for you, together with mattresses and bed linens too. We also have kitchen utensils and some other things you could use. When can you come for them? We've had to shut down our own boarding facility and we want to give you all the stuff we have." They had been forced to close their school because the Northeast Indian children in their orphanage had not been legally registered in the state of Karnataka. The legal advisors had misled this ministry, and their own so-called Christian staff had betrayed them and reported them to the authorities. They had been paid good salaries, but had been greedy for more.

When we got the 22 sets of beds, I went to the Lord and asked Him to direct me as to where I should send what I didn't need immediately. We gave ten sets to a Christian home for the mentally challenged and ten sets to a Bible college where the young men were stacked in a room like sardines in a tin—all sleeping on the floor. When God blesses us we must wait on Him until we hear what He wants us to do with what He has put in our care. I've learned never to hoard. When we give to others the best we have, better things will come back to us! "Give, and it will be given to you" (Luke 6:38).

From time to time God had laid it on our hearts to bless those who could not bless us in return. One year we were helping with the construction of a church just one kilometer or so from us. We needed a place to baptize those who had been saved in our services. So after helping Pastor Joseph and Sister Mary with their church construction we thought they would be open to the idea of building a baptismal tank behind their sanctuary. Next to their boundary wall is an open drain for sewage, but the Lord even told me the exact place to dig so sewage water wouldn't be seeping in. I called Pastor Joseph and told him that our ministry would provide the workers and material if he would only supervise the job. He agreed.

I sent workers and the main person was a Hindu gentleman. This man decided that the workers should wait for the truck strike to end to get supplies of cement, sand, and bricks. So the following day, nothing was done. We had already set the day for the baptismal service, following what God had prompted me. I sent for the pastor and said, "I'm very aware of the strike in the city. All you have to do is supervise the digging. We will manage the rest."

We had gotten bricks and sand, but no cement was available anywhere. I keep a busy schedule and had no time to run around and try to look for bags of cement here and there. I just sent a prayer up to heaven the next morning at prayer meeting and stated, "Just as God provided Abraham with a ram, He will provide the bags of cement today."

When I went home after the meeting, the phone rang. Mrs. Rita Paul, one of the teachers who was moving out of our area to build her own home elsewhere, was on the line. She said, "I have a feeling you need cement."

I replied, "How fast can you deliver it?" Even though there was a strike of all carriers, we managed to get all the cement we needed brought to the spot free of charge. Our God is only a prayer away. God had told Rita to give it to us and she asked her contractor to deliver it to us.

After eight years in India, David and I were taking a ministry trip to the US, traveling in Louisiana to our Gateway International Board meeting. As we rode down the highway, the Holy Spirit led me to say to David, "Pastor Dino Rizzo will fund our first building in Bangalore." He kept quiet and kept driving. By the end of the Board of Directors' meeting that day, no one had mentioned construction or funds for a children's home in Bangalore. Dino Rizzo, Secretary of the Board, had gone to the same Bible college as David. He pastors Healing Place Church in Baton Rouge. As the meeting concluded, he looked up with tears in his eyes and said, "David and Theresa, don't worry about that building in Bangalore. We will help you fund it." True to his word, his church sent $90,000 for the building we are now using for our home for children, a free school, and a sanctuary. We have a totally debt-free ministry. Our God is truly Jehovah Jireh. He provides more than we can ever dream or ask for.

While the Gateway Children's Home building was progressing, and we were using Gerald's penthouse apartment for our resident students, government officials surprised us at 4:15 one evening. The two men very graciously examined our records, attendance register, and food programs. Then they wanted to visit the children's living areas. So we went up to the penthouse where the kids stayed. The men said, "Even though they are minors, you must have separate accommodations for girls and for boys." So I told them we would do our best.

We had hit a snag. It would save us on staff if we could house the kids together. One of the reasons we don't hire staff of other faiths is that we don't close our school for all the Hindu or Muslim holidays. It was not always easy to have enough Christian staff working with us. Most of our kids had grown up on the streets their whole lives. They had a long way to catch up academically with what kids of their age should know. For years David and I have worked almost around the clock many days, each one doing the jobs of at least four people. God has been so good to grant us the physical and spiritual stamina to "run the race" this way.

At the prayer meeting the morning following the inspection, we asked God to open doors for us to have the next door penthouse apartment for our boys, so all could be on the same terrace level, yet separated. That flat was owned by Mr. Murthy, one of the big builders in the area. He knew my brother well. I discussed with Gerald the possibility of meeting with Mr. Murthy about his apartment. The man who had rented it previously, had moved to Chicago for a few months. He taught yoga, and would be returning to India soon.

That same morning, I went to meet Mr. Murthy. I told him we would like to have the use of his apartment for the boys we work with. He said, "OK, no problem. You can just bring me a check to purchase it and it's all yours. Anyway, why not just take the key and have a look at it?" He was asking a huge sum of money.

Gerald and I looked at the apartment and found it was ideal for our kids and staff. I went back to Mr. Murthy and told him it was exactly what we were looking for. "Have you brought the check?" he asked.

I said, "I have no check for you, but I still want the apartment."

He said, "I don't want to rent it; I want to sell it."

"Sir, I don't want to rent it nor buy it. I do want to use it for our work."

He put his head down; I wondered if he was shocked or what. When he looked up, tears filled his eyes and he said, "Madam, you can have it for as long as you like."

More people should trust the Lord and go out in boldness to do what He wants. The Book of Acts is not yet concluded. The Holy Spirit is still here with us to prompt us and teach us. He is our Helper, Intercessor, the One Called Alongside. He never fails to put the right words on our tongues, if we trust Him. We used that apartment for 13 months, free of charge. Then we heard he had an offer from a big buyer, so my brother decided to buy it from him and hand it over to us for as long as we needed to use it. God never fails to provide the resources if we have a heart for souls and if we have a vision.

Eventually the three-story stone building, erected on the property my sister Christine had given us, was completed. We were able to pay for the construction and all that was needed with God's help—mainly through Healing Place Church. In 2008 we moved in debt free!

CHAPTER 20

GATEWAY'S UNFORGETTABLE ONES

"Suffer the little children to come unto me" *(Mark 10:14, KJV).*

IN ORDER TO EVANGELIZE PEOPLE IN OUR AREA, WE USED A strategy God had given us. Three evenings a week the staff and older kids would meet in different locations in homes of kids who came to the free school. Not all were boarders, though all were very poor. Many went home for the night. Kevin, one of our boys, lived in the area. He was seven years old; his sister Jennifer, 5, and his brother Joshua, 3. Kevin was on fire for the Lord and wanted to go out with the evangelism team. One evening they had gathered with Veni, age 12 and Ravi, age 14 in the home of their parents. Their mom's name was Gouri and dad, Gopi, who was an alcoholic.

The one and only room was jammed with people. It had standing room for about ten, but 20 or more had crowded into the passage and outside the door. They had no faucet, no toilet area. Yet the power of God descended in that place. Kevin led in prayer and worship. Tears flowed as people experienced God's presence. Then Gopi came home drunk, smelling strongly of liquor. He squeezed through the crowd, but no one noticed him. They were so lost in Jesus. Kevin took them into the throne room of God. In His presence is fullness of joy; at His right hand there are pleasures forevermore. (See Psa. 16:11.)

That evening Gopi cried out to God, like a little child, in true repentance. He gave his life to Jesus. The Bible says,

"A little child will lead them" (Isa. 11:6), and "the kingdom of heaven belongs to such as these" (Matt. 19:14). There is power in praise and worship. When we offer a sacrifice of praise, God can make all things new. The following Sunday morning Gopi came to church to hear the Good News again.

Kevin's mom Maya and her family, all alcoholics, attended the Catholic church in the area at Christmas and Easter, but really had no faith. One day she fell in love with someone else, and in despair poured kerosene on herself at 11:00 p.m. Kevin's father, a humble man and not a drunk, had been outside the house, but came running in as she lit a match. He tried to put out the fire and burned his arms. Maya fell on the sleeping kids. Jennifer's legs were burnt, Joshua's private parts were burnt, and Kevin had burns too. A few days later Maya died in the hospital. All three motherless homeless children were being treated in the hospital as well. A year later Maya's drunken family demanded the kids from us and never brought them back. Only God knows where they are or what the future holds for these precious children.

Solomon Yusuf came to us through his grandmother, a Muslim convert. She had been thrown out of her village in Mangalore located in Karnataka State. She had come to Bangalore and worked at a wholesale vegetable market, sorting potatoes, carrots, and onions. At the end of the day, like Ruth in the Bible, she could take the leftovers and support her family with that. Solomon's dad had remarried; his new wife did not want to know about this boy. So the grandma and her unmarried daughter and son had been caring for Solomon. They had heard about Gateway through someone in Mangalore. He was eleven years old when he came to us.

At first, Solomon's grandma came to visit once a month on a Sunday morning. Then for two or three months she didn't show up. Solomon got anxious and wanted to go and look for her. One Friday he left the building without permission. We did not have his grandmother's address, but we had the phone number of a store owner in her area. He could contact her for us in case of an emergency. I could not even go to the police about this; for fear that the old lady would be in trouble for being a Muslim background believer. Solomon had never traveled on his own in a local bus. He had no money; he would have to beg. It took three or four bus rides to get to where his grandma was. He didn't know the way, only the name of the area.

When I discovered Solomon was gone, I sent staff and older students to look for him at the main bus station and the local railway stations. The long distance bus station was about a 45-minute drive from our place. They had seen no sign of him.

Friday evening I finally called the police to file a First Investigative Report (FIR), telling them a 12-year-old boy was missing. Then Saturday I went in and gave them all the information, including the only photo we had of Solomon wearing a yellow T-shirt with the word Jesus on it. I told them, "I just need to notify your office. I know the police force is under a lot of pressure today, because of what is going on in the state, and you don't have enough personnel to go around. We ourselves have been looking for him. He's not the type of boy who will live on the streets. He will come back to us. Can you wait awhile before you do anything?"

The police officer replied, "Right, we have a lot of pressure today. Why don't you come back tomorrow? We know you." I was relieved. But I knew I would have to give them his medical records, details of his family, and a more complete report the next day.

Saturday night about 11:00 p.m., I was pacing up and down in the living room of my home, praying in the Spirit for the Sunday morning church service. All of a sudden I knew in my spirit exactly where Solomon was that night. Early the next morning I called Sister Pushpa, one of our boarding staff, and asked her to go along with Michael to get Solomon. I told her,

"Right now, Solomon is sleeping on the floor of Emmanuel's home."

Emmanuel, Isaac, and Jacob were three brothers who had formerly been our students. I had asked them to leave because of their irregular attendance and bad behavior. We also had gotten no cooperation from their parents. Two of them were teenagers and would have been a bad influence on the other boys, had we kept them. Neither Pushpa nor I knew where Emmanuel's home was. Like the Book of Acts, where the Holy Spirit told Ananias exactly where to find Saul, or Cornelius' men where to find Peter, God showed us where to find Solomon. Our God is a God of details!

About half an hour's walk from where we were, through several streets, Pushpa found Emmanuel's home, as the Lord had directed me to instruct her. Just as God had revealed to me, Solomon was sleeping on the floor of that little room. They had no beds; everyone, including the parents, slept on the floor. The parents were in the village visiting relatives that weekend. The previous night Solomon had slept under a truck. We are grateful to God, who never fails us. I informed the police that Solomon was back. Case closed; praise the Lord!

Michael, one of our older boarders, was the son of big-time garbage sorters in our area. The whole Muslim family collected metal, plastic, glass bottles, cardboard boxes, and copper from electric wires. At the end of the day they would sell these things and use the money for alcohol and gambling. Very often the children didn't even get any food. Michael and his little brother lived on the streets and used to come to the school as day students.

One day Michael was nowhere to be found. Another staff and I went looking for him. He was a gentle, harmless kid, tall for his age. A woman in the neighborhood pointed us in the direction where the boys hung out. She also said Michael's mother had placed her foot on the boy's neck the night before in desperation. He had been wielding a small knife. Michael's mother was upset because he had joined a gang of boys his age and older. The gang stole merchandise from store fronts and clothes from lines, all the while drinking alcohol, smoking cigarettes, and getting high on local drugs. Finally we found him and took him to school. Ultimately Michael's mom handed him over to our boarding school.

I believed Michael was harmless and wouldn't have used the knife on anyone. He had never owned a toy in the ten years of his life. His father got drunk every day and Michael would see him lying in the street. One night Michael's dad beat his mom so badly that she was dead by morning. The dad got her buried and escaped to the next state, Andra Pradesh, where he had come from originally. The neighbors, mostly Muslims, hushed up the matter and no police case was filed. Sometimes the dad would come and ask for Michael. I would say, "First go get your wife; she's the one who admitted Michael to this home."

"She passed away," he answered.

"Yes, we know exactly how she died," I told him. So he would leave again. He used his younger son, age eight, to sort the garbage and get money for his liquor. The father would not let him come to school. If the dad ever came to the gate drunk, we would not let him see Michael. But when he arrived from out of state by train, he would be sober in the morning and stone drunk by evening.

One day Michael decided to go look for his older sister. He left the boarding home without permission. We felt anxious, because we didn't even know where to look for him. He was about 14 by then. My brother Gerald and I had to report this to the local police. We could not find him anywhere. I requested them not to broadcast it on TV, which they usually did when a child went missing. "Sir, he'll be back," I told the police officer.

That night I prayed, "Lord, you know exactly where Michael is. Please show us what is going on." When I awoke the next morning I sent for one of our male staff, Kamal. I asked him to take one of the older boys and hire an auto-rickshaw. "Go to Kanaka Nagar Street. Outside a storefront, on the steps, you'll find Michael sitting. Pick him up and bring him back; he'll be willing to come."

I must admit that I do not know anything unless I'm obedient to the Holy Spirit. If I open my mouth to speak the first sentence that comes, after that the second one is ready. I really do not know the whole thing until I'm obedient to start to say the first thing the Holy Spirit reveals to me. No human being told me where Michael was. It had to be God. Michael came back and stayed with us until he was 16 and finished the seventh grade. Then we handed him over to the Salesian Fathers of Don Bosco, a Roman Catholic organization that would give him vocational training. He had a very good memory. He could memorize whole chapters from books in all the languages we taught him. Recently we were able to reunite him with his widowed sister and her two little sons. We do visit him from time to time, pay for his training, and provide for his needs.

About five years after starting our work in Bangalore, the free medical clinic and boarding school, I got a phone call from the local police. They asked me to come and meet with them at the police station. They didn't say why. That afternoon we had planned a huge medical camp in a slum. Since it was impossible for me to be in two places at once, I decided not to go to the police that day. I knew I had not broken any laws or done anything wrong.

The next morning I asked my mom, who happened to be visiting from Canada, if she would go with me. She knows the local language. We dressed up very well in our best clothes and jewelry to go for this appointment. In general they respect people who are better off and mistreat those who are poor. When we got there some of the officers at the entrance were those who already knew me. They greeted me and asked us to go directly into the Inspector's office. He was available. They offered us tea and snacks, but we declined, having just had our breakfast.

I asked the officer why he had sent for me. He said, "Here's a letter from the Police Commissioner's office regarding your husband and you."

Even though my mother could read and write in Kannada, I replied, "Sir, I do not read Kannada. Would you mind explaining what the letter says?" So he explained to us that for the past five years the Central Bureau of Intelligence (like the US FBI) had been observing us both. They now wanted to know from me how we had managed to eradicate prostitution, drug addiction, garbage sorting, and begging in our area. They were asking if I could train them to do likewise in other communities of Bangalore.

I must admit that I was relieved. "Sir," I said, "We can only do one thing at a time. We've done everything because we love people." We were told that they would stop the kids on the streets and check with them about us. Formerly starving mistreated children were now excited to get food, naps, teaching, and even baths! We had about 150 kids and 16 staff at the time.

I thank God that He who calls us is faithful. "No weapon forged against you will prevail" (Isa. 54:17). "He who watches over Israel will neither slumber nor sleep" (Psa. 121:4); He is mindful of us in all our ways. (See Psa. 115:12.)

We had a boarder, Subash, whose mother committed suicide when he was five months old. A gang murdered his father when Subash was only a year old. He was cared for during the next seven years by his mother's brother, Milan, and his female friend, Jacinta, an older woman. Subash never went to school; he lived on the streets most of the time, till the two came home from work. When his uncle was not drunk, he worked as a painter. Jacinta worked as a maid in homes, cooking and cleaning. She brought Subash to us and gave me his story. I felt led of the Holy Spirit to admit the boy into our program.

Little did I realize what a handful he would be! He was the most violent kid I had ever known. He pulled the girls' pigtails and pinched them; poked boys with his pencil and bit some. He was always elbowing or hitting. He had a cousin, his mother's sister's son, named Satish. Satish's mother died when he was ten and his father was a drunk. He had already been going to school, but after his mother died his uncle put him to work as a carpenter's helper. When Satish came to visit Subash one Sunday morning, I asked him if he was interested in studying with us. He had seen how well Subash was doing in his studies.

Jacinta had not told us that Subash had a bleeding problem, an immuno-thrombocytopenic disorder. He bled profusely through his nose—huge clots of blood. The boy spent more time in the intensive care units of the Baptist and St. John's hospitals than in our boarding, which meant that one staff had to stay with him all the time. My kind brother Gerald went from one hospital to another to search for Subash's blood type—so he could buy plasma or blood for him. Gerald even donated his own blood to help. Subash's whole family were drunks and wouldn't come forward to help at all. Jacinta stayed at the hospital with him at night and our staff stayed in the daytime. His medical bills were sometimes greater per month than the food bills for the entire school. We have to use private doctors and hospitals for our boarders.

Finally God saw fit to heal Subash after three years of his being with us. One day after morning prayer, the kids all came to me and said, "Auntie, Subash was violent in the boarding last night." He had punched someone and bit his older cousin, who was double his height. The rule in our boarding school is if any kid raises his hand against another to attack him, I had the right to raise my hand against that kid. Subash was a great concern to us. We had tried everything—love, counseling, discipline, denying him his snacks, grounding him from privileges—nothing worked. He was being abusive.

That day I turned to the kids at the morning assembly and said, "From today onward, if Subash attacks any of you, whether you are in the right or wrong, scream out loud for attention. The rest of you go for him and give it to him where it hurts." That tactic finally worked. Subash did not raise his hand against anyone again. He had been taking advantage before, because we had asked the children to bear with him because of his illness. He stayed with us seven years, until he finished seventh grade. Satish studied with us up to the sixth grade. Then one Christmas when he went home, his uncle put him to work and he never returned to classes. He now joins us on Sundays for prayer and worship. As for Subash, he now stays with another uncle and aunt who are sponsoring his education. This couple does not have any children of their own.

One day I was teaching second graders their English lesson. We were short of staff for our eight grade levels of students. Sometimes I taught 28 subjects a day and marked books until 3 a.m. I was overworked, but I would not give up. My husband David was teaching English and Math, but he was also working hard with our construction projects as well as teaching at two other colleges. I was giving my best to these little ones, when all of a sudden, near where the class was meeting inside the building next to the boy's dorm room, I saw a huge angel momentarily standing alongside the stone wall. The outline was misty but the wing span was wide. The angel was alive and moving along the wall. All I could do was smile from deep within at such a confirmation that God was mindful of me. Every time I think of this, the memory is a healing balm that soothes and relaxes and blesses me. God is ever watchful of us. For days I felt a holy hush over that room; God's presence is always with us.

One evening our pharmacist, Claudia, and I were returning to our school from having ministered elsewhere. On the main street in one area we noticed, in the midst of heavy traffic, a young lady lying in the middle of the road. Her two-year-old daughter sat beside her holding a 100-rupee note (equivalent to two dollars) in her hand. When I observed this scene, I quickly parked my car along the side of this busy street and tried desperately to help this mom and child get out of danger, but to no avail. The mother looked like she had been beaten and raped. Her clothes had blood on them and she also had a black eye.

We swung the car around and went to get the local police to assist us. Two officers came on their motorbikes. After looking at the lady lying in the middle of the street, they just said, "Oh, it's this woman. Just leave her alone. We know who she is." Well, they knew that she was a prostitute and they didn't think she and her daughter were important enough to be rescued.

I looked at the two officers and as the old saying goes, "You never know what you're going to do when the anointing hits you." I told them if they weren't going to help us move this mother and child, I personally would bring all the traffic in the area to a halt by not allowing anyone to move beyond me. Immediately they got to work and did their best to move the woman.

Claudia and I also tried our best to tell the mother that if she came with us to our school, we could help both her and the little child, but she would not have it. Even though we had managed to get them off that busy street, we could not get them off our minds. That same evening we started praying to God, asking Him to give us that little child so that we could raise her up for Him.

A few days later both the mother and daughter were seen near our little school gate. Immediately we had our staff minister to the mother and encourage her. The little girl, Ammu, was taken in by our other staff, quickly given a fresh bath, changed into a pretty dress, given some sweets, put on a swing, and treated, in general, like royalty. Our kids started communicating with her in the Telugu language and made her happy. The mother was smiling to see her daughter look so clean and cared for. But after spending about two hours with us, it must have dawned on the mother that she was about to lose her breadwinner. If not for Ammu in her life, she would not be able to beg and bring in the money to take care of her boyfriends, her alcohol, or drugs. She grabbed the girl off the swing, threw the toys out of the child's hands, and left our grounds. We were very sad. We were learning that we had to first tie up the "strong man" who had held her captive, before we could rescue this mother and child from Satan's kingdom. (See Mark 3:24-27.)

Every day for the next two years we stormed heaven for this child, Ammu. Finally it was through another 12-year-old drug addict, Ankraj, whose sisters were in our program, that we were able to influence Ammu's mother to release her daughter to us.

When Ammu had been with us for a year or so and had seen her mother only on rare occasions, she began to long for her. One day as I marked my books, Ammu was playing church with a few other little girls under my table. She suddenly came up to me and said, "Auntie, these Christmas holidays I will go home to be with my mommy."

I hugged her, realizing that her mommy had never owned a home; she was a street woman. I replied, "Ammu, I'm going to miss you so much if you go, as my home is your home. When your mommy has her own home, we will make sure to see that you can join her."

She went back under the table and joined her friends. After some time little Ammu was back again. As the Lord says, revelation knowledge is hidden "from the wise and learned, and revealed … to little children" (Matt. 11:25). Her eyes were sparkling and with utmost confidence she said, "Auntie, I know what we are going to do. If I don't go home, my mommy surely will come here to look for me on a Sunday. Then you can preach to her and tell her about Jesus and she'll get saved." I am truly in awe of the work of the Holy Spirit in the lives of our kids. To David and me, each one is so special that for the first eight years of our married lives we took just two days of holiday in Thailand. We had traveled to preach in Singapore and Malaysia, and then stopped in Thailand to visit David's Thai friends. We proceeded on to Hong Kong and China to evangelize.

Having schooled Ammu for the first four years in our boarding school, we decided to move her to a private school along with some of our other orphans and semi-orphans. But without a birth certificate, it would be impossible for her to get admitted elsewhere. As we traveled to the new school for the admission test, I suddenly realized that Ammu had no birth date. While concentrating on the road and driving with a car full of kids, I began asking them to tell me what birthdates I had given each of them. They piped up, "Auntie, I have Nana's birth date," and "I have Papa's birth date." Someone else had my sister Mina's birth date, and so on. I was beginning to run out of birth dates of my immediate family to be given to my orphan kids. So I turned to Ammu, seated beside me, and said, "You can have Uncle David's and my wedding anniversary date as your birth date." She was all smiles to know that she too belonged to us. Yes, she was accepted at the school and is doing very well at her studies.

Not long after beginning her new school Ammu came to me and said, "Auntie, my mother has not come to see me for many months now. I wonder what's happened to her."

I looked at Ammu and, led of the Spirit, said, "Let's pray that your mother gets put into jail." The child was quite shocked, so I went on, "Ammu, if your mother gets put into jail, she won't be beaten and used by the bad men any more. Also, she will get a chance to hear about Jesus in the jail." Practically speaking, this kind of conversation is unheard of, but King David too said, "The Spirit of the Lord spoke through me; his word was on my tongue" (2 Sam. 23:2).

A couple of months later, a lady came to our school gate and introduced herself as an evangelist. She showed me her jail ID, saying she had ministered in the jail. She also had a picture of a group of women, among whom was Ammu's mother. She was sitting in the front row and in her right mind. We had never seen her looking so good and decent. When Ammu came home from school I told her about the evangelist who was waiting to meet with her. She was nervous and started crying. She begged me not to send her away from us with the lady at the gate. I said, "Ammu, all I want you to do is just see the picture of your mother in the jail receiving the Good News." I promised to stay with her and to keep her with us always. Talk about God answering prayer! Ammu, of course, is excited that God had to put her mom in jail in order to speak to her heart.

For several years I ministered in an AG church in Wilmington, Delaware, on my trips back to the US. The pastor, Edward Jones, then moved to Faith Assembly in Poughkeepsie, New York. Again he invited me to come and minister. On one such occasion, he and his son Ryan picked me up at the hotel to take me to church for the evening service. He told me, "Theresa, if there's ever a need; we're only a phone call away."

I turned round and said to him, "Pastor, God has been gracious. We are totally debt free and He has supplied all our needs. He is an on-time God." A year or so later, responding to our effort to acquire a half-acre property in India for the use of our Community College, Faith Assembly contributed $49,000.

One Christmas I decided, "Why don't we just bless the poorest of the poor, who can't repay us, with the $5,000 we had set aside for the building of our home. The work at the new site had been stopped for six months. The government was looking for land in that area to build an express highway to the new airport. Surveyors came, measurements were taken, but nothing seemed to be happening. David agreed, so we gave a thousand dollars to the Home of Hope for the dying and destitute. They ministered to 300 patients. We helped a few other desperate cases and similar institutions.

The very next day David's parents in Canada, Harry and Mary Greenhough, called and said they had 50,000 Canadian dollars they wanted to send to us for the construction of our home. They were in their 80s. They had already given generously toward the new house, plus buying the apartment we were presently living in for us from my sister. We never even asked God for anything. Miraculously, provision came in. The following day the contractor notified us that our new subdivision was the only one in the area not notified by the government. In other words, we could now proceed with the construction of our building. We have learned to be led by the Holy Spirit and not to hoard for ourselves. Remember, the Bible says that in giving, you will receive. (See Luke 6:38.)

CHAPTER 21

GOD'S CONTINUING FAITHFULNESS

"Jesus Christ is the same yesterday and today and forever" (Heb. 13:8).

IN THE YEAR 2000, DAVID AND I HAD PREACHED IN SINGAPORE and then in Hong Kong. We met David Balcomb there and then prepared to go into China for ministry. We planned to take along some Mandarin Sunday school material, tracts, and Bibles for the believers in the underground church. We packed these items in four of our suitcases. We knew that our bags would be checked by customs' officials at the China border. In those days no Bibles were allowed to be carried in.

As we pushed our luggage cart in the airport, we prayed in the Spirit. We exercised our spiritual authority before the devil had a chance to do anything. We asked God for favor. We claimed Matthew 18:19, "If two of you on earth agree about anything you ask for, it will be done for you by my Father in heaven." And, "whatever you bind on earth will be bound in heaven, and whatever you loose on earth will be loosed in heaven" (Matt. 18:18).

David placed the bags on the conveyor belt going through the X-ray machine. The Chinese customs' officer was staring into the screen. He didn't look to the right or to the left. His eyes were glued to the images on the screen. I looked at his face and saw his head start quivering, until all four bags had passed through. We quickly put the bags back on the cart and went on towards the exit. We didn't look back. I believe God sent an angel to distract him in some way. If we had been caught, the materials would have been confiscated and we could have been arrested. If one angel could put to death 185,000 of the Assyrian army (2 Kings 19:35), this was easy! God has a whole host of heavenly beings at our disposal. They walk with us and watch over us.

God helped us minister extensively to the Chinese believers. The people who organized the meetings would send messengers to us, strangers, to lead us to a different hotel each night. We would sit in the foyer and wait for a second stranger to come and give a message to us in code language. He would disappear, and we would follow the code and locate the correct meeting place. One evening we arrived at a huge auditorium with Chinese believers praising and worshiping and waiting for us. Many received the baptism in the Holy Spirit in the meetings.

David and I did tag-team preaching. He gave the theology and I gave the practical illustrations—meat trimmed with stories. One morning I was taken to the Beijing Medical University to speak at a conference for medical professionals. My coming had been arranged by two underground US missionaries. A three-hour session had been planned. A car came to the hotel for me. David was ministering to others at the hotel. The traffic was just like India, with bicycles and motorbikes cutting across all lanes—even the fast lanes. We came upon three major accidents that morning alone. Only 45 minutes of the conference remained by the time I arrived. I had already been informed that a government spy would be there and her description had been given to me. I was told to be careful of what I said and how I said things.

Meanwhile, I was having a tug-of-war in the Spirit. I wasn't sure of what message to bring. I prayed, "Lord, I'm available. Holy Spirit, you are let loose. God, use me in some way this morning." All the male and female professionals had been sitting and waiting over two hours. When I got into the building, I discovered it had no elevators. The meeting was on the fifth floor. I was out of breath by the time I got there. I still didn't know what to say, but I had a big smile on my face as I entered the room.

The Chinese very graciously welcomed me with flowers. I wasn't sure what to say, but I was led to say a little bit about myself. "I've been an educator most of my life. It would be nice for me to get to know you before we go further. How about telling me your names?" About 60 people sat in the room and everyone started talking to each other. "What's all the noise?" I asked.

One person replied, "It's impossible for you to remember Chinese names, though we don't mind telling them to you."

In the Spirit I said to them, "You'll be amazed. Just give me your names." I knew they were atheists, but I was available to speak whatever God said. He only gives me what I need. All I have to do is to be obedient and have faith.

Very graciously each person stood and gave me their Chinese names. Afterwards someone commented, "I wonder if you can remember even one name."

The Holy Spirit spoke through me at that instant and I began to call out each Chinese name, one by one, in the same order. In addition, I gave each person a word of knowledge. They were words of comfort and encouragement. They involved details of their lives no one else would have known about them—certainly not an outsider like me. These professionals started weeping, sobbing bitterly, but the Holy Spirit was doing a work in their hearts. In no time, like a wind going through, all were affected. No one felt the time passing, like a fast flowing river.

At last they asked, "How did you do that? Do you wear a computer chip? How could you tell us such deep things about ourselves?"

I told them that I was not wired; I had my own hair, not a wig; and no computer chip on me. I invited them to check me out. They were still questioning, "How then could you do what you just did?"

I went to the black board and wrote, "EVERY GOOD AND PERFECT GIFT COMES FROM GOD" (James 1:17).

"God?" they said, "Which god; what god?"

I gave them the salvation message and told them about the one and only true God. They cried more as the Spirit moved in our midst. They asked for my email address, my phone contact, and my mailing address. They offered, "We'll fly you from anywhere in the world. Will you come? We want our people to hear about the one true and living God."

"I've just sown the seed," I responded. "God has people here, on the premises, to water the seed. If you remain open and follow the leading of the Holy Spirit, He will instruct you. Then in turn, you will be able to instruct your own folk." Just as I finished, in walked the spy. She had also been held up by the traffic just like me, but only longer. She was very apologetic and described the traffic jam she had been caught in. Then I knew who had been responsible for it.

On another occasion, I was invited to be the main speaker at the Australian Assemblies of God National Convention for Women, which was to be held at the Melbourne Convention Center. On Saturday, the third and final day, the conference was open to all, men and women. Thousands had come; I preached on the baptism in the Holy Spirit and God's desire for all to receive the baptism. At the close of the service I asked all the pastors to come down to the altar to lay hands on all who had come forward to be baptized in the Spirit. People had filled the altar area and the aisles.

The platform was very high and I saw that the row closest to it had no one praying for them. So I jumped down to lay hands on them. Usually I close my eyes while praying, but I happened to keep them open this time. As I moved toward one gentleman, I saw an elderly woman about five rows behind him to the left, smiling broadly at me. As I anointed him with oil and prayed for him in the Spirit, he broke down in tears. I moved on to the next person until all had been ministered to.

The following morning, Sunday, I had been asked to preach at one of the main AG churches in the city. Afterwards, people again crowded around the altar waiting for prayer. The choir was singing softly, when the elderly woman whom I had noticed smiling at me the previous day came up to me. She spoke in a language I did not understand. Suddenly she slapped me twice on the cheek in frustration. The pastor came up and took her hands. "Pastor," I said, "I don't understand what she is saying."

Just then her niece came hurrying down from the choir, saying, "This is my aunt. I can interpret for you what she is saying. She says, 'Last evening you prayed over my husband, who wasn't a believer until last night. When you prayed, he was saved and filled with the Spirit. You spoke in our Greek Orthodox dialect, but now, why aren't you speaking to me in the same dialect?'"

I thank God that He can use our natural tongues to give Him glory in so many other languages. When the Holy Spirit comes in His fullness, let's not put limitations on His power.

A couple years later, another trip took David and me to the Philippines to join a team from Ron and Patti Marinari's church, Bedminster, New Jersey, for eight days of meetings. On the team from The Church of the Hills were two Filipinos, Marilyn and Rose, who had settled in the US. We planned to travel six to eight hours a day and conduct revival services in different towns each night. We traveled in one vehicle and a second van carried a musical team. I had decided to fast and pray throughout the journey. Sometimes I fast only from TV and the newspaper, but this time I fasted from all food items.

The first afternoon, we arrived at a hotel and I went to my room to freshen up. A banquet awaited us. I love fish and they were serving a huge stuffed one, but I decided not to go near it. I didn't eat at all, but just went into our room instead. Though I had sipped only water that day, I was vomiting and had diarrhea. I told David and the team to please go ahead and send a car for me a bit later. David and I were the main speakers for the services.

I had tried diarrhea medicine and antacids. Nothing was working. I was crying in the bathroom and feeling very weak.

I felt it was an attack of the enemy. Paul says in Romans that when we don't know how to pray, "the Spirit himself intercedes for us through wordless groans ... in accordance with the will of God" (Rom. 8:26-27). The Spirit led me to take authority over the attack of Satan in my body. I said, "Satan, I'm not taking this diarrhea and vomiting. You can have it, in the name of Jesus. The blood of the Lamb is against you, Satan." In an instant I was completely healed and strong.

I freshened up and went to the gymnasium grounds, only to find the 150 or so Filipino pastors very subdued and nervous. They had heard that the mayor had given instructions that no one should attend our meetings—the reason being that the speaker was a former nun and a heretic. The mayor had said that anyone who came to hear me would go to hell. The worship leaders and team were anxious too. They had heard that the place would be stoned that night.

When I arrived at the site, a group of basketball players—some of them drug addicts—were playing there. A section of the grounds was usually used as a basketball court. Just two or three rows of chairs had a sprinkling of people sitting in them. I got out of the car, went straight to the basketball court, and took the ball. I shot a basket from an angle that, humanly speaking, was impossible to hit. I used to play basketball as an athlete, off-season, when I wasn't training. I had represented my college in the sport. Having shot the ball into the basket, I went and retrieved the ball. Putting it under my arm, I asked the young men to follow me. Like lambs they did. I seated them on the front row and asked the organizers to begin the praise and worship.

We would wait on the Lord, not wait for the crowds. Halfway through David's turn to preach, we heard stones hitting the metal roof. David couldn't preach because of the noise, and the mayor had the electricity shut off. There was total darkness in that part of town. I asked someone for a flashlight. I took a metal chair and stood on it in front of the congregation. I kept the flashlight pointing at my face. Although the mikes were not working, I asked the people to go and park their cars on all four sides of the meeting area and turn their car lights toward us.

We had a Jericho march and stormed heaven, binding the spirits in the area that were obstructing the work of God there. We stood and prayed in the Holy Spirit, claiming that territory for the Lord. We rebuked the blind spirits of darkness holding the Filipinos captive. We asked God to release an anointing on the pastors and give them holy boldness to proclaim God's Word. For about 15 minutes everyone walked around praying, despite the stones landing on the roof. We cried out to God for victory that night.

Suddenly the lights came back on. I stood to preach and people started pouring into the seating area from all sides. A lady who had been paralyzed in a wheelchair, unable to walk, stood up and started leaping and running all over the place. That night the crowd stood by the altars for the longest while and saw the miracle-working power of a Holy God. Take authority over the spirits in your area. "Whatever you bind on earth will be bound in heaven, and whatever you loose on earth will be loosed in heaven" (Matt. 18:18). Stand in the gap; pray and fast. Take your eyes off your situation and turn them on God; He will be glorified!

While ministering in the US in Phoenix, Arizona a few years ago, I preached one Sunday at the Baseline Bible AG church. Pastor Brian and Jill Hartman pastor there. They asked me if they could include the children and youth in the evening service, since the Sunday school workers had missed the morning service. "Yes," I said, "Bring them to the front. I am excited to have kids around when I preach. They are so sincere and open to the gospel." So all the Missionettes and Royal Rangers came to the front at the end of the praise and worship time. That evening I preached on receiving the baptism in the Holy Spirit and said that anyone who had accepted Christ as Savior and Lord and welcomed Him into their lives could have constant communion with God. They could receive from the Father the anointing and the blessings of the promised Holy Spirit. When the Holy Spirit comes, we will be able to pray in a language that we have never learned and likely never heard spoken anywhere else. I could tell that the children in the congregation were all ears. When I gave an altar call for those who wanted prayer, they were the first to run up to the front. They were so hungry for God. Six of those children received the baptism in the Holy Spirit that night as the Spirit moved on all of us. That church still talks about that Sunday night when the power of the Holy Spirit fell and no one wanted to leave the sanctuary.

At another church on a Sunday morning, the service started at 10:00 a.m. The Spirit's power fell all over the place and no one left until 3:00 p.m. I was seated on the edge of the platform with my shoes off after standing for hours. A young lady came running up to me, crying. She said, "Of all days, I should have exchanged my nursery duty with someone else today. I missed everything God did in the sanctuary."

I answered with a little impatience, "It's the same Holy Spirit here. He would have moved in the nursery if given the opportunity." I could sense she was still feeling sorry for herself. I invited her to come and sit beside me, so I could share with her what I had preached. When I tried to give her the message, I started stuttering and stammering. I have never been known to stutter … and I broke down crying. I was convicted by the Spirit for my impatience. I asked God to forgive me and said, "Sister, I did nothing in this place. God did it all and He will do for you whatever you need from Him." To God be the glory!

Another Sunday morning I was to minister in a good-sized church. I was seated on the platform between the senior pastor and his associate during the praise and worship. I prefer to keep my eyes closed while worshiping, but I happened to glance up briefly. In that instant I saw three people—two men and a woman—dressed all in white. They came down the center aisle and sat midway in the sanctuary. That morning during the praise and worship, there was a real move of the Lord. It was a Spirit-filled church.

Then everyone stopped singing in tongues and praying in the Holy Spirit at the same time. One voice, however, did not stop. For some time I listened with my eyes closed; I did not feel this was of the Lord. I opened my eyes to see who and where the voice was coming from. It was that woman dressed in white I had seen coming in earlier. She stopped eventually as everyone waited uneasily.

After the ministry of the Word, people had rushed up to the altars to rededicate their lives to God and get prayed for. The Holy Spirit was moving in a powerful way once more. I could sense the hand of God touching the lives of the people and at the same time I could sense another spirit trying to operate in the sanctuary.

The trio in white had moved to the front pew at this stage. I had moved toward some folks in the pews that morning, even though the altars were crowded. God did not lead me to go near or to pray for these three. There was such a powerful demonstration of God that people were compelled to testify. I held the mike in front of each of them for about two minutes. I sensed they were truly touched and wanted to give God the glory. It was a large church; the altar service continued for quite a while.

I noticed a tall lady who had come in from the side aisle, sobbing bitterly and interceding in the Holy Spirit. I was not aware that she was the senior pastor's wife, who had been working in the nursery that morning. Led of the Spirit, she had come in to take authority over the contrary spirit that had been trying to take over in the midst of God's move and disrupt the service. The Lord led me to this woman, to tell her that God was in control of the situation. As I moved back to the front of the altars, the woman dressed in white came up and asked for the microphone. "I'll not give it to you," I told her, "But I'll hold it in front of you." I did not feel she had the right spirit.

She began, "This morning as I moved to the front of the sanctuary, Sister Theresa came and prophesied over me saying that I was a true prophetess of the Lord and that I had a word of knowledge for this congregation...." At that point I pulled the mike away from her face.

The anger of the Lord started burning inside of me. I said, "You are a false prophet. I did not even come near you this morning, because I sensed you had a contrary spirit. In fact, this morning you were at another church, where you disrupted the service and you came here hoping to do the same. God would not let you, because of the power of prayer in this place." She and the two men ran to the back door and exited. We never saw them again.

CHAPTER 22

THE ANDAMAN AND NICOBAR ISLANDS

"I will go before you" (Isa. 45:2).

ONE NOVEMBER I HAD JUST RETURNED FROM A MISSIONS trip and I was very tired. It was 2:45 a.m.; I had just finished praying. I had decided to go to bed, but I told the Lord, "I'm physically worn out, but if you want me to continue praying, I'm willing." Prayer is not tedious when you're so in love with Jesus. Prayer is just hanging out with the One you love. Don't let the enemy tell you prayer is boring. I just wait for moments to get away from people so that I can be with the Lover of my soul. It's so exciting to be with Jesus, especially when He confides in us the secrets of His heart. (See Psa. 25:14.) Whether you are sleeping or eating or walking, He is still in the business of making us His confidantes.

I used to think, "Wasn't it great for Adam and Eve to have lived in that beautiful garden—no pollution, no garbage, nothing of this earth's nonsense. Then they sinned. And God, you walked with them in the cool of the evening."

But then as I waited on the Lord, He said to me, "Theresa, you're more privileged than Adam and Eve were. Now I desire to live and move and have my being in you at all times. You don't have to wait until the cool of the evening to meet me." (See Acts 17:28.) Isn't that awesome to think that this great God lives in us? He says, "I live in a high and holy place, but also with those who are contrite and lowly in spirit" (Isa. 57:15). That's why David cried out, "A broken and contrite heart you, God, will not despise" (Psa. 51:17). The more humble I become the closer He gets to me.

So I cried out to God, "I would love to pray, but I know that in the morning I have to get up early. We have to take David to the train station, because he is going on another ministry trip. God, I have to go to bed, but if you want me to stay awake, I'm awake." The spirit God has given us is eternal. It is so important to allow our spirits to lean on God's Spirit, not on our own understanding. (See Prov. 3:5-7.) As we yield to Him, He will teach us to pray. He will pray in us with groans too deep for words. (See Rom. 8:26.)

Suddenly, about 4:00 in the morning, God started giving me a vision. In that vision I began to see the Indian map coming and then fading, but with the name Nicobar seemingly written in neon lights. I didn't understand, so I waited. A dream followed in which I saw myself back again in the convent. I was dressed as a nun and talking to one of the local tailors who happened to be a Muslim. I used to deal with him when I was principal of the school. He tailored all the uniforms the school students had to purchase. He was a sweet-natured and humble man and I used to pray that God would give that soul to me. Maybe God was telling me that he had gotten saved.

In the dream I called him by name, "Sammy, I hope you'll have all the school uniforms ready before the term reopens." Students would be coming a week in advance to pick up their uniforms, books, etc.

He said, "Sister, if you want any uniforms this year, you'll have to go to Nicobar," and he gave me the very name I had seen lit up in the vision. Then the dream ended and I slept again for a half hour. It was similar to Paul's dream of the Macedonian man calling him to come over and give them the Word (Acts 16:9).

When I awoke the next morning I knew I had to go and look at the map of India and see where that place God had shown me actually was. But my brother and I had to take David to the railway station to leave on his trip. While in the vehicle I said to them, "Guess what, guys. I'll be going to Nicobar." God had made me realize in my spirit that I had to start evangelizing in that place. There was urgency about the message.

They both said, "Where is Nicobar?"

I said, "I don't have the slightest clue," but I knew in my spirit that I had to go. When God gives you a vision, who cares whether you understand it or not? Don't get anxious. You don't need all the clues at once. You might collapse if God showed you your whole life from now until the end. Therefore, simply abide in the vine (John 15). God will direct your path.

The human mind cannot comprehend all God is doing, but as we yield to the Holy Spirit, He will take us one step at a time in faith and obedience. And He gives us enough grace to do what He's showing us to do. That's how you work when you receive visions and dreams. You cannot function in the natural when God is giving you the supernatural thing to undertake. It's superior to the natural. It cannot be done by might or power, but by His Spirit (Zech. 4:6).

So the two guys didn't say much. They knew better. If I've heard from God, I've heard from God! I went home and prayed for three hours as was my usual habit, but I didn't even bother to ask the Lord about this place. I was just doing my devotions. First things first! Again the vision came back to me of the Indian map and Nicobar written in bright letters. I went to my brother's home and looked for a map. My sister-in-law Maria and I couldn't find the place. So I returned home, took my laptop, and connected to the Internet. There I found three pages of information, more than I wanted to know. Foreigners were not allowed and no Indian could even go to Nicobar without permission. Only government officials were allowed. The Nicobaris were indeed a tribal unreached people group. So I said, "Well God, it's your agenda. I'm on board! I don't care what anyone else says, I'm there with you. I'm available, but Holy Spirit, you are in charge."

I called the travel agent for my air tickets and he asked me if I had a permit.

I said, "That's not your concern; just do what you need to do to get me my air tickets." He obliged by getting the tickets and I set out on this adventure with God. "What no eye has seen, what no ear has heard, and what no human mind has conceived—these things God has prepared for those who love Him" (1 Cor. 2:9). It would have taken at least 15 days to get a permit, and they would have looked into my background and possibly denied it anyway. If they had come to know that I am a Christian and doing Christian work, they might have arrested me for wanting to go to this people group. So, what I did was continue to wait on the Lord. He kept telling me to just be bold in the Spirit and go. And in the vision, I hadn't seen my husband David with me. My brother hadn't been with me either. God always makes it clear. So I was going alone.

I went to cancel my appointments for the next couple of weeks. Paul Yonggi Cho was coming into the country for the Indian Pentecostal Federation meeting. I was supposed to minister to the women at that conference. The Lord didn't give me a release to cancel that appointment, which meant I had very limited time to make this trip.

I flew the first two legs of the journey. No hurdle was going to stop me. As a child I had jumped over chairs, sofas, across the bed, and over fences and gates. My friends would send me into a field to get beautiful mangoes they had knocked from trees. I had to jump over the wall, grab the mangoes, and jump back before the watch dogs could get me. This was before I was saved. When I was 15, I had set the record in all of India for the high jump event.

When I arrived at the Port Blair airport in the Andamans, believe it or not, there was very tight security. I came out of the airport with my two bags—holding tracts and Bibles and anointing oil that were needed to help me evangelize. Officials were waiting to meet passengers. I saw police in uniform and plain clothes too, trying to see who was coming out of the plane. Sometimes it's hard for them to even see me as Indian, because

I don't dress in saris. You know why? Being an athlete all my life, I had told my mother, "Sorry, no saris." But I do wear the other Indian clothes, very graceful *salwar khameez* outfits usually. But it's just that I'm unique and when I travel I wear slacks suits or jeans and a T-shirt. I move around because I don't want anyone to even know who I am.

As I walked into the crowd I realized that the Spirit in me was connecting me with another group of people. So I just went up to these three men; they took my bags from me and I didn't say anything. They put me in a taxi with the instructions, "Don't say anything in the taxi. We've already registered you at a hotel. You don't even have to go to the front desk."

God uses different people to carry on His work. He has a mission and it's global! That's why He's not the God of one denomination only. Believe it or not, in heaven there are no denominations. I've ministered in Baptist, Methodist, Pentecostal, and Anglican churches—everywhere that God opens the doors, I'm there. Get excited about God using you, if you have no prejudices.

I then went to the hotel in the taxi with the three men and we didn't talk much. I didn't go to the front desk. The men told me they would bring my bags to the room. Even before I had arrived there in the Andamans, God had given a vision to a single woman by the name of Elizabeth, who was 47 years old. The Holy Spirit said, "You folks have been praying and fasting and believing for years for the souls in this place. Now the time is right. I'm going to release my missionary evangelist, Theresa Greenhough, in these territories. I will bring her and she will evangelize. But you need to pray; Theresa's life will be in danger. Intercede for her every day until she leaves the area." Elizabeth had seen my face in her vision and God had told her very clearly, "Go to your pastor and tell him to get the church together to pray and fast till she comes and until she leaves the island." He had given her the exact date and time of my arrival.

It was a small church, the only one of its kind in that whole area. They had seven women, five men, and eight to ten kids.

They had built their church on a hilltop. The pastor was only about 22 years old, but they had heard from God. I didn't know what God had told them, I only knew I had to be obedient to the Spirit. They had sent the underground missionaries to wait for me at the airport.

My instructions were, "Come out of your room only when you hear a certain number of knocks on your door. Otherwise, don't go near the door or even look through the peephole. Don't wear the same clothes you came in when you come out. Each time you go out on the island you must change your clothes. There might be someone spying on you." So I agreed and I wasn't afraid. When God gives a vision and you're obeying Him, you get excited to see how His plan is going to unfold. If you allow the spirit of fear to come in, you will worry, "Oh, I'm going to get arrested and they're going to find out I'm a missionary and that I'm married to a missionary...." It's Satan who puts those thoughts in your mind. It's time you send them back to him and let him know his end is near. He's a defeated foe. It's almost time for Jesus to come back. Are you ready? Have you completed the task Christ has given to you?

So I changed my clothes and walked up and down in the room praising God and praying in the Spirit. When you praise God, demons flee. When trials come and panic strikes you, put on a worship tape. Even if you can't sing, just join in with the choruses. Allow God to teach you to worship. When you praise God, you're praying twice. Double prayer is going up to heaven in word and song. And when you pray in tongues, no demon can stop that word from going right into the throne room of God.

After several hours I heard the knocks on the door. I came out and didn't say a word; I didn't know who was who. They hadn't told me their names. That's good, because if you are caught, you don't know who helped you. So we left the hotel and got into a three-wheeler. Now in the best of times I can't travel in a three-wheeler because of the pollution of the diesel and other vehicles. I usually start throwing up. But when you're working for God, He protects you. It was like He put a spiritual wall of protection around me. I wasn't coughing, sneezing, getting a rash on my skin, or anything! It was about 5:30 p.m., just beginning to get dark.

We traveled down some hills, up some hills, into little lanes and then we had to stop and walk a distance, so the man who owned the three-wheeler would not know where we went. When we came to a hillside, I felt the presence of the Lord all over the hill. Then I looked down where we had to go, down the slope, and you literally had to go by faith. The devil said, "You'll slip and fall and break your bones."

And I said, "Devil, you know that my bones will be intact because they are covered with the blood of Jesus. You're already broken."

You have to have a sense of humor in this Christian walk. You can't allow the enemy to mess with your mind. So we went down and started to enter a house. Everyone had left their shoes outside; it was holy ground. Inside was the living room of the woman who had received the vision of me. The room had sofa sets all around, filled with adults sitting and waiting expectantly. More people sat on the floor mats. The power of God—the unique and awesome presence of the Holy Spirit—descended on us. People were crying and praying in the Spirit. Someone would start a chorus and everyone would join in. The power of the Spirit just moved and took charge. It was like the Azusa Street revival when God was in control. He was orchestrating the whole scene. I went and sat down on the only available chair and the Spirit let me know it was time to preach.

I didn't have a Bible nor a note, but as a woman of God I am "prepared in season and out of season" (2 Tim. 4:2). When you have the Word of God in your heart and in your mind, He will put the words on your tongue. If you meditate on it daily in your devotions, He will take that, anoint it, and use it for His glory. So what did I preach on? I preached on God answering prayer! He's faithful when we cry to Him in humility. The people were excited because all that the woman had seen in her vision was happening. Here I was, the dark-haired Indian woman whom she had seen, whom God was going to use. After I finished they continued to sing and worship. Elizabeth had told them again that they must hold me up in prayer.

One man in the gathering went to the next room to make a phone call to his wife. He was one of the underground missionaries, and I still didn't know how many of them there were. His wife said to him, "Wait a minute; Sister Theresa is there, isn't she?" He said yes, not bothering to ask her how she knew, because when the power of the Lord is so strong, you don't ask questions. You just know that this is all the work of God. "Tell her that she is there at the right time in the right place—that she has to go and meet the archbishop of the Andaman and Nicobar Islands. Right now he has returned to the Andamans from Chennai where he had gone for medical treatment."

So the missionary came and told me that I had to go meet the bishop. He was the only one who could get me into the place God had called me to go. And I felt in my spirit immediately, that this was God's plan and direction. The others said, "No, you don't even dare go near the bishop. If he finds out you're a missionary, he'll be the first to have you arrested. And you won't even see your husband anymore."

Now these people pleaded with me not to go. But I knew that God was telling me to go, so I told them not to worry, but to continue praying and praising God. I went out, put on my shoes, and said to the two brothers who came outside with me, "Come, let's go to the bishop's house."

This man, Archbishop Edmund Matthew, was not Spirit-filled or Roman Catholic or even born again necessarily, but a leader in the Church of North India. In 1970, 23 years after the British had left India, the Disciples of Christ and the United, Anglican, Methodist, Baptist, and Brethren churches joined together to form the Church of North India (CNI). Bishop Matthew was stationed in South India. He is like a politician or gang leader; he clicks his fingers and things move. If he says you're excommunicated, you are. This particular bishop won't even smile. Even his wife has not seen him smile. He's that serious and shrewd.

That morning when I had arrived at the airport, one of the three men had handed me a ticket with another person's name on it for the ship leaving the following day. It's all about God's agenda. He goes before us. I had absolute peace and calm. When we don't know how to pray, the Spirit of Truth prays through us. So I knew that evening that I was supposed to meet the bishop of the area I was headed for. He was also planning to be on that ship the next day. He had received word that his sister back home had died. So as I went into the first building on my left I was stopped by a gentleman. He asked me what I wanted and I said, "I'm here to meet with the bishop."

The man told me I couldn't see him. I said, "OK, I'll be back."

He said, "No, you can't meet with the bishop. You have no appointment; no one meets him this way. We have strict security. The bishop sees no one."

"Where is he?"

"By the way, he's not here. He will come back very late and he's a very sick man. No one meets him."

"I'll be back later," I said. "He'll be very happy to meet with me when I tell him what I have for him." He proceeded to tell me the gate would be closed. Well, this man hadn't read Acts 12, nor could he have known that I had been a professional high jumper and could climb the gate if needed.

So I came out of the bishop's house and didn't know what to do next. The two missionary brothers who had brought me there were hiding in the bushes, because they didn't want to be seen at the bishop's house. We do have to be very careful and use a lot of wisdom and discretion. Every day I ask the Lord to give me wisdom.

As I started walking along the sidewalk the two brothers came out of hiding and asked where we were going from there. Walking with Jesus is walking in faith and obedience. When you fulfill the first step in faith, then He'll reveal to you the next step. If you don't take the first step, He's not going to unravel the next step of the journey to you. Suddenly the power of God fell on me and I said, "Right now, please take me to the intensive care unit (ICU) of the main hospital on this island. There's a three-year-old boy who is sick. I have to anoint him with oil and pray for him so that he will live."

One of the men, Peter, started crying. I asked him why he was crying. He said, "My little boy has been there for the last three days with vomiting and diarrhea. He's at death's door." Imagine, this man of God, an underground missionary, has a child in the ICU who is dying, and where is he? He's in the center of God's will—at the prayer meeting. He's at the airport to pick me up. He's at the hotel and in the three-wheeler. I want to be in the center of God's will like that, no matter what!

I said, "Peter, what happens after three days? You don't stay in the tomb; you rise! That same Spirit that raised Jesus from the dead will raise your child. (See Rom. 8:11.) You will see resurrection power. Your child will not die; he will live. Because you believe in Jesus, your child will live. I've got anointing oil with me; let's go and anoint your baby with oil and pray."

We walked into the ICU and the wife was crying her heart out. The baby was on IV fluids and had not opened his eyes for three days. He hadn't moved; he was very sick—just skin and bones. The doctors had tried everything and nothing seemed to be working. I went and patted the mother on the shoulder, saying, "Sister, don't cry; rejoice. The Bible says to give thanks in all circumstances. This miracle is God's will for you in Christ Jesus. (See 1 Thess. 5:17.) You're going to see resurrection life just now. Just believe!" I asked, "Do you believe?"

The child's mother nodded her head through her tears and I anointed the child with oil. The two men were praying with me. I prayed, "God, I just thank you." If Jesus is interceding and the Holy Spirit is interceding within you, you pray in accordance with the mind of God. I said, "I thank you, Jesus, that by your stripes this little child is healed. Thank you that this child is well and hale and hearty and on his way to victory. I thank you, Father, for victory in the name of Jesus!"

Suddenly, for the first time in three days, the child opened his eyes, turned, and smiled at his mother. The child was alive and kicking. I didn't know what I was to do next, so I stepped back and waited. You just learn to wait on the Lord and pray in the Spirit when you don't know what to do. God will take you on from there.

The two women dressed in white, a doctor and a nurse, who walked in at that moment, wondered what had happened. This child had not even been able to move for three days, and suddenly he had gotten back all his energy. I knew it was time for me to disappear. When you've done your part, you don't have to stay around. To God belongs the glory!

The nurse whispered to the doctor, loud enough for me to hear, "How I wish we could go to that part of the hospital where the Jarawas are placed—that group that has just been located in the jungles." That makes no sense to you or to me, but just then I felt the Holy Spirit moving inside me. I had never heard the name of that tribe before. I stepped out of the ICU into the corridor and signaled to Peter, the child's father, to follow me. I needed to talk to him. God was saying to me, "Go, it's time for you to go and meet the Jarawas. That's the tribe."

The child's father came into the corridor. We couldn't talk openly because this was a sensitive issue. I later learned that even the government had not known this tribe was in existence until the previous year. This was the story: A little boy in the tribe was hungry. He was about ten years old. This tribe moved around naked, the women covered their private parts with skins of animals and leaves. Their complexions were beautiful; their skin absolutely dark, their black hair short and curly. The boy started wandering in search of food. All they had were coconuts. They drank coconut water and ate the inside of it as well as using the shells for firewood. Their diet consisted of roots, betel nuts, and some small animals and insects. That's how they had survived for centuries.

The boy walked for days in the jungle. Finally he came to a wall. He had never seen bricks, cement, or a wall in his life. On the other side was a beautiful orchard, filled with fruit. He couldn't believe his eyes. He wouldn't have to go hungry anymore. So he started climbing, excited. He had never seen anything like this before. All at once he heard someone clapping. He didn't know there was another human being in this world that was different from those in his tribe. He saw a figure standing there, but he thought it was a bigger animal. Frightened, he lost his grip and fell out of the tree.

The man was the owner of the orchard. He thought the little black-colored boy was a baby bear or something, trying to get his fruit, so he was shooing it away by clapping. The little boy in the tree, while reaching out for the fruit, fell and broke his leg. The man heard his cry and realized it was that of a human being. He came running, picked up the naked child, and rushed him to the hospital. That's the first the government had learned of this tribe. Christ said, "This gospel of the kingdom will be preached in the whole world as a testimony to all nations, and then the end will come" (Matt. 24:14).

The hospital put clothes on the boy, such as he had never seen. For the first time he saw running water, electricity, different kinds of fruit and other foods, tall buildings, beds with mattresses and many other strange things. The staff pampered him, spoiled him. They took him on an airplane to New Delhi and brought him to the government headquarters. Those politicians who had brought him to the capital city said, "You've got to give us money to take care of this tribe." So they got the money, but everyone lined their own pockets along the way. Not much actually got to the tribe. Then the local government decreed that no one could go near the tribe. They did not want the tribals mingling with other people either. They wanted to keep their dealings with the tribe secret.

In India, some people are good at learning dialects. I know Hindi, Marathi, and Konkani very well and can understand Bengali, Nepali, and other closely related languages with similar vocabulary and structure. So the local government hired people to pick up the sounds and words, and to learn the boy's dialect. Following that, a team of officers went back with him into the jungles. A Jeep cannot go there; they had to walk for several days before the boy could introduce them to his tribe.

They brought 20-25 of them out and placed them in this government hospital to care for them. They asked the boy to tell his people, "They will do for you what they have done for me." Some of them had eye trouble, skin diseases, bloated stomachs, and fever from living in the jungles.

So I asked Peter, "Where in the hospital are the members of the Jarawa tribe? I've got to meet them."

He said, "Sister, don't even go there. The local government doesn't want anyone to even know that they are in this hospital. It's very straightforward; no one can mingle with them. Everyone here knows that. Even the doctors and nurses have been brought from other islands, so no one here can know anything about them."

"Peter," I replied, "I don't even want you to go with me. I'm just asking you to point out the building in which the tribe is being kept."

"No, Sister Theresa, please. You'll be arrested by the police and everything will come down on the rest of us. We'll be caught."

I told him, "No, I know the Holy Spirit wants me to go to these people."

Peter, though frustrated with me, came out of the building with me and only looked in the direction of one of the distant buildings. Then he turned and ran for his life. He did not even want to be seen with me. If I got caught, they all would get caught.

So I started walking toward that building. Having God's anointing means you have no spirit of fear, but power, love, and a sound mind (2 Tim. 1:7). You can't depend on your human ingenuity or talents. I was banking on God's faithfulness to see me through, though I didn't know what to do next. Security guards had surrounded that building. As I walked that long path, a nurse dressed in white came alongside me. She was trying to walk fast without looking at me. I tapped her on the shoulder and she was surprised, as I called her by the name God gave me for her. I said, "Listen, Sister, you're not here by chance. You're just on time. I know you love the Lord; you're a believer. I'm a missionary evangelist and my name is Theresa. God wants me to evangelize the Jarawa tribe that's being kept in that building. I want you to make a way for me to enter that building." She freaked out!

"No, no, I'm not even allowed to speak to anyone. I'm not even from this island; I'm from another place. The doctors and nurses are not allowed to say a word to anyone from outside, so please don't be seen with me. My family's lives will be at stake and so will your family."

Then I spoke to her with authority, "Sister, why are you so frightened when you have the call of God on your life? Listen, there's one thing for you to do. I'm not asking you to go with me. Just do what I say, or you'll answer to God. All you have to do is go to that man who is sitting on that high stool, the chief security officer, and ask him to go for a tea break." It was about 8:00 p.m. You don't tell anyone to go for a tea break at that time—maybe between 3:00 p.m. and 5:00 p.m., but not at that hour. When God puts words in your mouth, to the natural mind it may be nonsense. God's ways are still higher than our ways, His thoughts higher than ours. (See Isa. 55:8-9.) She was only a nurse and couldn't really order this man. She couldn't wait to run away from me.

The nurse asked me if that was all. Then she ran quickly toward the man, not wanting to be seen with me. She spoke to the man in spite of her fears. I don't know what transpired, but he immediately jumped off his stool, clapped his hands, and all his officers followed him around the building on the far side.

It worked! The plan of God has to work. It's from above. The Holy Spirit sent me shooting into the building, unhindered. I was being led of the Spirit, because I had never been in the area before. I had never been to that island or that hospital before in my life. I ran up a flight of steps and into the passageway. I saw 10-12 tribal people just staring at me. They seemed to be all different shapes and sizes, but all dressed alike in loose clothes of different colors. I couldn't tell who was male and who was female, who was young or who was old. I suddenly got nervous, my head spinning and my stomach in knots. They stared as if to say, "You can't come close to us; we'll eat you alive." I didn't know whether they would bite me, claw at me, or tear me to bits. The tribe was known to kill people with poisonous arrows. I was afraid they would jump on me if I stooped down. When you don't know what to do, pray! When you don't know what to pray, the Holy Spirit prays through you. (See Rom. 8:26-27.)

The Spirit told me to do what comes naturally, love them. I love children. So I got down on their level and picked one of them up. I thought the "child" was unusually heavy; though I'm used to picking up children. Immediately I put that one down. It may have been a grown man; I don't know. So they all looked to see the reaction of that person. He was all smiles. For the first time he had felt the love and warmth of another human being outside his tribe. It had felt good to him. Next, they all wanted to be carried. I couldn't carry them, so I was huffing and puffing. The Holy Spirit was saying, "Move, do what you have come here to do."

I took the anointing oil I had in my hands and started praying for the one near me. It is so fascinating when you walk with God. I continued to be prompted by the Holy Spirit. I then waited to see the person's reaction. I usually close my eyes, but I was waiting to see if he would pull my hand away or bite it or what. These were uncivilized people. I expected them to pull at my clothes or hair. But I was led by the Spirit and prayed in the Spirit for them. Then I moved to the next person, but I noticed that the first one was crying lots of tears. What happened was that the whole group started breaking into tears—tears of repentance. I realized I was speaking to them in their own dialect, by the power of the Holy Spirit, not my power. Some of them were trying to go into the room to bring out the others. I used sign language. The sounds coming out of my mouth sounded like grunting and groaning to me, but they understood what I was saying to them. I went into the other two connecting rooms and placed my hands on those who were really sick. In the Spirit I saw fevers leaving, tumors gone, people being born again, and tears running freely.

As I left the second room I saw that the people in the passageway had joined their hands together and they were dancing in the Spirit, giving glory to God. The Holy Spirit confirmed to me that I had evangelized these people in their own tongue. Oh, the faithfulness of God!

Then I felt in my spirit that I needed to run out of there. I went back to look for the two brothers near the ICU. I motioned for them to follow me again, and said, "Let's go."

They asked, "Where to?"

I said, "The bishop's house, even though it's late."

So we went there, the two guys hiding behind the trees again. It was very dark outside. When I had gone there earlier that evening, I had been told that the gates would be locked, that the bishop was a sick man, and that he would not want to see me. But closed gates mean nothing to Christ, who is "the Gate"! As I approached, the big gate seemed to be opening of its own accord. I entered the building and turned left down the hallway. I saw a short Indian man dressed in a *lungi* (a long Indian wraparound cloth that men wear at home). He had no shirt on.

I tapped him on the shoulder, saying, "Bishop, would you mind going in and putting a shirt on? I'll be waiting out here." The hallway opened into a living room. I sat on a couch. Once dressed, he came and sat on the next couch.

"Yes, what do you want?" he asked gruffly. He was serious, not exactly polite.

I told him about my vision and dream. I told him God wanted me to go to the Island of Nicobar and help him. "I will not be a burden. I'll pay my way and any expenses necessary." That morning when I had arrived at the airport, one of the three men had handed me a ticket in someone else's name.

The bishop said, "You can't travel; you have no ticket. The ship leaves tomorrow." The ship went to Nicobar only once every 10-12 days.

I said, "But I do have a ticket." I didn't say that it was in someone else's name.

He persisted, "But you don't have a permit to enter."

I said, "Bishop, you are my permit." With his head bowed down he told me he would see me at the ship the following day.

With God's help I was smuggled onto the 800-1000-passenger ship. I knocked on a particular cabin door. I entered to find 12 people worshiping and interceding for me. The Holy Spirit had led me to that place. Twenty-two hours later there came another knock on the door. It was the bishop's elderly attendant. Only the Holy Spirit could have guided him to that particular cabin. He said the bishop wanted to meet with me in his cabin. I gathered my things and followed him back.

The bishop was in his 60s, but his wife was 48 years old and very petite. Their young son sat there too. The previous evening I had offered to pay for a hotel and expenses. Little did I know that the place had no hotels, only a government guesthouse for officials. The bishop had clout, but he said, "You will be my guest and stay with us."

Now it was unheard of for a non-Nicobari to stay in the houses of the local people. It was against their custom to welcome a stranger into their home. He went on to say it was too risky for me to stay in the government guesthouse. I spent the rest of the journey in the bishop's quarters on the ship. When we got close to the harbor, a huge raft came alongside the ship. People started jumping onto it—a 5-6-foot leap. The bishop was carried down on the shoulders of some attendants. The raft tossed on the waves as huge boxes and bags were piled on it as well. I jumped onto the raft and sat on a case between the bishop and his wife. I wondered how God would get me to land without getting nabbed. I looked tall compared to the local people, even when I was sitting down. I was the only different-looking person in the crowd.

As we neared the pier, a little boat came and took the bishop's family and me to shore. His attendants stayed behind on the raft with the baggage. How would they hide me? Just then came a heavy downpour of rain, unusual for that time of year. The bishop put up an unusually large black umbrella. I rode from the seaside to the waiting vehicle on the shoulders of the bishop and his wife, my head hidden by the big umbrella. God surely has a sense of humor!

The vehicle had tinted windows, but I could see that most of the homes were all the shape of half a coconut, built on stilts. They had no windows or doors, just access via a ladder from below—for fear of wild jungle animals entering. Each little dwelling had slatted bamboo flooring for ventilation and a thatched roof. They had no running water, no power, no beds or sheets. They slept on the floor.

They gave me my own separate little house. The bishop and his wife had a larger cottage with a big bed. After we arrived, the wife suddenly became ill, seriously ill, even at death's door. About 15 witches and warlocks came into the large bedroom chanting around her. They had needles piercing their noses, ears, and mouths. They were tattooed, wearing only loincloths and carrying spears. They had feathers on their heads and bells on their ankles and wrists. They had beaten their drums in a wild rhythm since early morning.

The bishop's sister-in-law told me that the people were saying her sister was at death's door because the bishop had brought a foreigner into their home. I came down the ladder from my hut and into the bishop's dwelling. The house was packed with people. The bishop sat outside in a chair, unsmiling. He was a man of very few words.

"I hear your wife is not well. I have anointing oil with me. If I anoint her and pray, she will be healed," I said.

"What is that?" he asked. I explained the passage in James 5, and he said, "Give me that."

I told him I had more and that I could give him some. "But this doesn't work until people have faith in Jesus. I've got to explain how this works."

"Go, do it."

"But I've got to teach them first."

"Go, teach," he said.

Lots of men were inside; the bishop's wife lay on her stomach on a long low bed. The atmosphere was tense. They wanted to kill me, but couldn't because the archbishop supported me. His wife was vomiting green seaweed-looking liquid into a basin. Her head hung over the end of the bed, her hair matted and wet. I began, "The bishop has given me permission to pray and anoint his wife with oil, but first I have to teach you about it." There were no smiles, no yea or nay. "Jesus is the only way to eternal life," I continued. "Whoever believes in Him will live forever with God." I explained the principle of divine healing and the instructions of James 5. No one moved. I sat down next to the woman and rubbed her back with my left hand. I anointed her with my right hand. More green vomit came out. I closed my eyes, interceding in the Spirit. Most of these people understood English; this had been a vacation spot for the British. They knew Hindi too.

All of a sudden, the bishop's wife jumped up and, pointing to the witches and warlocks, said, "Get out and don't enter here anymore. I had a vision of the Lord and He told me to listen to this sister. It's time to celebrate life! Bring the fattened pig and roast it"—this from a woman who had been at death's door a moment before!

The next day was the one-week anniversary of the death of the bishop's sister. He had come back from the mainland for this service, planned for the graveside. The bishop asked me to pray and say a few words. They had lit candles and incense sticks and had slaughtered a chicken or goat to apply blood on the gravestone.

Everywhere I went for those ten days, I preached about Jesus. They took me to the huge cathedral one evening where 250 boys and girls, the youth, were practicing Christmas carols in English and in the local dialect. It had a high stairway leading to an elevated pulpit. The bishop said, "Go, preach." No woman had ever ministered from that pulpit before. I preached about the Holy Spirit coming on people for power, but that it was necessary to first receive Jesus as Savior, and then the Spirit would help the young people sing even better. I asked them to repent of their loose morals and wicked ways. They had many teen pregnancies. Many people followed as I led them in the sinner's prayer. After their response, I instructed them that they must be filled with the fullness of the Holy Spirit.

The next day the bishop, his wife, and his sister-in-law toured the island with me. I saw huge churches, all with the pagan rituals—smoke, incense, the blood of chickens or goats on the altars. The bishop would say, "Go, tell!" I would step forward and teach. Some places the tribals were celebrating and waiting for us to come. They were very hospitable. One woman had only one fish, salted and drying on her roof. She wanted us to have it, so she brushed off the red ants and gave it to us. Their food was meager, no eggs, milk, or butter; no provision stores. What they had included coconut, papaya, and betel nut. No buildings except the church steeples rose higher than a few stories. The people wore few clothes, because of the heat.

As we traveled, I laid hands on the sick. The bishop's two nephews were demon possessed. Handsome young men, they had dropped out of school and had shredded their books, notebooks, and clothes. I prayed and God cast the demons out of them. One of them went and got a Bible from home and started reading it in front of me. The goodness of God began to come out of them.

Though that place had many mosquitoes, I never felt ill or got malaria. I ate many strange foods, but never threw up once. God took care of me. When I had to leave by ship, the bishop managed to get me a return ticket in my own name. I still had to be "smuggled" back on the ship, since I had no permit.

Wedding party—October 17, 1998

CHAPTER 23

AN AMAZING JOURNEY

"See, I have engraved you on the palms of my hands" (Isa. 49:16).

ONCE ON THE SHIP LEAVING NICOBAR, I OPENED THE DOOR of my cabin to find it brightly lit. What relief to again have a mattress, pillow, and clean white linen on the bed! I put my two bags on one of the top bunks. A Muslim government official, his sister, and two children, occupied the bunk below me. The children were already seasick. Two other men lay on the opposite side, a Hindu government school teacher on the lower bunk and a Hindu naval officer on the upper one. About midnight I wanted to put out the light, but decided not to disturb the others by getting down. I turned my face to the wall, preparing to welcome sleep (after ten days with little rest). The Holy Spirit said to me, "It's not time to sleep. Go down and pray. Do your devotions." I had already spent ten days in Nicobar, trying to do my best to follow the Spirit's direction—evangelizing, casting out demons, raising a woman who was near death, and now I needed rest. But I had to do the Spirit's bidding. God said, "Pray in the Spirit." So I started praying. Then He said, "Take your Bible and sit down."

There was a little couch between the two bunk beds, and a window above the seats. I didn't have the guts to go open my bag to get my study Bible, but I did. Then I became lost in the Word for a couple of hours. All three men in the cabin were staring at me. I looked up and got a little nervous. My stomach started twisting into knots. I wondered whether these officials would hand me over to any authorities if they discovered that I had no permit. When Peter looked at the wind and the waves he began to sink. As long as his eyes were on Jesus, he was walking on the water. When he took his eyes off Jesus, he was sinking. (See Matt. 14:29-31.) So I resumed reading my Bible again.

The Hindu gentleman said to me, "You not only read your Bible, you live it too, don't you?" I didn't know whether he was trying to trap me. I just looked at him and then looked back into the Bible. Then the Muslim gentleman said, "Tell us about your Jesus." I thought maybe he intended to report me, but I was led to look at them with great compassion in my heart. They were like "sheep without a shepherd" (Mark 6:34). And the Word of God in Hindi just started flowing out of my belly. I had studied Hindi as a second language 25 years earlier as a schoolgirl, but hadn't really used it much since, and then only for common everyday communication with mainly non-English speakers. In fact, I haven't memorized even one verse of scripture in Hindi.

The Holy Spirit anointed my tongue and many prophecies pertaining to the times just before the Second Coming of Christ started coming out of my mouth. I explained the prophecies that have been fulfilled already in this generation, yours and mine.

Tears started flowing out of the Muslim gentleman's eyes. He said, "Sister, I knew that you would tell me the truth. There's a pastor who lives near my home. He's a good man, a solid man. He doesn't beat his wife, doesn't drink alcohol, and doesn't gamble. One day he invited me to his church, and I went. Those people are very loving, very friendly. Now that you've told me the truth, I'm going back there when I get home."

The main thing is that you have to stop looking at yourself. Know that you can do all things through Him who strengthens you. (See Phil. 4:13.) I continued talking to these men about the things of God from His Word. They said, "We are government employees. We have a dining hall upstairs; we want to treat you if you will join us." At lunch we ate a sumptuous meal of chicken biryani and all that went with it, including dessert. As we stood on the deck I gave the naval officer an English Bible and ministered to him. He said he would read it. My cabin-mates went out of their way to make me comfortable.

Late that evening a voice on the loudspeaker told all of us to get our tickets and permits ready for disembarking. I had been so busy ministering to my friends that I had failed to realize the time was passing. We had reached the harbor area and could see the crowds gathered. I noticed lots of police vehicles and officers with dogs. They ran up the gangplank with chains and whips, as soon as it touched the dock. The scene horrified me, nervous and scared as I was.

The Muslim brother with whom I had shared the Scriptures stood beside me. In the crowd on shore I suddenly saw the faces of the three brothers who had met me at the airport previously. I had my bags with me and said to my Muslim brother, "You see those three men. They are my brothers. Can you give these two bags to them for me?" He agreed to do it.

I started praying in the Spirit and moving toward the gangplank, very relieved that I was able to pass this far without getting stopped. Others were getting handcuffed, chained, or whipped. This was the only way off the ship, just one exit, as they had closed all others. I prayed, "Lord, you're not going to dump me now, are you? There's no way I can jump or swim away from this ship."

When it was my turn to pass the exit point, the ship's official bellowed, "Your ticket and your permit, please?" All I had in my hand was my ticket. Just then a naval officer, dressed in white, stepped between my hand and the official. I left my ticket in the official's hand and ran the rest of the way down the gangplank without looking back. I went to the three men holding my bags and said, "Get me out of here." They wanted to wait for a taxi, but I insisted on going with one of them on a motorbike. He took me to a hotel where they had again booked me under another false name. It was a different hotel than I had stayed in before.

That evening when I met the underground missionaries again, I said, "What will I do? I'm carrying ancestral shells from the island of Nicobar, which I'm really not meant to be seen with. They were gifts from the bishop. I did not want to offend him by not taking them. How can I get through security?"

These brothers said, "If you have carried them this far, the Lord wants you to have them. God has been faithful to you; don't doubt Him. And by the way, no one will see you off tomorrow morning. We'll be there on all four sides of the airport praying for you, but you won't see us. Go out of the hotel in the morning, get a taxi, and go to the airport. Tip the driver well."

I prayed most of the night for my safety. I knew God had work for me to do yet. I followed my friends' instructions. As I took my bags from the taxi I wondered how God was going to help me. At the airport entrance I was to put my bags on the conveyor belt for a security check. Some policemen and security officers were on duty. The moment my feet touched the first step of the airport building, however, the power in the airport failed. The security men were taking all the bags off the conveyor. I was still holding onto my two bags tightly.

Two very tall officers, dressed in white uniforms bearing the badges of Jet Airways—the airline I was to be flying with—stood beside me and asked me for my bags, saying, "Follow us, sister." I obeyed. One officer went and stood on the other side of the ticket counter; the other stayed behind me. The officer behind the counter took my ticket and worked on my boarding pass. He said, "Sister, you will not need the bag on your right shoulder. Just take your wine-colored book (my Bible) and your water bottle from inside that bag. You can keep your purse. You will not have to claim your bags at the Chennai airport when you disembark to take the connecting flight. You will get all three at the Bangalore airport." The bag on my shoulder had a big shell wrapped in a scarf so it would not break. When he handed me the boarding pass, I looked to see if my own name was on it. When I looked up to thank the two men, no one was in front of me and no one was beside or behind me. I went to the ladies' room and cried, thanking God for the angels He had sent my way!

As I sat in the boarding area, praying in the Spirit and waiting for the plane, some policemen came up to the persons on either side of me and asked to check their purses. The officers appeared not to see me. God had given me His peace; I was not afraid. I had seen the hand of God working on my behalf.

While at Chennai, I had an appointment with the founder of a prominent Christian organization. I met him in the transit area, and then had to hurry off to change airlines. I had just enough time to board the second flight. When I got off the plane in Bangalore, I had almost forgotten the bags and was walking towards the exit. I was surprised to see all three bags, sitting at the exit unattended. They were inside the airport, but placed at the exit, not in the baggage claim area—just as the angel had said!

About two years later, I visited the Andaman Islands again. After preaching three or four services on the Sunday I was there, I was scheduled to go to an island where some lepers were kept in seclusion. The altar service lasted longer than expected as the Holy Spirit's power fell. The pastor informed me that the ferry to the island where the lepers were would have already left for the day. Just then I saw a vision of the ferry coming back. I insisted on taking a taxi to the wharf. Sure enough, no ferry was in sight. I told those with me, "The ferry will come back."

The people said, "No, we know the timings. The ferry can't reverse; impossible!" Four men standing there shook their heads. The harbor area was some distance from where the taxi dropped us. I would have to walk down to the edge where there was a broad bare area. I prayed for the others to have faith. Suddenly the men started shouting, "The ferry's coming back!" It neared the shore and having passed my purse and Bible to those in the ferry, I had to jump a six-foot gap to get on. The four men had no choice but to do likewise.

When we got to the island where the lepers were I had to climb a steep hill and walk quite a distance in my uncomfortable dress shoes. About 20 lepers sat on their beds in a low building. I sat on one bed at a time talking to them. They told me I was the first visitor to come there in 20 years. Most of them had not seen any of their families all those years. I had brought them bananas and biscuits. I prayed with them and ministered to them and went back by ferry that evening.

Jesus said in Matthew 7:21-23 that it is only those who do the will of God that will enter the kingdom of heaven. Of my own accord, it is impossible to do God's will, but with God's grace and strength, all things are possible. At the end of my life's journey I don't want to hear the Master say, "Depart from me," but I want to hear Him say, "Come and share your master's happiness!" (Matt. 25:21).

CHAPTER 24

EPILOGUE

"Your kingdom come, your will be done, on earth as it is in heaven" (Matt. 6:10).

GOD'S WORK, DONE IN GOD'S WAY, WILL NEVER DECAY. NOT only His mercies, but His strategies are new and unique. What He is calling each of us to do; He will not create another to do it. As we move in tune with the anointing, the Holy Spirit who comes with all His gifts will abide in us and teach us. The Holy Spirit will not only instruct us, but also enable us to fulfill the dream that God has dreamt for us. Let us learn to yield 100 percent to the will of God for our lives so that His kingdom will come and His will be done in and through each of us.

David and I are still running the race under the guidance and instructions of the Holy Spirit. A week after we got married in New Jersey, we left America to come and toil in the mission fields of India. Through Gateway International and Gateway Ministries, both of which are registered with the government of India, we feed, clothe, medicate, and educate street kids, garbage pickers, and children of prostitutes, jailbirds, and lepers.

We are excited about the passion He has given us for the lepers of North Karnataka, from where we have been able to bring children and educate them in more ways than one. Jesus said in Matthew 24:14, "This gospel of the kingdom will be preached in the whole world as a testimony to all nations, and then the end will come." Praise God, for we are truly living in exciting times! This gospel continues to go forth in power and in boldness, bearing fruit in abundance, and God keeps getting the glory. May He who called you to a walk of faith and "began a good work in you" (Phil. 1:6), bring it to completion on the day you stand in front of Him and hear His eternal voice saying, "Well done, good and faithful servant!" (Matt. 25:23).

CHAPTER 25

A PRAYER THAT CAN CHANGE YOUR LIFE

"I write these things ... so that you may know that you have eternal life" (1 John 5:13).

THIS VERSE TELLS US THAT WE MAY KNOW THAT WE CAN HAVE eternal life. Yes, God can give each one of us an absolute assurance in our heart that we are His children. How does a person receive this assurance? By doing what the Bible tells us to do. This is God's blessing for every person—whether Jew, Catholic, Protestant, or any other faith. God does not favor one person over another.

On our part we simply need to say a special prayer in agreement with Scripture concerning what Jesus Christ has done, and believe that the words being spoken are true, and when we do this we will receive the gift of eternal life.

Some people may have said many prayers throughout their lives. But this prayer is unlike any other prayer he or she has previously prayed. It is a prayer that provides the inward assurance that we are His children.

We must know that without the shedding of the blood of Jesus on the cross, there would be no forgiveness of sin. And we must believe that Jesus loves us and washes us from every sin with His own blood when we come to Him in repentance (with a change of heart).

If you desire to receive the gift of eternal life, I encourage you to pray the following prayer. This prayer can be called a prayer of thanksgiving. You are praying to God what you believe in your mind, what you believe God has done for you.

Dear God in heaven, thank you for Jesus Christ. Thank you for sending Jesus Christ to die for me. I repent of my sins. I believe Jesus died for me so that all my sins could be forgiven. I believe in my heart that the blood of Jesus cleanses me from all my wrongdoing. Thank you for the gift of eternal life. Thank you, Jesus, that you are my Savior and my Lord. Thank you, God, for giving me absolute assurance that I am your child and that I will be with you forever. In the name of Jesus I pray. Amen.

It would be good to continue to thank Jesus each day for what He has done. Thank Him that His blood has cleansed you. Thank Him that you have received the gift of eternal life. God will then speak to you personally and tell you that He has given you His Spirit and His nature, thus making you His child.

If you have just now confessed Christ as your Savior, we would like to hear from you. Send an email to education@gatewayindia.org, and we will do our best to respond to you with some words of encouragement.

May God's abundant blessings be in your life as you live for Christ!

CONTACT US

As a result of friends who have partnered with Gateway International, we are able to continue our work for God in India. Thank you for praying as God continues to expand His ministry. Please pray for us to have wisdom and protection in all that the Lord would have us accomplish for Him.

If you would like to invite Theresa for ministry or to know more about Gateway, go to our website at www.gatewayindia.org or send an email to education@gatewayindia.org. You may also make contact through one of the following addresses:

Gateway International
P. O. Box 3211
R.T. Nagar, Bangalore 560032
INDIA
Ph: 91 98 86184662

Gateway International
P. O. Box 77514
Baton Rouge, LA 70879-7514
USA
Ph: (225) 324 6091

Gateway International
P. O. Box 80001
Peterborough, ON K9J 3T5
CANADA
Ph: (705) 743 3752